CW00665165

Advance praise for the book

'*India Versus China* is a brilliant book that combines deep knowledge, analytical insight and elegant prose. Its conceptual framework – the four master categories of Perceptions, Perimeters, Partnerships and Power – is highly original. Written with assurance and authority, the narrative ranges widely over history, economics, politics, leadership, military strategy and social structure. The book is a model of its kind, taking the lessons of a lifetime of scholarship to the intelligent general reader. And on a timely and very important topic too.' **Ramachandra Guha**

'In *India Versus China* Kanti Bajpai, one of the most perceptive of India's international relations experts, traces the origins and development of the modern India–China relationship and astutely considers how the balance of power between the two giants has evolved and shifted with time. At a time when tensions are at a historic high, Bajpai's book is a lucid, timely and important intervention; policymakers and China watchers alike would do well to pay heed.' **Shashi Tharoor**

'At a time when Sino-Indian military conflicts have once again risen to prominence, Kanti Bajpai's *India Versus China* provides a superb overview of why their deep differences in visions, interests, affiliations and capabilities promise to persist, with troubling consequences for both states. There is no better tutorial on this strained relation than this book.' **Ashley J. Tellis**

'In this essential read Kanti Bajpai, a foremost Indian thinker on international relations, uses his scholarly insight to clarify the roots of India–China tensions and crises. Analysing the two countries' differences in perception, of power, on the border, and in their foreign policy practice, Bajpai writes in limpid language that often sparkles, about what is probably the most complex and consequential relationship in Asia. He concludes that India and China are unlikely to find their future less challenging than the present. A deep and readable book on India's greatest foreign policy challenge.' **Shivshankar Menon**

'Kanti Bajpai presents his deep knowledge of the subject with clarity, objectivity, eye-opening facts and acute insights. This book is a must-read for anyone who wants to understand the immense scale of India's China challenge.' **Prannoy Roy**

'Kanti Bajpai's insights as well as his incisive writing style makes this book both compulsively readable and exceptionally informative. He has a clear and precise view and communicates it pithily and forcefully. You will learn a lot from this book which will add immeasurably to your understanding of the India–China relationship.' **Karan Thapar**

'Kanti Bajpai, one of India's finest minds on international affairs, must be commended for producing a scholarly yet fluently written account of the conflicts that have bedeviled the relationship between India and China. In December 1988, the two countries had decided to intensify engagement while taking steps to manage these conflicts. Over the past year, however, that paradigm has been severely damaged. Why and how did this happen? Why is the India–China relationship so conflict prone? What lies ahead? Can cooperation and competition replace confrontation and conflict? These questions are uppermost in our minds and therefore Bajpai's latest offering is both timely and relevant.' **Jairam Ramesh**

India Versus China

India Versus China

Why They Are Not Friends

Kanti Bajpai

JUGGERNAUT BOOKS
C-I-128, First Floor, Sangam Vihar, Near Holi Chowk,
New Delhi 110080, India

First published by Juggernaut Books 2021

10 9 8 7 6 5 4 3 2 1

P-ISBN: 9789391165086
E-ISBN: 9789391165093

Typeset in Adobe Caslon Pro by R. Ajith Kumar, Noida

Printed at Thomson Press India Ltd

For Gayatri, Rudra, and the rest of my family

Contents

Introduction

India and China comprise nearly forty per cent of the world's population. Their relationship is vital for three billion people. It is also consequential for the countries in their neighbourhood and for the world at large. After the war of 1962, the two countries had managed to preserve a high degree of military stability along the Himalayan border. Then, in June 2020, a melee at Galwan in Ladakh left Indian and Chinese soldiers dead and injured. Both sides rushed military reinforcements to the area. Despite a series of negotiations, they were unable to disengage the nearly fifty thousand troops amassed on either side of the border – as many troops as they had deployed in the entire 1962 war. Six decades of relative calm between the two countries collapsed in a matter of weeks. The Ladakh crisis suggests that India–China relations are darker and more complex than most observers appreciate or acknowledge. It is tempting to ascribe the current difficulties between them to the memory of the war and to the unsettled border. Clearly, those do affect Delhi's and Beijing's thinking. Yet Galwan suggests that we need to dig deeper. Why did these two societies become locked into a conflict that has stubbornly refused to go away?

Post-imperial India and China started well. India was one of the first countries to recognize the communist government and support its right to a seat in the United Nations. From 1950 to 1953, Delhi mediated between Beijing and Washington during the Korean war. Jawaharlal Nehru, who would go on to be India's first prime minister, had twice visited China before India gained its independence and had helped arrange for a group of Indian medical personnel to go there in the late 1930s. In *The Discovery of India*, he recorded his admiration for Chinese society that continued after rising tensions in the 1950s: 'the vitality of the Chinese people astonishes me. I cannot imagine a people endowed with such bed-rock strength going under.'[1] In 1954, he made a highly publicized trip to China, was greeted by large crowds, and met Chairman of the Communist Party Mao Zedong and Prime Minister Zhou Enlai. When Zhou visited India in 1960, Indian crowds cheered, 'Hindi Chini bhai bhai!' – Indians and Chinese are brothers! – as he drove through the streets. Two years later, though, India and China were at war. India lost the war, and despite the withdrawal of Chinese troops from most of the areas they had captured, the relationship between Asia's giants never fully recovered. Countries fight and become friends, but India and China, sixty years after fighting a short war, are still not friends, as the bloody encounter in Galwan showed.

India and China are not friends for four key reasons: deep-seated differences over their *perceptions* of each other, their territorial *perimeters*, and their strategic *partnerships* with the big powers, as well as the asymmetry of *power* between them. The two societies' perceptions of each other, especially influential Chinese perceptions of India going back to the nineteenth century, have been negative. This may in part account for why India and China cannot agree on their perimeters – their borderlands. Negative perceptions of each other and profound differences over their perimeters are compounded by the fact that they have never been strategic partners. They have both partnered the Soviet Union/Russia and the US at various times but have never been in partnership with each other and have no history of working closely together. Their differences might not have mattered had it not been for the power gap between them, which particularly since the early 1990s has grown relentlessly in China's favour. As a result of the gap, India cannot concede, for fear of appearing weak, and China will not concede, as it does not see the need to do so.

Are there other factors that bear on their relationship? What about a fifth P – Pakistan – which is often identified as a source of conflict? Pakistani Prime Minister Yusuf Gilani rather blushingly described his country's friendship with China as 'higher than mountains, deeper than the ocean, stronger than steel and sweeter than honey'. The quasi-alliance between the two powers clearly irks India, which sees Islamabad as a pawn in Beijing's geopolitical moves. In the end, though, the close China–Pakistan relationship is more effect than cause: it resulted from the India–China conflict, not the other way round. India and China are also divided by a number of other differences – growing Chinese influence among India's other neighbours in South Asia; India's coalition building with Japan and Vietnam in China's backyard; their diplomacy in other parts of the world and in multilateral forums; international status-seeking by both powers; India's huge trade deficit with China; and Chinese dam-building on the Yarlung Tsangpo/Brahmaputra river. These are important elements of the troubled relationship, but again they are more effect than cause. They are not the fundamental causes of their conflict. Rather, they have become additional points of friction driven by the four more basic causes.

This is a book about the India–China conflict examined through the two countries' perceptions of each other, their differences over the border and Tibet, their partnerships with the Great Powers, and their growing power asymmetry. The two countries do also have a record of cooperation, primarily in preserving military stability along the borderlands. Despite serious confrontations in 1967, 1975, 1986–87, 2013, 2014, 2015, 2017, and 2020, the total number of Indian battle-deaths in these eight episodes is just over a hundred (the Chinese figures are not public).[2] For a 'live' border quarrel between such large countries, this is a small number. On the other hand, India and China have had five major confrontations in the last decade alone, after nearly twenty-five years of military stability, confrontations that could have escalated. In a paper I published on India's China policy in June 2018, I concluded with the thought that India was 'faced with the possibility of more Doklams around the corner' – this after the 73-day stand-off between the two militaries near the trijunction of India, China, and Bhutan in 2017.[3] The Ladakh crisis of 2020 was much more than a Doklam, but the prediction was correct in so far as it suggested that relations were increasingly brittle and prone to crisis. The 2020 confrontation may be resolved more or less peacefully, but it is a good bet that there will be more Ladakhs.

India Versus China makes four broad arguments. First, while India and China at various times looked up to each other until about the fifteenth century, their modern perceptions of each other, from the late nineteenth century onward, have been largely negative including during the Covid-19 pandemic. The influence of colonial thought on their mutual perceptions but also ignorance and racism on both sides have produced feelings of disdain and disrespect. When I say Indian and Chinese perceptions, I refer largely to elite perceptions. How ordinary Indians and Chinese regard each other is mostly unknown, though they are probably far more occupied with the challenges of everyday life, even survival, than they are worried about trans-Himalayan realities. Elite perceptions matter, and it is vital that we understand them.

Secondly, differences over perimeters – the borderlands and Tibet – are at the heart of much of the India–China conflict. Some writers blame India and others China for the original quarrel. I suggest that Delhi's and Beijing's handling of the border problem between 1949 and 1962 suffered from mirror-image difficulties – hesitations in engaging on the issue; contradictions and inconsistencies when they engaged, leading to suspicions on both sides; and an inability to accept the other's basic principle on colonial boundaries (India thought colonially inherited boundaries were legitimate and China thought they were not). Differences over the border were compounded by doubts about the other's commitments on Tibet. India concluded that China had reneged on its commitments on Tibet's autonomy, and China concluded that India wanted to undo Tibet's post-1950 status. Each side also thought the other to be aggressive rather than defensive militarily. Differences over the border, Tibet, and military moves in the Himalaya continue to complicate relations.

Thirdly, if India and China had been partners internationally, they would havc had a history of strategic collaboration to draw on, to balance against their negative perceptions of each other and their conflicts in the perimeters. They would have been better placed also to reassure each other when disagreements occurred. Instead, in seventy years of engagement, they have almost always been on opposite sides of world politics. They have never been partners against a common foe, though their interests sometimes ran parallel, particularly in resisting American hegemony. The moments of diplomatic convergence were ephemeral, and the two leaderships, civilian and military, have lacked robust structures of trust and communication. This pattern looks set to continue.

Finally, since the early 1980s, India has fallen increasingly behind China in terms of economic, military, and soft power. While the economic power-gap is enormous and insurmountable in the foreseeable future, the military power-gap, while real, is tempered by geography: the intervening mountains and oceanic distances between India and China mean that war and the use of force will at best be limited. India can defend against an attack on its land borders. China lacks sufficient naval power projection to overcome India's natural advantages in the Indian Ocean. The military balance is not static though. If India does not galvanize its indigenous arms industry and if China forges even further ahead in the development of key emerging technologies, the current military balance will turn more decisively against India. As for soft power, China bests India. Overall, on a rough estimate, China may be seven times as powerful as India in terms of comprehensive national power.

Negative mutual perceptions, differences over perimeters, rival partnerships, and the power asymmetry affect each other. The book presents these four drivers of conflict as orthogonal – at right angles to each other, as unrelated – but as suggested above they are intertwined. To show how the four constantly interweave would be a massive task, well beyond the scope of what is intended to be a relatively succinct and accessible account of the relationship between India and China. The reality though is that in combination the four magnify each other and make the conflict even more complex and enduring. My sense is that mutual perceptions and the power asymmetry may be the most serious problems between the two countries. If India and China looked at each more respectfully and if they were on par in terms of capabilities, the border quarrel would probably have been resolved by now. Being in rival partnerships might not have mattered all that much. This is hard to prove of course; it is just an intuition.

It is important to say a few more words on what this book is and what it is not. As noted above, it is about four key drivers of conflict between the two Asian giants. It is not a book about the latest developments in India–China relations, in particular the events in Ladakh since April–May 2020. We are too close to those developments. Also, while I argue that India must reduce the power-gap with China if the two countries are to move to a more accommodative stance, the book does not say much else about how they should resolve their deep and growing differences. Nor is it a book that assigns blame. Holding leaders, processes, and entire societies responsible for actions and inactions is justified, even necessary, and there are writings that do so – some very partisan, others more measured and careful. This book tries to explain how India and China got to be so fractious despite their attempts at cooperation. In doing so it is probably clear enough where I attach blame even if I do not raise a red flag.

Finally, this is a work of synthesis which draws on existing scholarship. I am particularly grateful to five authors: Ranjit Singh Kalha, John Garver, Srinath Raghavan, Tansen Sen, and Reshma Patil. Anyone writing on the India–China border will profit, as I did massively, from Kalha's encyclopedic *India-China Boundary Issues: Quest for Settlement*. John Garver's massive volume, *Protracted Contest: Sino-Indian Rivalry in the Twentieth Century*, is masterful in its measured, even-handed analysis. His article 'China's Decision for War with India in 1962', published in 2006, is invaluable as a source on Chinese decision-making. Srinath Raghavan's two chapters on the India–China conflict in his *War and Peace in Modern India: A Strategic History of the Nehru Years* are fluent, rich accounts, and informed the chapter on perimeters. If it is possible to write a single volume on the history of India–China relations from the earliest times to the present, Tansen Sen's *India, China, and the World: A Connected History* has set the standard. It was never far from my reach. So also, on contemporary Chinese views of India and Indians, Reshma Patil's perceptive and often wry *Strangers Across the Border: Indian Encounters in Boomtown China* is indispensable. Time and again, I turned to these works for facts, stories, and interpretation, and I have done my best to acknowledge them. They of course bear no responsibility for how I deployed their information and insights.

1

Perceptions: From Regard to Disdain

A place to begin thinking about why India and China are not friends is their perceptions of each other. For a brief moment in the mid-1950s, the two countries seemed to celebrate each other in the slogan 'Hindi-Chini bhai bhai'. Since then, the tone has been more sober, at the best of times. In the worst of times, it has been harsh. The Himalaya limited India–China interactions, especially between the centres of political, social, and economic power, but Buddhism and trade above all brought them into contact. From the fourth to the eleventh centuries CE, it is fair to say that China looked to India culturally as a result of the spread of Buddhism. From the eleventh century CE to about the fifteenth century CE, the relationship was reversed: parts of India paid material and political tribute to the Chinese court. During the colonial period, their perceptions were filtered through the views of the imperial powers and the experience of subjugation, and in the late nineteenth century Chinese perceptions of India turned negative. India's perceptions of China also turned negative, most bitterly after 1962. Contemporary images of each other in many walks of life, in the media, in popular culture, and in surveys are mixed, but negative, even racist perceptions abound. In addition, the two societies hold to a set of broad frameworks within which they cast themselves and their place in world history. These worldviews are not explicitly about India–China relations, but they have implications for how they perceive each other.

Pre-Modern Perceptions

Before the nineteenth century, India and China had limited contact but had respectful views of each other. The high point of contact was when Buddhism thrived in China. This was followed by a period of some Indian kingdoms paying tribute to the Chinese court: the relationship was reversed, and Indians looked up to China. With the coming of the European colonial powers to India, the relationship between the two societies came increasingly to be mediated through imperialism, and from it developed a Chinese attitude of disdain towards India.

China Looks Up to Buddhist India

While Buddhism first came to China from Central Asia and Iran, not directly from India, the golden period of India–China interactions resulted from Chinese Buddhist pilgrimages to northern India, starting in the fourth century CE and extending up to about the eleventh century CE. The flow of influence was not all one way. Chinese Buddhist ideas and practices flowed back to the land of the Buddha, but it is fair to say that India was looked on as the *Madhyadesha* or Middle Kingdom.

The origins of the relationship

As every Indian schoolchild learns, the Chinese Buddhist monks Faxian and then Xuanzang came to India in the fifth century and seventh century, respectively. They are the best-known chroniclers among Chinese visitors, but hundreds of other Chinese monks and pilgrims came to India to venerate and to learn. The great era of Chinese pilgrimage came to an end in about the eighth century, though Chinese inscriptions discovered at Bodhgaya are dated as late as the eleventh century.[1] When Central Asia passed out of the hands of the Chinese, making travel difficult, and possibly also as a result of the decline of Buddhism in India, the pilgrimages ended.

However, in the meantime, Indian monks were invited or on their own decided to go to China. Indian missionaries probably arrived there in the first century CE. The most famous early Indian missionary – his father at any rate was of Indian descent, his mother was Central Asian – was Kumarajiva, who was taken prisoner to China from his home in Central Asia in 401 CE. Hundreds of Indian Buddhist scholars went to China carrying learning and texts not available there. Chinese records show that Kashmiri Buddhists played an important role, but other parts of India sent monks as well, sometimes by the sea route. The monks not only taught and preached, they also helped in the massive project of translating the texts they took with them. In the fifth century, Nalanda, the great ancient seat of learning, had opened its doors. By the seventh century, it was a major centre for Chinese scholars. The last Indian monks, according to Chinese records, came to China in 1036, by which time Buddhism in India was deeply in recession.[2]

Chinese responses to Buddhism

Contrary to the popular view in India, it was not all one way. Chinese Buddhism flourished and sometimes came back to influence Indian thought. Tansen Sen notes that 'localized beliefs evolved to such an extent that they were transmitted back to India'. He gives the example of the cult of Mount Wutai in China's Shaanxi province that by the sixth century was attracting Indian monks.[3] The Cinacara ('practice of China') cult had Indian followers. Some Taoist influences may have come to India from Buddhist monks returning from China. Xuanzang apparently worked on a Sanskrit translation of the *Dao de jing* in the Tang period for the edification of an Assamese king.[4] Chinese scholarship was not just religious and philosophical. Xuanzang's accounts of his India days include a detailed description of the rule of Harshavardhana of Kanauj. Indeed, along with the writings of Bana, it is one of the key sources on those times.

The introduction of Buddhism in China had a great impact on Chinese society, but it was not all friendly and reverential. In his survey of China–India interactions from ancient times to 1939, Rudolf Wagner writes: 'The massive Chinese absorption . . . of basic Buddhist ideas and concepts, social institutions, and ritual practices was not to be accommodated within the existing system.'[5] Inevitably, there was resistance and repugnance in China. For one thing, Buddhism 'assigned it [China] a place as a "land at margin"'. India was the original (or co-equal) Madhyadesha or *Zhongguo* ('Middle Kingdom'). For China, this was difficult to accept. Buddhism, with its view of 'life as suffering', also went against 'a culture devoted to long life and prosperity'. China before Buddhism emphasized that young people should be 'productive, take care of their elders, and have children in order to continue the ancestor cult'. The new religion encouraged an existence marked by donations, a monastic life, and celibacy.[6] Chinese responses included creating a 'Buddhist narrative for China' or 'sidelining Buddhism' by older faiths and practices.[7] Daoism launched a strong attack, even arguing that its founder, Laozi, was the Buddha. In 842 CE, Emperor Wuzong declared Daoism as a true

Chinese religion and 'proceeded to a systematic suppression and expropriation' of all 'foreign' religions. As the state came to control religion, Buddhism became a Chinese faith alongside Daoism and Confucianism.[8] That Buddhism had more or less collapsed in India by this time only helped in the Sinification of the religion: the land of its origin had ceased to be an inspiration.

India Looks Up to Imperial China

From here on, for seven hundred years from the ninth to the sixteenth century, it was trade, especially maritime trade, that came to mark India–China interchange: the material came to replace the spiritual. China's growing naval reach peaked in the voyages of Zheng He to Asia and Africa from 1405 to 1433, and parts of India became tributaries or felt the sharp end of Chinese power.

Towards a new relationship

The asymmetry that marked cultural relations was supplanted by a perhaps more reciprocal relationship in the exchange of goods – 'perhaps' because we have no records of the volume of trade. Tansen Sen in his wonderful synoptic history of India–China relations from ancient to modern times presents a vivid picture of the material economy that replaced the spiritual economy. After the tenth century, an array of goods, beyond Buddhist relics and paraphernalia, went from India to China: exotic and other animals (including horses from Arabia), plants and plant products, spices and foods, drugs and herbs, precious and semi-precious stones, gold and silver objects, pearls, ivory products, incense, textiles especially cotton, and even slaves. In return, Chinese rulers sent silk and, in one case, slaves, musk, robes, jewels, quivers, and swords. They also granted traders the right to sell their wares in

China and offered tax exemptions. Chinese traders sold silk and other textiles, spices, and porcelain.[9]

Sen reminds us that Sanskrit texts of the pre-Buddhist period had contained references to products that are suffixed by the word 'cina' including *cinani* (peaches), *cinasi* (hides), *cinarajaputra* (pears), and *cinaka* (camphor) and of course *cinamsuka* or *cinapatta* (silk). However, this did not imply that the two societies knew a great deal about each other: most of the products that came from China were through intermediaries in Central Asia.[10] During the period of intense spiritual encounter, Buddhist paraphernalia were the mainstay of material flows. Later, diplomatic gifts were part of the flow. Later still, tributes to China from maritime polities in the Indic region including Ceylon dominated material exchange.

Indian tributes to China

These tributes did not necessarily signify subordination, though Song China and Yuan China under Kublai Khan tried to control maritime trade in the Indian Ocean – and Kublai Khan threatened and then sent punitive missions.[11] More famously, Admiral Zheng He, in the early fifteenth century, led seven expeditions into the Indian Ocean region including to the Malabar coast and Bengal.[12] Some contemporary Chinese interpretations portray Zheng He's voyages as a benevolent exercise in which a hegemonic navy controlled piracy, managed local conflicts from Southeast Asia through South Asia to the Gulf and east coast of Africa, and laid the basis for a cosmopolitan trading environment which worked to everyone's benefit. In other words, China delivered what economists call a 'public good'. More accurately, though, Zheng He was sent to enlarge tributary relations, to expand China's imperial and private trade, and bring home exotica of various kinds. Often enough, his navy intervened in local affairs, siding with one ruler against a rival, and using the threat if not actual use of force to settle the matter – including in parts of Kerala and Bengal. This was Chinese imperialism, plain and simple. As Sen notes, 'many of the features of the Zheng He expeditions were similar to the activities of the European colonial powers subsequently'.[13]

By the early fifteenth century, interactions between India and China had declined. This was in part due to the Song dynasty's decision, at the height of its maritime imperialism, to discourage the voyages of Zheng He and other Chinese naval expeditions. Tribute to China continued sporadically, mostly from the South China Sea area and from parts of India and Sri Lanka through intermediaries in Southeast Asia. With the disappearance of Chinese maritime control, the Portuguese, the Dutch, and the British in turn adopted and adapted Zheng Ho's network and maritime order. Chinese imperialism was replaced by European imperialism.

From the fourth to the end of the ninth century, with the spread of Buddhism, China – or at least some Chinese – had looked to India as a spiritual centre. From about the eleventh to the early fifteenth century, Chinese reverence for India was replaced by Indian reverence for China in the form of tributes from various Indian kingdoms. The next four hundred years saw the Portuguese, Dutch, and British insert themselves into the relationship. India and China no longer dealt with each other in the direct if limited sense that had marked the period from the fourth to the fifteenth century. Neither side looked up to the other or looked down at the other – at least until the nineteenth century when British interventions in China led to Chinese resentment and disdain towards India and Indians.

Perceptions in the Nineteenth and Early Twentieth Centuries

The commodities trade between India and China expanded and the nature of relations between the two changed during the colonial period. The Dutch linked India and China through the opium trade. They took opium from production centres in Patna and Malwa to China. From its original medicinal and aphrodisiacal uses, it became a recreational drug.[14] The opium trade would go on to have enormous consequences for India–China interactions over the next three hundred years or so. Under the British, Indian cotton and opium were increasingly traded for Chinese tea, silk, and sugar ('chini' or crystalline white sugar from China, as against the original dark sugar made in India). A financial system too sprang up, of credit bills, loans, and insurance. In addition, India–China economic interactions mediated by the British led to Indians working in China and the establishment of a Chinese community in India, around Calcutta mostly. As Chinese intellectuals reacted to the intrusions of the Western powers, they turned their attention to British rule in India, its antecedents and consequences. The interactions with Indians in China and the conclusions they drew about India were often negative.

Chinese Perceptions of India and Indians

Two sets of negative perceptions of India and Indians were formed as the two societies were interlinked by British rule. The first came out of Chinese encounters with Indians in China. The second grew out of Chinese intellectuals reflecting on India under British rule.

Perceptions of Indians in China

After the Opium Wars (1839–42 between China and Britain, and 1856–60 between China, Britain, and France), the Indian community in China grew substantially. Indians had largely lived in Guangzhou, Tibet, and Xinjiang, but after the wars, they spread out to Hong Kong and Shanghai as well. They were largely traders but also Sikh policemen and watchmen.[15] Their presence led to an increase in disputes and resentments. Parsi traders violated an agreement with Chinese authorities not to sell opium in 1839. They also helped finance the Opium Wars and loaned out ships to the British. In Xinjiang, Indians were involved in various commercial and fiscal disputes. In Shanghai, Sikh policemen and watchmen developed a reputation for being fierce and violent. They and other Indians attracted various racist descriptions referencing their appearance and colour. Indian soldiers under the British fought in the Opium Wars and helped suppress the Taiping and Boxer rebellions. They too attracted all kinds of invidious names and descriptions.[16]

Chinese intellectuals view India

This disdain was to become evident, too, at the level of China's intellectuals and its political elite in the late nineteenth century. The source materials for their knowledge of India came largely from European and Japanese writers (the latter's views often drew on European writings). Wagner in his survey of Chinese attitudes concludes: 'The trope of the unchanging Indian national character that was unable and unwilling to adapt to changing circumstances was already well established in the West by this time [i.e., the early nineteenth century] and became firmly established in the Chinese discussion.'[17] Chinese writers and thinkers got a picture of a timeless rural population, 'divided into castes, addicted to ascetic superstition, religious suicide, and abstruse philosophy'.[18] Indians were feudal and disunited, unable to stand up to foreign invaders, and willing to serve anyone who ruled. Indian ('Hindu') servility came from a history of living under 'despotic' rule without rights and without regard for truth and honesty. This was an image that the British would propagate about China as well: the rulers of these Asian societies in effect had deserved to lose control of their territories to outsiders because they had failed to look after the security and welfare of their subjects.

By the 1890s, Wagner shows, the Chinese were getting 'a steady stream of mostly commercial and political news about India'. After China was defeated by Japan in the Sino-Japanese war, the British missionary journalist Timothy Richard wrote about the benefits of crown rule in India (when it supplanted the East India Company) – he had been asked to submit to the Chinese imperial government ideas about governance reforms. Robert MacKenzie's *The Nineteenth Century*, which reflected similarly on British rule in India, was made compulsory reading for Chinese officials in 1898.[19] Emerging Chinese intellectuals such as Kang Youwei and Liang Qichao, fearful that a backward China would be partitioned after it was defeated by Japan, set up reform newspapers and became loud and critical voices for change.

Wagner's fascinating study of the period shows that the young reformers urged China to emulate Japan, Russia, and Germany in their reform process and not to go the way of societies like India. At the heart of their view was that internal weakness more than imperialism was the cause of Indian national decay. For Liang, China could avoid the fate of India (and others) because the 'yellow' races were as talented as the 'white' – by implication this was not the case with the other races. Liang and others also had access to Japanese writings about India. These writings, too, blamed India's internal weakness, not imperialism, for its decline and colonization.[20] A group of Chinese students in Japan ran a series of articles on India in 1903, titled 'The Causes for the Demise of India'. Drawing on Japanese sources, the articles produced a damning picture of India. The tone of the writing is by turns contemptuous, exasperated, and melancholy:

> [T]he word 'India' is in fact nothing but a name from history. Aya! Their land is all smashed to pieces . . . this brown race will be forever enslaved . . . Looking at China today, it is like India in the past . . . As a matter of principle, it were the Indians who brought about the demise of India . . . The character of the race is chaotic, their languages topsy turvy, their religions all separate from each other . . . there is no unified spirit, no patriotic thinking, the elites are drowning themselves in song and dance, and know nothing of great purpose . . . Alas, India is lost![21]

For some in China, among the causes of India's decline was Buddhism, with its metaphysical abstractions and non-violence. In 1937, Hu Shi, a Kuomintang ambassador to the US, in a speech at Harvard University's 300th anniversary, attributed China's lack of resistance to the Japanese to the 'Indianization of China' which had seeped into its culture thanks to Buddhism. As Wagner points out, he made these remarks even as the Kuomintang was trying to cultivate Indian nationalist support against the Japanese invasion.[22]

Wagner shows that news and analysis of India during this period was extensive. Between 1872 and 1938, *Shenbao*, a leading Chinese-language newspaper, published 1629 news and lead articles on India. A number of them were from Reuters, the British news agency. This amounted to an average of 24 per year or 2 per month. From 1921 to 1938, the average was 71 per year or nearly 6 articles per month. The Chinese-language periodical press, in addition, featured 9363 articles with the word 'India' in it. Initially, the reform press of Liang Qichao and Kang Youwei dominated India-related publishing. But after 1908, the more commercial press featured India materials. The average per year went up to 120 'dedicated articles' on India in the period until 1928 and then 540 articles per year thereafter.[23] This is quite extraordinary coverage and has probably never been repeated. Not all the coverage and commentary was negative: much of it may simply have been factual news of the day. Yet Wagner concludes, 'The increasingly rich and diverse knowledge about India available in China . . . was not able to undo the basic narrative of India being a country for the demise of which its own people were responsible . . . It had become a trope already by 1900, and it was revived time and again ever since.'[24]

It was in this context that Rabindranath Tagore visited China in 1924 after a trip to Japan. He was already famous for being the first Asian to get a Nobel Prize (in Literature) and arrived in China with his brand of non-violent, 'spiritual cosmopolitanism'. His reception was mixed. He had his admirers among intellectuals, artists, and students, but as in Japan, he came under criticism. The trip left him somewhat bitter and must be counted a failure if the intent was to propagate a sense of cosmopolitanism and non-violent emancipation.

Whatever Tagore's intent, he was roundly denounced and ridiculed, particularly by leftist/communist revolutionaries, old and young, including former admirers and translators of his work. He was seen as extolling traditional, feudal Asia and romanticizing the Orient against the material, industrial Occident. His critics argued that China had to emulate the West in respect of science and reason, not fall back into tradition and spiritualism. Ramachandra Guha quotes the Chinese scholar Wu Chih-hui's scathing and cruel judgement: 'Mr Tagore . . . a petrified fossil of India's national past, had retreated into the tearful eyes and dripping noses of the slave people of a conquered country, seeking happiness in a future life, squeaking like the hub of a wagon wheel that needs oil'. Guha notes that in a poll of over a thousand students at Peking University in 1923–24, over 700 students wanted revolution in China. Nearly half admired Soviet Russia over the US. And in a list of international leaders that they most respected, Lenin got the most votes by far (227), with Tagore getting a mere 17 votes and Gandhi receiving only 9.[25]

Indian Perceptions of China and the Chinese

What about Indian attitudes towards China? The short answer is that we have no detailed picture of their perceptions of the Chinese in the nineteenth and early twentieth centuries. On the other hand, we do have some evidence relating to the Chinese communities in India and of elite Indian views of China.

The Chinese in India

We know much less about Chinese communities in India than we do about Indian communities in China. In 1871–72, there were about 1100 Chinese in Calcutta and Bombay. By the Second World War, though, the numbers had grown to 15,000.[26] The largest number were in Bengal, around Calcutta, and in parts of Assam. The first immigrant came to Bengal as early as 1778. He brought tea and got a land grant in return for setting up a sugar mill. He then imported Chinese labour. Added to this were 'runaway sailors and indentured servants'.[27] By the early nineteenth century, the Chinese had built community life in a residential area in Calcutta's Bowbazar. The immigrants were tradespeople – 'shoemakers, opium-sellers, carpenters, cabinet makers, and lard manufacturers'. By the end of the nineteenth century, their numbers had been fortified by new immigrants, and they established new businesses, associations, temples, and schools. In addition to carpentry and shoemaking, they set up tailor shops, tanneries, restaurants, tea stalls, dental clinics, pharmacies, grocery stores, and they sold silk and paper flowers.[28]

This suggests that Chinese immigrants led a reasonably productive and peaceful life in India. However, it was not all sweetness and light between the immigrants and host communities in Calcutta, Darjeeling, Kalimpong, and Assam. A nineteenth-century British official recorded that sections of the Chinese hated the local population 'in all intensity of Chinese hatred'. Thc Chinese apparently felt that they depended on British protection and that the colonials were 'better paymasters than the local Bengalis'. In his account of the community, Sen notes 'the preference to work for the British in India continued to be expressed by Chinese migrants up through Indian independence . . . indicating the uncomfortable existence of the ethnic Chinese among the Indians'. This would come back to haunt them in the late 1950s and early 1960s when India–China tensions sharpened.[29] Particularly from 1959, sections of the Chinese were spied on and eventually had to register with the police. Anyone who failed to do so lived under threat of deportation. According to the Chinese scholar Xing Zhang, bank accounts were 'confiscated', remittances to China halted, and 'Chinese shops were pillaged by mobs and forced to paste words against the Chinese government on their doors'. Not everyone was under suspicion or pressure. Xing tells us that some 'continued to flourish, open new businesses, and even came out in support of the Indian government' and donated to the National Defence Fund.[30] During the war of 1962, matters worsened, though, when many in the Chinese community were interned in camps and dispersed to places like Deoli in faraway

Rajasthan. In some cases, they were deported to China even if they were born and raised in India and were dispossessed of their properties without compensation. The travails of the Chinese community have been poignantly fictionalized in the Assamese writer Rita Chowdhury's *Chinatown Days.* Reflecting on the book, she writes: 'Those who were young during that turbulent time had all grown old now. The rest of them, deeply embittered by the dreadful memories of the time and its insufferable aftermath, migrated to different parts of the world . . . The agony that had maimed their psyche forever still ran deep in their spirits . . . What moved me the most was their unflinching love for Makum – the place of their birth [in Assam] . . .'[31]

Elite views of China

We will get a flavour of Indian elite perspectives on China and the Chinese when we deal with Indian worldviews later in the chapter. Suffice to say here that among the moderate-liberal nationalists of the nineteenth and early twentieth centuries, China may well have appeared in the way that the British saw it: like India, it was big but brittle, internally divided and weak, and governed by aloof despots. Among the emerging Indian nationalists including Mahatma Gandhi, Jawaharlal Nehru, and Subhas Chandra Bose, China was a fellow Asian victim of imperialism trying to oust the European powers and reform its own society – much as India was trying to do. It was also a potential partner in the project of Asian unity, along with Japan (at least until Japanese militarism reared its head) – this was most famously Tagore's message but is evident in Gandhi, Nehru, and Bose. Among Indian socialists and communists, China's growing revolutionary spirit was an example and inspiration, its society to be emulated and actively helped during a time of massive social and political transformation.

This is by no means a full picture of Indian attitudes to China and the Chinese during the nineteenth and early twentieth centuries – that would be another book. In any case, as things stand, Chinese attitudes towards India and Indians are better documented. On Indian attitudes, there has been much less research, though historians such as Sen have written about Tagore, his pan-Asianism, and his efforts at India–China artistic and intellectual collaboration at Cheena Bhavan.[32] Rahul Sagar's *Ideas of India*, a massive online archiving of Indian writings in English from 1825 to 1950, suggests that China did feature fairly extensively – unfortunately, I became aware of this trove too late to access its content.[33] On the whole, it is safe to say that the views of key Indian nationalist leaders and personalities were positive if not admiring of China's classical culture but also of its modernizing impulses, including its resistance to Western and Japanese imperialism.

Perceptions in More Contemporary Times

How do Indians and Chinese see each other in more recent times? The short answer is not very positively. Since 1962, Indian admiration and affinity for China has been replaced by a sneaking/fearful admiration of its rise to power mixed with a sense of betrayal/humiliation as a result of the war. In China, the negative views of India have continued: nineteenth-century disdain combined with a degree of indifference. The Chinese increasingly see their country as a great power with no peer except the US, and Americans are their main reference point. This mutual alienation between Indians and Chinese somewhat overstates feelings on both sides. There are those who see something to like and engage in the other, and there is curiosity, even respect. Yet, the negative views of each other's society and at the same time ignorance of each other is palpable.

How can we access these views? First we turn to the insights of three Indian writers who lived and travelled in China beginning in the early 1980s (there do not seem to be equivalent writings by Chinese travellers except for Hong Mei's *The Farther I Walk, the Closer I Get to Me*, which is only available in Mandarin). Beyond these writings, two academic studies of Indian and Chinese attitudes in the mainstream and social media reveal the extent of racist and jingoistic views, particularly in China. A third source is survey and polling data of Indian attitudes which depict the extent of fear and mistrust towards China, especially after the Doklam confrontation in 2017. Finally, Indian dispositions towards the ethnic Chinese in India and towards China in the wake of Covid-19 show that racism and jingoism are alive and well south of the Himalaya too.

Chinese Perceptions of India: Through Indian Eyes

We can begin to get a sense of more contemporary Chinese views of India through three writers who spent time in China – Vikram Seth, the Indian novelist and poet, Anurag Vishwanath, an Indian scholar who travelled widely in the country as part of her doctoral and postdoctoral studies, and, Reshma Patil, an Indian journalist who reported mostly from the big Chinese cities.

'From Heaven Lake'

In 1981, Vikram Seth, the writer but at the time a doctoral student from Stanford University studying in China, hitchhiked from Xinjiang to Tibet on his way home to India. He records his arduous journey and his encounters with ordinary Chinese people along the way in a candid, affectionate book, *From Heaven Lake: Travels Through Xinjiang and Tibet*.[34] It is a revealing account: the Chinese clap to Bollywood songs, are curious about India, soothe Seth over the 1962 war, and display a cheery ignorance about Indian society. In Turfan, Xinjiang, he is asked to sing an Indian song in front of a small audience. He sings the theme-song from the classic Bollywood film *Awara* and finds that the local musicians on stage immediately play the instrumental accompaniment to the song. Seth notes this is to have a happy consequence the next day when he applies for official permission for his trip to Tibet. Someone who was in the audience the previous evening is present during his application for the enabling permit. They get talking about *Awara* while the official considers the application. The local official knows Bollywood films and is drawn into the discussion, and Seth soon gets his permit.[35]

On a train ride, Seth is engaged in innocent and friendly conversations by curious fellow passengers. He is asked forthrightly about his marital status, a family photograph is examined, and questions are asked about his father's kurta and his mother's bindi. The 1962 war, he is told, was 'an unfortunate incident, the fault of governments, not of peoples, and anyway a very short period of hostility when looked at in the perspective of such a long friendship'. Discussion turns amiably to Raj Kapoor, Seth's job prospects, and India's birth control programme.[36] In Liuyuan, he tries to get a truck ride for the next stage of his journey. A rather comical exchange with a truck driver ensues, with the driver trying to guess Seth's nationality: Mexican, Sri Lankan, Pakistani, Nepalese, Iranian, Russian? He is playfully steered to the right answer. The driver clearly has no picture in his mind of the physical appearance of an Indian – or at least a north Indian.

Seth also describes an evening spent with a local official who had served in the army in the 1962 war. You can almost see the rueful headshaking of the man as he recounts: 'A strange task [being a border soldier in 1962]. You couldn't tell where the border was. One day it was here, another day there. We retreated, they [the Indians] occupied, and *vice versa*. We just did what we were told. I'm glad things have improved in our relations.'[37]

On the evening before India's annual Independence Day celebrations, Seth reflects on the two countries. It is 1981, China's extraordinary economic reforms and rise have not yet occurred, yet there is already much to be admired in China's development story: 'One overwhelming fact is that the Chinese have a better system of social care and of distribution than we do. Their aged do not starve. Their children are basically healthy. By and large, the people are well clothed'. Would it be better to be born Indian or Chinese, Seth asks himself? If he were among the lucky two-thirds on top of Indian society, he would choose India, 'But if I were born to the inhuman, dehumanising misery in which the poorest third of our [Indian] people live, to the squalor and despair and debility that is their life, my answer would not be the same.'[38] India has its assets – given the climate, Indians need less, they have more arable land and sunshine and (potentially) irrigation – and the country is democratic. Yet, it must be granted that the average Chinese is better off.[39]

What, then, of mutual feeling between the two countries? Seth concludes his book rather gloomily. Ignorance and lack of a shared history typify their relationship: 'friendship rests on understanding; and the two countries, despite their contiguity, have had almost no contact in the course of history . . . the heartlands of the two great culture zones have been almost untouched by each other . . . Unfortunately, I think this will continue . . . The fact that they are both part of the same landmass means nothing. There is no such thing as an Asian ethos or mode of thinking . . . The best that can be hoped for . . . is a respectful patience on either side'.[40]

'Finding India in China'

Two decades later, the Indian scholar Anurag Vishwanath travelled to the remotest corners of China as part of her doctoral research on Chinese reforms and poverty alleviation. Based on fifteen years of travels, she penned an engaging book of encounters that she intriguingly titled *Finding India in China: Travels to the Lesser Known*.[41] In fact, though there are moments in China that evoke a memory of India, the book reveals the opposite: China and India seem economically, socially, and culturally miles apart. Mostly the book is about China and the matter-of-fact interactions she has with Chinese people in remote parts of the country. Yet here and there the narrative provides glimpses of not-so-positive views of India and Indians.

Among the places Vishwanath visited was Gansu province, widely regarded in China as one of its poorest – at least by Chinese standards. In a revealing aside, Vishwanath reflects on the province and Chinese attitudes to India: 'Gansu is generally considered *luan* – an oft-used Chinese word which narrowly means "chaotic" . . . Of course, it does not help that the average Chinese categorises India as *luan*, too – disordered, chaotic and not given to easy navigation.'[42] Vishwanath describes an encounter with a drunken local official who suddenly asks her, 'Are all Indians as black (dark skinned) as you?' She and the other Chinese at her table try to quell the offensive official 'but then there was no stopping his running tongue as he slid into a nasty diatribe on India as a place of filth and poverty'.[43] In *vino veritas* – in wine, truth? Probably not quite. Vishwanath's encounter is unusual – Indians in China are unlikely to experience something as nakedly racist and derogatory. Yet the episode reveals an element of Chinese attitudes towards India: a *luan* place inhabited by dark-skinned people.

Later in the book, Vishwanath recounts more charming encounters. Among them is one in Inner Mongolia, in the town of Hohhot, with Professor Fun Wen, 'a die-hard fan of Rabindranath Tagore' who emotionally recites Tagore all morning long for her. She later dines with Fun Wen, a sociologist working on India, and the local Party Secretary, a 'dashing' man, and no mere party apparatchik. The functionary is knowledgeable about India and 'effortlessly' turns the conversation to Rahul Gandhi, among other topics.[44] These Chinese are not racist. They are admirers of Indian culture, or they are cool-headed interlocutors interested in India's modern development.

'Strangers Across the Border'

This duality is not uniquely Chinese. Every society harbours ambivalences about other societies. Reshma Patil, the *Hindustan Times* correspondent in China from 2008 to 2011, renders both the denigrators and admirers of India in her candid, perceptive book *Strangers Across the Border: Indian Encounters in Boomtown China*.[45] More than Seth in the 1980s or Vishwanath in the 'lesser known' in the 2000s, Patil deals with urban, developed China and Sino-Indian encounters in more upmarket settings. Here, ironically, the ignorance of and disdain for India is far greater than knowledge of and admiration for things Indian.

Patil's account opens with an encounter over cricket – the Indian game 'accidentally invented by the British', in the sociologist Ashis Nandy's famous quip. She finds herself among budding young Chinese players at Tsinghua University in Beijing. Their ignorance about and lack of engagement with India are rather baffling but also amusing. No one at the field shows any interest in Indian cricket. They are blithely unaware that the Cricket World Cup is being played at the time. And they evince little interest in wanting to discuss China's relations with India. When, out of her cricket encounter, she invites two Chinese students to watch the film *Slumdog Millionaire*, she is taken aback. One professes ignorance of Mumbai and the other mortifyingly asks, 'Where is India? Is India near . . . Nepal?'[46]

Ignorance mixes with disdain for India. When a Chinese foreign policy expert at Shanghai's Fudan University asks his students if they like India, they respond with four opinions: 'India is dirty', 'India is poor', 'India invaded and seized China's land', and 'India hosts the Dalai Lama'.[47] Patil reports a similar encounter at Peking University. Here the students 'expressed no interest in the Indian economy growing second fastest after China's'. Nor are they interested in 'Indian tourism and Bollywood movies'. Instead Patil is peppered with questions on 'caste discrimination, poverty and Hindu–Muslim distrust'.[48] When talk turns to *Slumdog Millionaire*, a student asks, 'Is it true that people [throw] dead bodies in the river and bathe in it too? But it's so dirty!' Few see India's rise as 'peaceful'.[49]

When a Chinese broadcasting executive in Chongqing meets Patil and is pressed to reveal his real views of India, he mentions the poor transportation system and inequality. He adds: 'Children in India are naked. They piss on the streets'. And then somewhat soothingly (or perhaps snidely) he adds: 'but all Indians have inner peace'.[50] A Chinese interlocutor who has been to India tells Patil that before his trip his friends wondered if India was near Africa and had black people. The head of a Chinese consultancy company that produces a report on India shares the response of Chinese interviewees: 'They don't think India has good leadership. They don't think India is rising . . . India is not a Buddhist nation . . . India is another world. Another planet.'[51] In Nanjing, Patil finds that 'Chinese cultural interest in India is limited to movies and fashion' and little beyond.[52]

This popular level of ignorance–disdain is evident among people who should know better. Foreign Minister Wang Yi – the same urbane Wang Yi who negotiated the five-point troop disengagement agreement with External Affairs Minister Subrahmanyam Jaishankar in Moscow in September 2020 – characterizes India as a 'tribal democracy' whose future was uncertain. The future of Indian democracy might well be uncertain, but to describe it as tribal was clearly intended to demean and hurt.[53] Patil is repeatedly asked why the Indian media is so hostile to China and why the Indian government does not rein it in – as if the Chinese elite, which avidly follows the processes of American democracy, is unaware that governments in open societies may be both legally unable and morally unwilling to control journalists.

There is ignorance and disdain too of India's economic capabilities. At a meeting in Changzhou, in the midst of senior company executives from blue-chip Indian companies, a local trade official expresses surprise: 'Manufacturing in India? We have only heard of Indian IT [information technology].' As the meeting progresses, Patil notices that the local officials have left and other attendees are in 'deep sleep ... mouths agape, in danger of sliding to the carpet'. Patil notes that this is typical of meetings with visiting Indian business delegations: 'The snooze button was pressed in business seminars everywhere I shadowed India in China.'[54] Even Indian IT is largely unknown and ignored. In other areas where India has strengths – pharmaceuticals, agricultural products, and engineering goods – it has failed to make inroads into the Chinese market. Chinese buyers simply do not see Indian products as competitive.[55] Shockingly, in surveys conducted between 2000 and 2010, Chinese consumers identify the Indian economy at the bottom of a list of significant economies. While the US and Japan top the list, Patil notes that India comes in below North Korea and Pakistan. Clearly, this reflects China's close alliance-like relationship with the two countries. Yet the cognitive disconnect between the reality of the Indian economy and its significance in the perception of Chinese consumers is oceanic.[56]

Chinese dismissiveness extends to India's military and strategic importance. Throughout her stay in China, Patil asks if India is regarded as an enemy or a friend. The response usually consists of 'uncomfortable silences, blank stares, frowns and skyward gazes'. India apparently does not merit either category! Mention of the 1962 war does not excite much interest either. Here and there, particularly among the military or in the strategic community, there is a view that India needs to be taught a 'lesson' again, as in 1962.[57] A fairly widespread view is that its great power pretensions are just that – a mere 'figment of the imagination'.[58] A student engages Patil in conversation: 'your national day parades . . . in China we roll out impressive tanks and soldiers smartly holding guns . . . but your soldiers hold their rifles backward'. On a Chinese internet site, India's military modernization is described as 'loud thunder, tiny rain' and its forces on parade as looking like 'dancing clowns'.[59] The *Global Times*, the hard-line English-language newspaper, intones that 'India needs to consider whether or not it can afford the consequences of a potential confrontation with China'.[60] The newspaper will repeat the warning during the 2020 confrontation in Ladakh.

Patil's account of her China days does feature admirers of India – or at least of (some) Indians and things Indian. Tagore and Gandhi still attract Chinese interest and respect (Nehru does not). The Nobel laureate's works continue to be read: as late as 1985, a translation of his *Glimpses of Bengal* is sold out in a day in a Beijing bookstore. Patil's encounter with a Tagore scholar reveals that 'no other foreign poet has been translated, studied, forgotten and resurrected in China as much as Tagore'.[61] A section of Chinese dissidents seems to particularly admire Gandhi, seeing in his political practice a non-violent pathway to opposing authoritarianism. A sculpture of him in a Beijing park, near the posh Palm Springs high-rises, gradually attracts more visitors including local schoolchildren who 'bring flowers' on Tomb Sweeping Day (Qingming Festival) to mark the beginning of spring but also to pay respect to ancestors.[62] Gandhi is not a Chinese ancestor, but he draws veneration.

Indian culture – its classical and popular culture – has its admirers. Yoga flourishes in China. The indebtedness to Buddhism still exists. It is probably the basis for the Chinese saying, which allegedly even Mao pronounced on occasion, 'If a man lived a good life then he would be reborn in India'.[63] A student, contrary to most of his peers, says, 'I like India. It has many things we never see in China or any country, and I think Hinduism is a very tolerant religion.'[64] Sa Dingding, a popular musician who 'promotes Sino-Indian fusion', charmingly and sincerely tells Patil, 'I believe I was a soul in ancient India in my past life. Everything in India feels so familiar.'[65] Sa has studied Tibetan and Sanskrit texts, but eagerly follows Indian popular culture – its films and contemporary music and dance – as well. She informs Patil that the 'melody and rhythm of ancient Indian music has influenced Chinese music and Buddhist chants'.[66]

Patil's interlocutors on the whole though are more interested in present-day India. Here and there, Indian democracy, economic advances, and social policy win plaudits. A student declares, 'In future, China will be a democratic nation. In this aspect, China should learn from India's experience.'[67] The Anna Hazare campaign against corruption in India catches the eye: 'How come there's no one like Hazare in China? Look forward to that!'[68]

India's new economy also garners admirers. A vice president of the China Institute of International Studies sees progress over twenty–twenty-five years since a visit he made in 1990.[69] The resilience and capabilities of Indians impress. One interlocutor confesses, 'We in China often wonder why Indians look happy ... even those who are not so rich.'[70] Indians are complimented for being 'good at learning', Indian factory workers and vocational workers are thought to be better than Chinese counterparts, and the international success of Indian managers both puzzles and inspires.[71] Even Indian social welfare policies get a positive review. Ren, a Chinese journalist, returns from a trip to India and reports on the ease of buying railway tickets and subsidized medical care for migrants.[72]

Chinese and Indian Media Representations

Vishwanath, Seth, and Patil provide a set of vignettes and snapshots of Chinese attitudes towards India. Is there more systematic data? As it turns out, there is, in the form of some interesting studies of Chinese media representations of India and Indians and also some Indian views of China.

Chinese racism

In 2011, Simon Shen, a professor at the Hong Kong Education Institute, published a fascinating study of Chinese online comments on India and Indians.[73] He tabulated opinions posted in various chat forums and concluded that Chinese netizens have a fairly 'monolithic' view of India. In the case of Japan and the US, perceptions vary a fair bit, but when it comes to India there are two dominant, negative perceptions across liberals and nationalists: 'India as the "yellow sick man" and its depiction as a trouble-maker for Beijing'.[74]

Shen's research shows that racial ignorance and stereotypes run deep. For some Chinese, Indians are the same racial type as Africans because of their skin colour. Both are placed at the lowest rung of the racial rankings. Among the racist stereotypes is that Indians are dirty and smell of 'curry'. In some of the commentary, because Indians wash themselves with the left hand after defecating, their hands are described as disgusting. Words associated with India include 'the rubbish nation' and 'dirty, messy and bad'. The disdain extends to India's economy. Shen notes that virtually all commentary places India as part of the poor 'Third World' which cannot compare with China. India is full of slums and beggars, the distance with China is growing, and its economy will be left behind even by laggards such as Vietnam. Shen notes that Indian achievements in IT receive no credit. The overwhelming view is that 'India is crawling behind China, eating the Chinese dust'. Why so? The answer is its chaotic democracy and its religious and social attitudes.

India is also inferior militarily and strategically – yet capable of making trouble for China. Shen shows that Chinese netizens have little regard for India's military. India lost the 1962 war and its military performance since then has not impressed Chinese online opinion. India, in this view, would lose devastatingly to China if it chose to fight, its military being no better than China's in the Second World War.[75] Strategically, India is seen as being in league with Japan and the Western countries. Among the more nationalist-minded Chinese netizens, India is seen as a 'servile' follower, with little independence. At the same time, it is a troublemaker: it refuses to negotiate on the border and supports Tibetan separatism. Not surprisingly, a good proportion of the online posts think that a punitive war against India is inevitable.[76]

Jingoism . . . and Bollywood

A decade after his seminal study of online Chinese opinion, Shen teamed up with the Indian journalist Debasish Roy Chowdhary to untangle more recent attitudes towards India but also Indian views of China. Their study focused on mainstream and social media commentary on military issues, the Indian media's coverage of economic relations, and Chinese social media views of Bollywood films. At a broad level, they found that the Indian media's coverage of military affairs is 'marked by shrill jingoism and distrust reflecting the paranoia at the heart of India's elite perceptions'. The Chinese media is more sober, because it is under the watchful eye of the government, but it has increased its coverage of India and feeds off what it reads in the Indian media to produce its own brand of 'self-righteous anxieties'.[77]

Shen and Chowdhary's analysis of the Chinese social media during the Doklam crisis of 2017 gauges more popular opinion. Strikingly, most of the themes that Shen had identified in his 2011 study feature again. Indians are derogatorily referred to as 'ah san' (a racist term). India's actions at Doklam show that 'Indians are arrogant, inefficient, have been uncompromising on border negotiations, and filled with hatred and suspicion since the 1962 war'. Indian 'bullying' must be opposed – and more: 'While facing India, we should not just defend, but also make a strategic plan to dismember it.' India's moves in Doklam are evidently part of a China containment strategy in league with the US and Japan: 'Indians listen to whatever Captain America says.'[78]

On the other hand, Shen and Chowdhary suggest that Indian business reporting and Chinese social media on Bollywood films contain more positive messaging. In the second decade of the new millennium, as the economic relationship deepened, Indian newspapers increasingly featured positive stories about the benefits of trade and the theme of 'partnership' between the two countries. By the end of the decade, even this positive message had frayed, as the trade deficit was portrayed as another form of Chinese predation. In response, the *Global Times* dismissively urged Indians to complain less and 'work harder if you want to catch up'.[79] While there is little Indian engagement with Chinese movies – perhaps only martial arts movies with Jackie Chan draw an audience in India – Shen and Chowdhary show that Bollywood has a following in China. For example, the Indian film star Aamir Khan has achieved crossover appeal. His Weibo account has 1.25 million followers and garners largely positive posts. His hit film *3 Idiots* sold 11 million tickets. Despite some resentment over depictions of China and over India's growing soft power, a segment of Chinese viewers commended films such as *3 Idiots*, *Dangal*, *Secret Superstar*, *Bajrangi Bhaijan*, *Hindi Medium*, and *Hichki*. For some Chinese viewers, the films opened a window into Indian life, stimulated comparisons with aspects of China, and engagingly portrayed the contemporary social challenges facing both countries.[80]

Indian Perceptions of China and the Chinese

This chapter has so far dealt quite a lot with Chinese views of India. In fact, there is data, both quantitative and more impressionistic, of Indian views of China and the Chinese.

The China threat

The Pew surveys of Indian and Chinese opinion of other nations show just how consistently negative the two are about each other. Between 2014 and 2019, when Indians were asked if they had a favourable attitude towards China, on average only 27 per cent said yes. In 2018, the year after the Doklam confrontation, that number fell to 12 per cent. This was more negative than US views but less negative than Japanese views of China. Between 2014 and 2016 (there are no Pew surveys in China beyond 2016), when the Chinese were asked the same question about India, on average only 26 per cent said they had a favourable view. In 2019, 40 per cent of Indians also said that China was having a negative effect on their economic conditions, 61 per cent responded that China's growing economy was bad for India, and 73 per cent thought that China's growing military might was also negative for India. In 2017, 44 per cent of Indians polled thought that China's 'power and influence' was a major threat to India's security (though the terrorist threat of ISIS and climate change were ranked as greater).[81]

Indian racism and jingoism

While no one seems to have done a systematic study of Indian attitudes towards China and the Chinese, we know that racism and disdain in India exist in plenty. Chinese references to 'ah san' are matched by Indian references to 'chinky' among even elite and educated Indians. It would be unusual to see Chinese nationals on Indian streets, but Indians from the North-East who are thought to look Chinese are routinely referred to as 'chinky' or 'chichi chu chu' (and asked if they are 'Chinese'). The Indian badminton star Jwala Gutta, whose father is Indian and whose mother is Chinese, recounts how in online forums she has been called 'China ka maal' ('made in China'), 'half Chinese' (why not half Indian?), and 'Chinki', especially when she is trolled. With the Covid-19 outbreak, she was called 'half Corona'.[82] During the early days of the outbreak, Indians from the North-East living in other parts of the country were yelled at and sometimes shunned for being associated with 'corona'.[83]

Liu Chuen Chen is a journalist with the *Indian Express* newspaper. She is Indian Chinese, born and raised in India. Early in the Covid-19 outbreak, as a regular customer she rushes to 'a familiar store for some purchase'. A member of the staff accosts her to 'pass some unpleasant remark and walk away'. Though he is forced to apologize by the store owner, Liu decides never to return to the shop. Soon afterwards, the Ladakh crisis blows up. Liu worries that she will have to prove she is not a spy. She recounts that when she tweeted 'something in favour of Indian Chinese', she was 'cornered for being a "Chinese agent" with a few people tagging the National Investigative Agency'. She accepts that most of the time she and others of the Indian Chinese community are 'treated with respect', but in times of conflict with China 'we are looked upon with suspicion'. She knows no Mandarin and speaks Hindi and Bengali, but someone suggests to her that she should 'wear more of ethnic clothes and wear a bindi to "prove" my nationality'. She wonders: 'Am I not just one of the 1.35 billion Indians out there? Why must minorities change culture to be seen as citizens?'[84]

As Jwala Gutta and Liu Chuen Chen saw and heard during the Covid-19 outbreak, everyday racism towards people who look Chinese is never very far away on Indian streets. The pandemic reinforced prevailing Indian attitudes not just towards Chinese-looking people, though; it also deepened negative images of China. The Takshashila Institution's survey of China's role in the spread of the virus, conducted in April 2020, indicated that 67 per cent of the Indians surveyed blamed China for the pandemic. About 18 per cent thought that it was caused by Chinese biowarfare and 48 per cent thought that it was due to China's failure to stop the illegal trade in wildlife. The survey noted that Indians frequently used terms such as 'Chinese virus', 'Wuhan virus', and 'Made in China pandemic' to characterize the origins of the pandemic.

Nearly 53 per cent did not think it was racist to use these terms. Rather, it was vital to do so, to ensure that China did not 'escape responsibility'. Two-thirds of respondents said that Beijing's response to the pandemic was 'draconian and opaque', though a third felt that it had done a good job since the outbreak. Fifty-six per cent regarded Chinese assistance to other countries cynically, as China's way of 'projecting power', and 19 per cent thought it should be doing more to help internationally given that it was responsible for the crisis.[85] The Congress politician Manish Tewari used his Twitter account to suggest that the 'CoronaVirus is a bio-weapon that went rouge [sic – rogue] . . . It is an act of Terror.' Kunal Purohit wrote in the *South China Morning Post* that many Indian social media posts about Covid-19 had 'xenophobic and racist undertones, including remarks mocking the diets of Chinese people'. Fake videos of Chinese government actions circulated and 'images of homeless people on the streets of Shenzhen were passed off as being dead bodies on the streets of Wuhan'.[86]

In the tragicomedy that is so often India–China relations, the Indian media, on 17 November 2020, ran a story about a pre-print of a paper submitted to the respected medical journal *The Lancet*. Three researchers seemingly from China – all three have Chinese names but one of the authors is from a US university – suggested that the 'Indian subcontinent' and specifically India and Bangladesh may have originally incubated the coronavirus in the summer of 2019, months before it arrived in Wuhan. A heatwave, diminishing water supplies, monkeys fighting over scarce water, subsequent animal-to-human transmission, poor healthcare systems, and 'imperfect' hygiene were posited as the causes. The animal-to-human transmission may have occurred, the paper argued, via Malayan pangolins in Southeast Asia – which, the paper helpfully pointed out, neighbours India and Bangladesh. While this was not altogether implausible, weeks later the paper was withdrawn.[87]

What the Indian media failed to tell its readers was that Indian scientists too had made misleading claims about the origins of the coronavirus as early as February 2020, just weeks after the outbreak of the disease. A pre-print of an article by Indian researchers suggested that Covid-19 'may have been deliberately engineered using the HIV [virus]'. This 'fed conspiracy theories that the new virus might be a bioweapon' – perhaps it fed Manish Tewari's imagination. It quickly elicited criticism from Chinese researchers based in the US and China. Days after it appeared, the Indian scientists pulled the paper from the website where it had been originally uploaded.[88]

~

We are brought up to think that mass education, the growth of international travel, the exchange of goods and services across borders, and modern communications bring societies closer together: they learn more about other peoples, develop an appreciation of foreign cultures, discover common interests, and, in the end, find ways to live harmoniously (or at least peacefully) side by side. Our review of recent Indian and Chinese perceptions suggests that the people of the two countries see the other society in increasingly negative ways. Are there other 'ways of seeing' (to use the critic and novelist John Berger's famous phrase) which take a kinder view?[89]

Worldviews

India and China engage each other and the rest of the world via 'worldviews' – lenses through which they see themselves, the future of world history, and, by extrapolation, each other. Societies have all kinds of lenses by which they organize reality, and the three described here are not the only ones that influence India's and

China's perceptions. Yet, my sense is that the three we deal with capture quite a lot of Indian and Chinese ways of seeing.

Indian Worldviews and China

India has three big worldviews – a classical, a modern cosmopolitan, and a Great Power view. The classical view goes back to its Hindu past, to the era of Kautilya's *Arthashastra* and Kamandaki's *Nitisara*, which were most likely composed somewhere between the third century BCE and the second century CE. Beginning in the early twenty-first century, the *Arthashastra* in particular has drawn increasing interest in India (and elsewhere), with several interpretations of it. The modern cosmopolitan view can be traced to Indian thinkers from about Vivekananda onward to at least Rabindranath Tagore and Mahatma Gandhi. The Great Power view is evident in the thinking of a range of social thinkers including Nehru and M.S. Golwalkar and contemporary strategists such as Bharat Karnad.

Kautilya

The Kautilyan view is of states (or state-like entities) operating in a world of other states, constantly eyeing each other preparing for war. It is a world of contention and conflict, with a potential *vijigisu* ('conqueror') aspiring to expand the realm. In this world, the big fish eat the small fish, the strong conquer the weak. When the vijigisu expands to the limits of the known world, he or she becomes the *chakravartin* or universal ruler – in a modern setting, this probably means regional hegemony rather than global dominance. In the *mandala* world of Kautilya, other states are enemies, allies, neutrals, and mediators, with neighbours usually rating as enemies. Expansion may be brought about by various means: '*sama* (conciliation or alliance), *dana* (placating and winning over with gifts), *danda* (punishing through the use of force), and *bheda* (sowing dissension)'. Danda is only to be deployed when all else fails.[90] Not every ruler wishes to expand his or her realm, but the vijigisu does harbour that ambition. Expansion sets in motion a dynamic of strife. This is a hard-bitten world, but not necessarily an amoral world. Rulers, including vijigisus, are guided by dharma, by a sense of righteous duty – otherwise the unending quest for expansion would be megalomania and sadism. The vijigisu must bring dharmic rule to the world and thereby eventually deliver integration and peace.

Cosmopolitanism

At the opposite end of the worldview spectrum is modern cosmopolitanism. India has an older tradition of cosmopolitanism: this is typically evoked by the Upanishadic phrase *Vasudhaiva kutumbakam* ('the world is one family'). It is in Vivekananda, Tagore, and Gandhi that we get the modern renditions of cosmopolitanism. Clearly there are differences between the three thinkers. What is common is an insistence that the world is plural, with each society and civilization defined by different values and practices. Yet a conversation between peoples is possible and desirable: each brings its own unique contributions and world mission to the table. Key to the ecumenical dialogue across culture and faith is tolerance and an ability to integrate diversity. India, in this view, has a unique message of tolerance and integration of different peoples and religions: it has received and absorbed many peoples in its long history, without exterminating or enslaving them (unlike the West). It therefore has its own special role.

The more radical element of Indian cosmopolitanism is its scepticism towards the state and nationalism upon which modern international relations are built. Especially for Tagore and Gandhi, nationalism is both emancipatory (from colonial rule) and oppressive (it encourages individuals to sacrifice their creativity and moral sense for the collective and to make excuses for social violence). States built on nationalism are inevitable, but for Tagore and Gandhi individual self-restraint and moral behaviour are the key to peace and order: if we all respected certain norms of behaviour towards each other, irrespective of nationality, governments and states would become largely irrelevant. Gandhi argues in the end for a global order built on small, self-sufficient communities – village republics – with only a loose relationship to central governments.

Great Power

The third Indian worldview is of India as a Great Power. India has been shy talking about itself in grandiose power terms. Virtually all Indian references to India as a Great Power are qualified, the most frequent being the qualifier 'rising'. Prime Minister Narendra Modi and External Affairs Minister Jaishankar have stopped using the term 'rising power' to describe India but do not go further than to refer to India as a 'leading power' – even though deep down they may believe it should (will) be a hegemonic *vishwaguru* or 'world teacher'. The Indian strategist Bharat Karnad, the most outspoken proponent of India's Great Power destiny, titles his book *Why India Is Not a Great Power (Yet)*. The title gestures towards the inevitability of India as a Great Power but admits it is not in the top bracket. The sense that India will inevitably be a Great Power is widespread among the chattering classes. Pratap Bhanu Mehta, the political theorist, summarizes the inevitability view: 'Almost by virtue of her population, resources, and location, India would be a great power; if India were to be left free to be itself, greatness would come to it. But it would be a greatness that would not depend on the projection of power . . . it would be a great power without global objectives.'[91]

India's first prime minister had little doubt that India was already, or would become, a Great Power and not just for the reasons of population, resources, and location. India, for Nehru, is uniquely a bridge and a crossroads, culturally, politically, and geopolitically. With its Islamic cultural heritage, it links to the Gulf and Middle East and other Muslim societies. With its Buddhist past, it connects to Southeast and Northeast Asia. And its Hinduism is a bond to its South Asian neighbours and to Southeast Asia. Beyond the religious-cultural linkages to others around it, India has a larger Asian identity arising out of migration, invasions, trade flows, philosophical thought, the arts, and even colonialism. The Indian diaspora in Asia and around the world also gives India a global cultural presence that perhaps only China can match. Politically, as the world's largest democracy, India shares values with modern Western civilization and other parts of the world. Geopolitically, India's non-alignment positions it as a bridge between the two Cold War blocs. Nehru makes the point that non-alignment is an active stance. It is not neutrality. India and other non-aligned countries are bound to intervene in the quarrels between the two blocs to help manage conflict in the interest of international peace and stability.[92] As the biggest of the non-aligned, India has a special responsibility: in a world torn between contending Great Powers, India's approach 'will continue to be not only to keep aloof from power alignments, but [also] try to make friendly co-operation possible'.[93]

The Nehruvian view of India as a pivotal, bridging Great Power is still widely shared in Indian strategic circles even if Nehru's policies are under increasing criticism. For instance, Modi's and Jaishankar's formulation of India as a 'leading power' has nothing Nehru would find troubling. Nehruvians are not naive about power, but they think that an international order based on an overly active striving for power must eventually collapse: the balance of power in Europe failed to prevent a world war twice in the twentieth century. Better than the striving for power is the pursuit of international cooperation. The Hindu right shares the Nehruvian belief in India as a potential Great Power. Yet its view of international order is suggestive of a different kind of pathway to power. M.S. Golwalkar, the second chief of the Rashtriya Swayamsevak Sangh (RSS), articulates a Hindu nationalist view. He sees international order as inescapably one in which each state single-mindedly cultivates and pursues power: 'When we . . . read the world correctly, we are forced to arrive at the conclusion that the only basis for our free and prosperous national life is invincible national strength – a strength that will strike terror into the hearts of aggressive powers . . . Strength is the very elixir of national life.'[94] Nehru quietly prepared the ground for India to become a traditional military and economic Great Power but emphasized the possibility of using its capabilities to forge cooperation. Golwalkar was less coy about India's Great Power pathway and more cynical about international cooperation.

China in Indian worldviews

What do these worldviews mean for Indian attitudes towards China? Strictly speaking, the *Arthashastra*'s advice is directed at a ruler (or a country) aiming to be a vijigisu. It is hard to imagine India aiming to be a vijigisu in relation to China. China's size, the stopping power of the Himalaya, the massive Tibetan plateau, and the plains of China beyond Tibet make any thought of conquest in a literal sense impossible. Yet as a powerful neighbour, it must be regarded as a rival. Its neighbours are potential allies of India.

However, many neighbours of China are also neighbours of India. Bhutan, Nepal, and Pakistan are therefore simultaneously potential rivals of India *and* China. Given their location between the two powers and given their size, they are probably better thought of as neutrals and mediators. In fact, though, they appear increasingly like allies of China against India. This has certainly been the case with Pakistan since 1963. Nepal and Bhutan could conceivably change their stance too.

From the Kautilyan point of view, then, it is only China's distant neighbours that are possible allies of India – primarily Russia and Japan. Unfortunately for India, while a Kautilyan view may suggest that Russia should see China as its greatest worry, the Russians regard the US and European powers as their biggest concern. Moscow has therefore made common cause with Beijing even as it remains friendly to Delhi. As a result, Russia appears as a mediator between India and China rather than as India's ally against China. In September 2020, at the trilateral summit of Russia, India, and China, Moscow played just such a mediatory role. What about Japan? It does fear China, but it has limitations as an ally, in part because of the stopping power of the sea between it and China but also because of its economic and military weakness relative to its giant East Asian neighbour. Taking a broader view of the Kautilyan strategic framework, the US and its Western friends would be potential allies of India: they could open up a diplomatic and strategic front against China. The US, with its capabilities, more than any other power is consequential for India. Not surprisingly, India views America increasingly as an ally against China.

The *Arthashastra* is suggestive of another potential resource for India: dharma. From India's point of view, the spread of dharma to China might alter the relationship. If China were to adopt a dharmic polity and a dharmic view of international relations in which righteous conduct governs both domestic and external policy, India and China could find a way to live together in peace as two morally guided neighbours. Golwalkar has written that India could spread dharmic values peacefully. While Kautilya sees the vijigisu spreading dharmic values as it expands and conquers, the RSS supremo envisages the willing adoption of dharma based on the appeal of the moral codes themselves as also India's exemplary dharmic behaviour.[95] An India that is consistently, even obstinately, dharmic might manage China by means of non-strategic instruments. Indian policy towards China since 1949 certainly could be said to have attempted to resolve differences by invoking legal and moral codes.

How does China appear in India's modern cosmopolitan worldview? India and China might have quarrels over territory and their standing in the world, but more important than these mundane, conventional matters is the possibility of a dialogue on values and norms, on larger questions about human existence and organization. For Vivekananda, Tagore, and Gandhi, modern (Western) industrialism has impoverished the spiritual life of humanity. Yet that transcendent life is still available to us and could unite India and China – not in the political sense of merging territories and governments but rather in the quest for a more wholesome, just, and sustainable existence for humankind.

India and China, in this view, appear as co-leaders of a possible pan-Asianism. Important to this view is the notion of a 'Chindia' that is *for* the world not *against* the world: it is an alliance not for India's and China's betterment at the expense of others but rather for everyone's betterment. In the cosmopolitan view, the two societies would bring to global conversations an alternative to the dominant Western view of historical possibilities. Tagore and Nehru are the prophet-voices of such a view – and particularly Tagore. Tagore was one of the key figures in the discussions on pan-Asianism in the 1920s and 1930s which above all involved Indian, Chinese, and Japanese intellectuals and artists. In India, he more than anyone in modern times gave life to engagement across the Himalaya. In 1924, he visited China (to a mixed reception) to promote the idea of India–China engagement and pan-Asianism. In the 1920s, even as he was travelling in China, his school, Santiniketan, began hosting Japanese, European, and Chinese scholars interested in India–China interactions. In 1937, Tagore set up Cheena Bhavan at Santiniketan (with mostly Chinese money – Indian donations were meagre), to reinvigorate contact between the two kin civilizations. At any rate, the cosmopolitan view is of China as a partner in a new post-colonial world, reviving historical ties with India and deepening not just their mutual relations but also the world's moral and spiritual progress.

What, then, of India as an aspiring Great Power? Where does China appear in this worldview? Nehruvians and Hindu nationalists have their differences but neither viewpoint regards China as India's friend (though Nehru once did hope they could be): Great Powers are fated to mistrust and fear each other. In the Kautilyan view, India and China are rivals by virtue of geography: they are neighbours. In the Great Power view, it is not primarily geography that makes them rivals, it is the dynamic of power. As Great Powers they would be rivals, regardless of their location; geography merely adds to their rivalry. China can be expected to resist India's ascent and entry into the select club – just as the US seeks to resist China's ascent. Beijing would attempt to undermine Indian power materially but also symbolically deny it recognition as a Great Power. A key token of Great Power status is permanent veto-bearing membership of the United Nations Security Council. So far, China is the only major power that has not endorsed India's membership.

How should India as an aspiring Great Power deal with China?

One way is broadly the Nehruvian: India rising to become a full-fledged Great Power, by stealth, nuancing its rise, cultivating the image of a different kind of ascending power – a bridging or shaping power. This is the image of an India that looks after its interests, to be sure, but also leads coalitions of weaker states to create a more secure and emancipated world. India's External Affairs Minister Jaishankar in his recent book, *The India Way*, captures the orientation: 'The India Way, especially now, would be more of a shaper or decider than just be an abstainer . . . India must be a just and fair power as well, consolidating its position as a standard bearer of the global South . . . [it must] express its brand with growing confidence, whether in its civilizational attributes or in its contemporary achievements.'[96] Bharat Karnad, who has written two big books on India's Great Power ambitions, has a more traditional answer to what India must do: declare a 'Monroe Doctrine' in the ocean space around it; organize a coalition of rimland and offshore states surrounding China; access US capabilities in Asia; draw India's neighbours on the Asian landmass into its economic sphere; and 'build up versatile, strategically-oriented conventional military forces able to take the fight to China'.[97] The current chief of the RSS, Mohan Bhagwat, has the bluntest and simplest answer. India must beat China: 'In our military and economic preparations, in forging relations, internationally and with our neighbours, we will need to be bigger than China'.[98]

Chinese Worldviews and India

We can distinguish between three broad Chinese worldviews as well. The first is what might be labelled the *tianxia* ('all under heaven') view, the second is the republican and communist view, and the third is the Great Power view. The tianxia view draws on ancient Chinese philosophy, the republican and communist view is about a hundred years old, and the Great Power view is even more recent, being no more than two decades old. The differences apart, what is common to the three perspectives is the idea that the world is organized hierarchically.

Tianxia

China's modern tianxia view has gained considerable attention since the Chinese philosopher Zhao Tingyang's writings began to appear in 2005. Zhao's influential work *The Tianxia System: An Introduction to the Philosophy of a World Institution* spread an awareness of the ancient philosophy of tianxia and provided a modern interpretation relevant to China's governance but crucially also the conduct of its external relations and the nature of international order.[99] As with any great philosophical system, differences exist over its meaning: is tianxia a cosmopolitan view of the world that emphasizes justice in governance provided by a powerful moral authority (irrespective of whether that authority is China); or is it the rationale for a strong China resuming its place as the centre of the world and dispensing order to lesser entities? In either case, is the central authority, whether Chinese or other, an object of reverence or fear? Does authority depend on its moral superiority and munificence or on its material inducements and coercive abilities?

The operational part of tianxia in international relations is the idea of a tributary system. A dominant power receives 'tribute' from smaller powers and dispenses legitimacy, order, and even material benefits to its tributaries. It does not demand tribute; it attracts it by its splendour. In whatever way tianxia is conceptualized, at base it as also the tributary system is a hierarchical organization of political and international life. The most telling argument for hierarchy, one that exists everywhere and not just in China, is that by slotting people and groups and assigning clear obligations and expectations, it produces stability and satisfaction. In modern political life, hierarchy is regarded with suspicion, but in tianxia and the tributary system and other graded systems, it is the basis for justice and peace.

Republicanism/communism

A second source of international thought in China arises from its republican and communist heritage. It may seem odd to club republican and communist views together. Common to both streams of thought is a rejection of traditional authority and, most importantly, the rule of kings and emperors. The republican movement that ended with General Chiang Kai-shek's defeat on the Chinese mainland in 1949 and the triumphant communist movement share a revolutionary legacy. Both movements were dedicated to the end of imperial rule in China if not the destruction of the royal household. The Son of Heaven in a tianxia world would be replaced by secular authority backed by people power. Today, China is supposedly a communist country because it is run by the Communist Party of China (CPC). In fact, it is less communist ideologically than republican – with a president who is not popularly elected but who claims his legitimacy from the will of the people. In short, China is a republican country with a communist past.

The communist past has provided a view of international relations, like tianxia, which is hierarchical. While communism envisages a world in which capitalism is overthrown and an entirely new world order is born – one that Karl Marx refused to describe, saying it was impossible to know what would emerge after the revolution – those who brought the revolution in Russia and China had little doubt that their countries would live in an international system in which capitalism was still rampant. The global struggle of communism would be a long one. In the struggle, Russia and then China would be central. Here too there were debates between internationalists who wanted to actively propagate the struggle against capitalism and those who wanted to secure the revolution at home before embarking on a global crusade. Those who stood for consolidation at home were convinced that given the size of Russia and China they would be at the centre of global revolutionary thought and praxis. They would stand as examples for other revolutionaries and would provide guidance if not material aid. This suggests another hierarchical view, a more tutelary view, but quite compatible in a broad sense with tianxia. Revolutionary tributaries, even if they were not communists, would come to Russia and China for inspiration, legitimacy, and help to oust Western colonial powers and local ruling classes. Eventually, a Russian- or Chinese-led global revolutionary struggle would confront world capitalism and its defenders, mostly Western powers.

Great Power

The third source of thinking about China's place in the world is its Great Power view. Perhaps the most celebrated statements of this view are the trilogy by a former interpreter of Deng Xiaoping and now a professor of international relations at Fudan University, Zhang Weiwei. Beginning with a book in Mandarin (which is not available in English), he published three books for a Chinese audience, two of which he then translated for a wider audience – *The China Wave* in 2012 and *The China Horizon* in 2016. The former book is emblazoned with the claim that it sold more than half a million copies in China. The subtitles of the two books are triumphalist: 'Rise of a Civilizational State' and 'Glory and Dream of a Civilizational State'. Zhang celebrates China's arrival as a Great Power, indeed as the greatest power on earth: the first chapter in *The China Horizon* is called 'From Catching-up to Surpassing' – that is, surpassing the current greatest power, the US.[100]

Summarizing his trilogy, Zhang can hardly contain himself: 'Concerning China's rise, my primary viewpoint is that the rise of China is that of a civilizational state, and it is the world's longest continuous civilization amalgamated with a huge modern state. This civilizational state has at least eight features, namely, a super-large population, a super-vast territory, super-long traditions, super-rich culture, a unique language, unique politics, a unique society and a unique economy'.[101] This breathless description, almost every part of which is contestable for its truth-value, nevertheless captures a widespread if not always publicly articulated view: most Chinese would not offend foreigners by saying these things in their hearing, but many would hold to much of the Zhang formula privately. At any rate, here is another hierarchical view: China as the greatest power on earth, 'returning to the preeminent status it once enjoyed in the past' (in Zhang's categorical words) and unmatched in its super and unique features.[102] Chinese exceptionalism is reminiscent of American exceptionalism. Yet Americans could hardly claim to match China in terms of being the longest continuous civilization, the largest population, or the inventors of a unique language. China is, therefore, on this view, a very special superpower.

India in Chinese worldviews

India has a slightly different place in each of these Chinese worldviews, but what is constant is that it, as much of the world, is placed in a grid in which there are gradations and ranks. From a tianxia view, India is another smaller neighbour on the periphery of China. It is by far the largest of the 'smaller' neighbours, so it ranks above others in Asia, but it is a potential tributary. In a social setting, smaller entities must understand their place, which means knowing their entitlements and obligations. China too must comprehend its own size, entitlements, and obligations. Because China is the moral and political centre in a tianxia universe, those on the periphery including India would be drawn to it for protection and symbolic and material rewards. Historically, tributaries would send tributes or would personally appear to kowtow at the imperial court with their tributes in order to be recognized by the Son of Heaven, the Chinese emperor. They would bear gifts and submit to certain norms and obligations. The emperor would in return give personal gifts, trading rights within China and in the region, and protection against rivals, domestic and international. Tributaries are not humiliated or punished, unless they violate norms established in the relationship or fail to pay tribute. As the largest of China's Asian neighbours, India would qualify for somewhat different treatment from the treatment given to other tributaries. India–China relations might be marked by a special degree of Chinese benevolence and indulgence. For its part, India would be expected to give China its loyalty and support on issues that matter to Beijing.

China's communist perspective on the world also would have India in a secondary or subordinate role. For all the talk of fraternal relations between socialist partners that communism trumpets, some revolutionary partners are more important than others in the global struggle against capitalism. They guide and lead; others follow. While the CPC is no longer much of a communist party ideologically, in this perspective China is the leader of the developing world. It is revealing that despite its spectacular economic advance over the past forty years, Beijing continues to insist on being recognized as a developing country, a status it clings to for political and diplomatic reasons. India in this view is a junior partner in the international system, though once again a junior partner with heft of its own. As a major economy and as a long-time member of various developing-country coalitions in multilateral forums, India has influence in ways that other developing countries do not. It can stand with China on issues such as climate change, trade, humanitarian intervention, and internet and cyber protocols, where Beijing is often in contention against the Western powers.

In this hierarchical view, China would expect to lead in formulating the developing world's positions on global issues, just as in the early years of the Cold War it sought to be the leader of the global communist movement. Its split with Moscow beginning in the 1950s was partly over the withdrawal of Soviet assistance to its nuclear programme. More importantly, though, Beijing regarded Moscow as increasingly timid in confronting Washington. In Mao's view, the Soviets were wrong to believe that nuclear weapons necessitated strategic caution and a tempering of socialist radicalism. Almost from the beginning, and certainly after Josef Stalin's death, China wanted to lead the communist movement, just as it now wants to lead the developing world. Beijing certainly cedes no ground to Delhi as a leader of the global south; indeed, it has gradually increased its influence among the various coalitions of the non-aligned/developing countries.

The tianxia and developing-country leadership perspectives are increasingly backed by China's Great Power self-confidence. Chinese thinkers place their country in the same league as the US, especially since Xi Jinping's leadership. In 2014, under Xi, Beijing began to mention the possibility of a 'new type of great power relations' with Washington – which President Barack

Obama pointedly ignored. Looking forward, Xi has made clear that his 'China Dream' is a dream about being number one in the world, not coeval with the US. Deng Xiaoping, who led China's economic reforms and its extraordinary rise, urged China to 'hide your strength, bide your time, never take the lead'. Xi's China Dream has effectively buried 'hide and bide'. Publicly Chinese policymakers dismiss any ambition to replace the US as the pre-eminent power and to restructure the reigning international order, but the ambition is clear enough.

Clearly, China does not see India as a fellow Great Power. This is not particularly surprising, in part because India itself does not use the term 'Great Power' to describe its status. India is trying to change its image from 'rising power' to 'leading power', but it has resisted staking a bigger claim. In a backhanded compliment, Beijing has periodically referred to India as an 'important power' (usually when India has pressed its claims for a permanent seat in the UN Security Council) but has refused to go any further. Zhang, the exponent of China as a unique civilizational state referred to earlier, dismisses all of India's claims to greatness: 'Although many in the West wish India to outperform China, arguing that India's democratic system is its trump card . . . this trump card is of dubious and poor quality, and India's gap with China is likely to grow further . . . China is a much better governed country.' Holding India back are five key weaknesses (most Indians would probably go along with the list): 'politicization of everything . . . populism prevails . . . India's 'soft state' . . . short-term politics . . . [and] schisms and disunity'. As a result, 'the gap between the two Asian giants could not be larger'.[103]

At the height of the crisis in Ladakh in June 2020, the editor of the *Global Times*, Hu Xijin, wrote scathingly about India: 'Some Indians arrogantly believe that the modernization of Indian troops will allow them to defeat the Chinese People's

Liberation Army and take revenge on China for India's defeat in the 1962 border war. I'd love to tell them that there was not much difference between China and India in terms of economic strength in 1962, but today, China's GDP is about five times that of India and China's military expenditure is over three times that of India according to Western estimates. If India escalates the border dispute with China into skirmishes or even local wars, it would be like an egg dashing itself against a rock.'[104]

In sum, from three perspectives, China affirms a hierarchy in world politics, with itself at the top. India features at best in the second tier of Asian countries, perhaps not even in the second tier globally, where Beijing would likely place Russia, Japan, the UK, and France. Zhang's depiction of China in terms of superlatives is indicative of the Chinese view. This is not just an elite's triumphalism. In 1998, some weeks after South Asia's nuclear tests, I was invited to give two lectures at Fudan University in Shanghai to a group of Chinese, Indian, and Pakistani students assembled for a month-long workshop on nuclear arms control. Before and after my own lectures, I attended some of the other sessions. During one of these, an Indian student commented that in the middle of the twenty-first century India would surpass China in population terms. She quoted a United Nations estimate to make her point. It was a casual remark and not the burden of her intervention. However, as soon as the words were spoken, a Chinese student asked to be recognized. I remember her matter-of-fact words: 'On China and India's population, I would like to say that China can never be behind India. That is impossible. It is not based on facts.' She was an affable and pleasant young woman, as we discovered in the evening's social gatherings, and there was no animosity in her voice – it was more a mixture of shock and exasperation. The idea that India could surpass China in any way was a childish fantasy to her – and fantasy was not admissible in the rational setting of the conference hall.

At the same workshop, when discussion turned to nuclear weapons, we were reminded of the Chinese attitude to India's size. When a Western expert criticized India's nuclearization, an Indian student aired the view that India had a right to develop nuclear weapons at least to the level of the second-tier nuclear countries of China, France, and the UK. India, he reminded the audience, faced two nuclear-armed rivals on its borders. A Chinese expert, a scholarly and restrained man seated beside me, quickly responded: 'But India is such a small country, and China is such a big country. You cannot compare the two.' It was clear that he was sympathetic to the comparison with France and the UK, but to mention India in the same breath as China was hard to accept. Like the Chinese student who had intervened earlier, he was a genial host and good company over a beer, and there was no hint of a put-down in his manner. It was simply incomprehensible to him that India could be compared to China.

~

If these are the two leading sets of worldviews of China and India, is there any area of convergence? India sees China as an implacable rival neighbour, as an Asian co-partner in a cosmopolitan world, and as a hurdle to its own aspirations as a great power. China sees India as a tributary, as a junior partner at best in a socialist world, and as an *arriviste* power in the second tier below the US and China itself. A stark conclusion is that their worldviews do not converge and are a source of friction. Only one worldview among the six is positive about the relationship – the Indian view of a cosmopolitan world not obsessed with the nation state, in which

China is an Asian partner. This view is also the least likely to have any resonance in contemporary India and China. If there is convergence today, it is in the Great Power–aspiring power view. Indians and Chinese converge on the idea that China is a Great Power. They also converge on the idea that India is an aspiring power. However, India sees China as actively thwarting its rise by threatening its borders and by turning India's neighbours against it. China would say that it is not seeking to stop India's ascent: Indians are doing a good job of retarding their own progress by tolerating bad governance and economic failure.

Conclusion

How have Indians and Chinese regarded each other historically, and how do they see each other's contemporary politics, society, and culture? The data, admittedly, is scarce, and so this chapter of the book rests on far more impressionistic evidence. Nonetheless, it does tell us a story about how Indians and Chinese assess each other. The broad conclusion is that they have gone from a respectful relationship in ancient times to a less respectful view of each other in modern and contemporary times. This may well reflect two changes: increasing communication and, at the same time, incomplete knowledge of each other; and the border conflict and power asymmetry between them.

Until the nineteenth century, India and China had limited contact. Buddhism was a point of engagement, but the spread of the faith to ordinary Chinese was a Sinicized version and did not lead to a terribly intimate relationship between the two 'heartlands'. Trade as well as social and cultural interactions between Indians and Chinese in other places such as Southeast Asia certainly was a bridge between the two societies after Buddhism declined in significance, but it was British imperialism in the nineteenth century that reconnected the two, mostly in negative ways related to the opium trade and the creation of foreign enclaves in China. It is in the twentieth and twenty-first centuries, with modern technologies of communication and travel, the spread of mass media, and public education, that the two peoples at large have become more aware of each other. Even then, the extent of mutual understanding has been quite thin. It also seems to have complicated the relationship. In 1709, the British poet Alexander Pope wrote: 'A little learning is a dangerous thing'. Pope's insight applied to India–China interactions is not that the two societies should know each other less but rather the opposite. Yet the signs are they are increasingly looking elsewhere for inspiration and edification.

2

Perimeters: From Cooperation to Conflict

Perceptions matter, but India and China are also not friends because since 1949 they have not been able to agree on their perimeters – on the definition of their boundaries, on the status of Tibet which sits between the heartlands of the two societies, and on the nature of their military presence and actions in forward areas. In October 1962 when they went to war, the Indian and Chinese leaderships were deeply suspicious of each other on all three issues despite attempts to cooperate. The war seemed to bring to a climax their antagonism. This might have led to a resolution of their differences. Or it could have resulted in an alienation so complete that any form of normal intercourse would have become impossible. In fact, after some years, Delhi and Beijing returned to a process of cooperation on the border, Tibet, and military relations. By the summer of 2020, when the two armies fought on the Galwan heights, a second period of cooperation closed, once again in a violent encounter and the threat of war, eerily reminiscent of 1962.

Background

To understand the quarrel between India and China over their perimeters, a little background is vital on the border, Tibet, and military relations in the Himalaya. The India–China border stretches from Aksai Chin in the west, through a so-called middle sector, to Arunachal Pradesh in the east. The dispute in the western sector is over Aksai Chin, bordering Ladakh. In the middle sector, the contestation is over relatively small strips of territory along the Himachal Pradesh and Uttarakhand borderlands. In the eastern sector, China lays claim to all of Arunachal Pradesh (Zangnan or 'South Tibet' in Chinese parlance). In total, the conflict has come to be about 130,000 square kilometres of territory – 36,000 in the west, 2000 in the middle sector, and 90,000 in the east.

Why should 130,000 square kilometres excite such antagonism given the continent-size expanse of India and China? The total disputed area represents about 4 per cent of India's land and less than 2 per cent of China's vast expanse. We must recognize, though, that a country – a nation – is defined by land. A society may be attached to a parcel of land for historical and symbolic reasons, regardless of its size. People carry around representations of their national boundaries in their heads from their schooldays, and it is hard to shed those images. An area may have people in it that are cultural kin with those just across the boundary line and may want to (re)unite with them. Control over land is also a sign of sovereignty. Sovereignty is the freedom to do what you want in a piece of territory. When societies liberate themselves from imperialism, they imagine they will once again exercise that freedom. Not surprisingly, post-imperial countries are very jealous of their territories and boundaries. Countries can also have material interests in a section of land even if it is relatively small. The land may have valuable natural resources – oil and gas, minerals, forests, and water. It may be important by virtue of its geostrategic location – for example, as a buffer zone against a powerful rival neighbour or a connecting zone between two larger parts of national territory. It could also be a crucial basing area for the military.

In the case of India and China, all these apply, in some measure – it would be another book to describe all the meanings that Indians and Chinese associate with their territorial possessions. But it is worth underlining the military-strategic interests. In the western sector, between 1951 and 1957, China built a road from Xinjiang to Tibet across Aksai Chin, at a time when Beijing's political and military control over Tibet was tenuous. The road was vital in allowing the Chinese military to move men and supplies from bases in Xinjiang to reinforce its Tibetan garrisons. India by contrast had very little material interest in Aksai Chin, which is largely desert and scrubland. In Arunachal Pradesh in the eastern sector, the situation is reversed. India is determined that China cannot have a presence south of the McMahon Line because Chinese forces could 'break out' from there into the plains of the Indian North-East. On the other hand, it is unclear why China wants to occupy the southern slopes of Arunachal: militarily, it is a challenging place to hold, as the supply lines will be long and difficult to maintain. Beijing's real interest is probably the Tawang monastery there, a site with symbolic and therefore strategic significance. The monastery is under Indian control, but China regards it as important for the integration and stability of Tibet.

Beyond the quarrel over boundaries, India and China have differed on the status of Tibet. In the 1950s, India held a view that it had interests in and responsibility towards Tibet, given its presence there from the days of the British Raj. The historical link with Tibet through Buddhism and trade reinforced that view: India had cultural–moral obligations towards a kin civilization and was the main source of vital supplies including food. After Tibet's integration into China in 1950, Delhi's aim was to ensure the province retained a degree of cultural and social autonomy. With its defeat in the 1962 war, India concluded it could no longer play a role in backing Tibetan autonomy: the dangers were too great, and in any case the 1954 treaty with China, which had committed Beijing to maintain Tibet's autonomy, had expired by 1962. India's involvement in Tibetan affairs could now only be to host the Dalai Lama and the exiles.

While India sees itself as a passive guardian of the Dalai Lama and exile community, China thinks that Delhi is active in supporting him, stirring anti-China sentiment in the exile community, and interfering in Tibet itself. In Chinese thinking, the border quarrel with India and Beijing's continuing struggles with Tibetan integration are linked. The border between India and China is essentially Tibet's border with India. So, it must be delineated in a way that ensures India cannot militarily or politically influence Tibetan affairs. The reverse is also the case. Stability in Tibet is vital for China's border control with India. A Tibetan insurgency or rebellion could undermine Chinese defences at its frontiers. In sum, for China the border is not just about 130,000 square kilometres of land. It is about stable control over the 1.2 million square kilometres of the Tibet Autonomous Region (TAR), roughly one-eighth the total land area of China. Any discussion of the India–China conflict over their perimeters is unavoidably, then, one that must include the status of Tibet.

In the late 1950s, the India–China border area became increasingly militarized. Both sides increased their troop presence gradually prior to the war of 1962 and have remained vigilant since then. This was a historic development: over hundreds if not thousands of years, the border was notional and soft rather than demarcated in hard lines. Local people lived in a region without clearly defined boundaries, and pilgrims and traders moved both ways without strict controls, at least until the British tried to tie imperial China down to firm delineations in the nineteenth century. The militarization of the area gives both governments an illusion of control and sovereignty when in fact given the mountain heights, valleys, passes, glaciers, vegetation, and waterways it is almost impossible, even with modern technology, to maintain troops and patrols in the farthest reaches of the borderlands up to India's and China's claim lines. Modern states have a fairly absolutist view of borders, yet in this region they are unable to exert the kind of exclusivist control that they promise their publics. Not surprisingly, India and China are exceedingly sensitive to charges that they have lost control and that the other side may suddenly grab its land.

~

In December 1971, days after the Bangladesh war ended, I was on a train to Siliguri and then Bagdogra on my way to Gangtok, Sikkim. As the child of a foreign service officer, I got to see my parents only once a year – the Indian government had decided it could not afford to unite families more often than that. The winter holidays usually saw me packed off to relatives in Delhi and Mumbai, but in 1971, I was sent to Gangtok, where my uncle, the diplomat Katyayani Shankar Bajpai, was the Indian Political Officer (as it turned out, the last Indian Political Officer before Sikkim joined India). On the train, perhaps near Siliguri, I was in a compartment with Indian troops returning from Bangladesh. War is hell of course, and the soldiers were grey-faced. I was entering my last year at school. The officers were not much older than me. We got talking about the war, and one said, 'It is our problem now' – referring to Bangladesh. It was a sobering moment. A week later I would have another sobering moment, this time at the India–China border.

Gangtok to Nathu La is about sixty kilometres by road, about a two-hour journey. My elder brother and I, getting restless in the palatial residence of the Political Officer, were dispatched on a day trip to the pass. Nathu La is where India and China had fought a blood-filled battle in 1967, with hundreds of casualties. Along mountain switchbacks and climbs, we were nauseated and clutched ourselves against the cold. Gangtok is at an elevation of 1650 metres, but Nathu La is at three times that height. It is a fairly rapid climb to the pass, and for plainspeople the ascent can leave you breathless and slightly dizzy. Like most Indians, I had never been to a border area: borders were lines on a map I could draw by rote from my geography classes and not much else – shadow lines, to use novelist Amitav Ghosh's words. As we climbed, I was beginning to see what a border might really be, in the Himalaya at any rate. The first indications we were closing in on Nathu La were large signs painted on bare mountainsides warning us we were within various calibres of gunfire. The last sign, as the army jeep slowed, said: 'You are now within small arms fire.'

At Nathu La, after some bread dipped in sweet black tea, we were led out towards a post. It was not far, as I recall. The scene was bleak: it was windy and grey, and I think there were a few huts and trenches. At some point, as we perhaps showed disappointment at standing around the post and looking across at China, a young officer pointed to movement on the other side and handed us binoculars. When my eyes got used to the binoculars, I found myself looking at a gaunt Chinese soldier in an overcoat, stamping his foot and hugging himself against the cold. He was smoking a cigarette. All of a sudden, he saw me looking at him and gesticulated at the hut behind him. He was quickly joined by another soldier who now raised a pair of binoculars to stare back. I was about to wave when the young Indian officer next to me enclosed my right hand: 'Don't do anything sudden. Slowly bring the binoculars down to your side.' Which I did.

This was the line on the map, where a naive sixteen-year-old schoolboy could spark a violent incident by raising his binoculars and waving to the enemy. Borders matter to all societies, and they are usually defended to the death. In the last days of 1971, I got a glimpse of what India's Himalayan borderlands really are. Wars are hell even when you are winning (as in Bangladesh); for the young men on both sides, with nothing to do in the harsh temperatures and thin air, determined to defend a line they could hardly define, this was hellish enough even if they were not at war.

The Border, Tibet, and Military Conflict, 1949–1962

The story of the India–China quarrels in the high Himalaya has three inter-related parts – their border negotiations; their interactions over Tibet; and their military worries and moves along the boundaries. It is a story spanning two broad periods of time: from 1949, when the CPC took power, to November 1962 when the India–China war ended; and from 1963 to the present. The first period is a particularly complicated story, with partisan accounts blaming one side or the other for the disputes and, in the end, for the war and subsequent rivalry. In fact, the two governments tried, and to some extent succeeded, in cooperating on the border, Tibet, and military stability before succumbing to conflict and eventually to war.

The Border

From 1949 to the outbreak of war on 20 October 1962, India and China tried to settle their differences over the border. Much of the writing on the period suggests one side or the other was determined to stick to its view of the border, was deceitful in negotiations, and was spoiling for war. In fact, none of those propositions is particularly correct. Charles Glaser, the American political scientist, has suggested that international conflict often arises because of 'greedy' countries that are aggressive-minded and expansionist.[1] All countries want to protect their territory, are sometimes deceitful, and will take decisions to go to war, but India–China interactions in these thirteen years were not the interactions between two greedy countries or even between one greedy and one more moderate country. Instead, they were both security-seeking countries that, as in a Greek tragedy, came to see the other as greedy, expansionist, and aggressive.

Contrary to a now quite prevalent view on both sides that the other was looking for a fight over the border, India and China were initially hesitant to raise the issue of conflicting territorial claims. When they finally did engage each other directly on the subject, they saw contradictions and inconsistencies in the other's statements and actions. Delhi and Beijing also had deep differences over imperially defined boundaries that tipped them into outright disagreement over the border: India wanted to honour inherited boundaries whereas China wanted to renegotiate them. The border problem was intimately connected to the status of Tibet. Both countries concluded, particularly after the Tibetan rebellion of 1956–59, that the other had failed to honour its commitments. India felt China had reversed course on Tibet's autonomy, and China felt India had reverted to a policy of interference in the province. Finally, both also regarded their own military moves in the Himalaya between 1949 and 1962 as being defensive and the other side's moves as being aggressive.

Hesitations

India's prime minister Jawaharlal Nehru and his foreign policy team are often faulted for being dreamy-eyed idealists in international affairs, with a penchant for thinking about what should be rather than what is and failing to adopt even normal precautions on the border with China. In fact, though, even before the communists had come to power, Indian decision-makers were aware that they would have a problem with China. As early as 1948, the new Indian ambassador in China, the historian and geopolitical thinker K.M. Panikkar, had written warningly to Delhi. He noted that as the successor state to British India, independent India had inherited rights in Tibet. It should expect the new Chinese government to fully integrate Tibet, and in doing so challenge the validity of the McMahon Line in the eastern sector.[2]

Shortly after the communists took power, Girja Shankar Bajpai, Secretary General in the Ministry of External Affairs, had a more general worry about China, namely, its communism and strategic views. He confided to the British High Commission in Delhi that 'Chinese Communists, like any other Communists, reacted well to firmness but would exploit any sign of weakness'. In a letter to Nehru's sister Vijaya Lakshmi Pandit, he noted he was trying to curb the prime minister's 'enthusiasm' over China. In October 1950, British diplomats reported Bajpai to have said that with the end of the civil war in China, India would have a 'militaristic and aggressive nation' on its borders – in other words, a greedy country.[3]

Unable, he felt, to curb Nehru's enthusiasm, Bajpai penned a long note on relations with China. He sent the note to – in his view – the more hard-headed deputy prime minister, Sardar Patel, on 31 October 1950. With some amendments, Patel transmitted the letter under his own signature to Nehru. This is the now-famous 7 November 1950 letter on China policy. In it Bajpai/Patel underlined the concern that China would have a military and political presence right up to India's borderlands and to the small, vulnerable Himalayan states of Nepal, Sikkim, and Bhutan as well as Burma. Given the difficulties with Pakistan over Kashmir, India would face a two-front challenge. This necessitated both internal and external security reforms and a review of India's diplomacy with the Anglo-American powers and China. Patel died soon after sending the letter to Nehru and never got a reply. While Bajpai and Patel did not quite urge immediate negotiations on the border, the letter argued for greater attention to border security.

With Patel's death, it was left to Bajpai and Foreign Secretary K.P.S. Menon to get Nehru to engage more fully with the threat they saw from China. They urged that a Tibet accord should be linked to Beijing's settlement of the borders with Delhi. However, Panikkar disregarded their instructions.[4] He explained his view later to Bajpai. If India raised the issue, China would either accept the McMahon Line or refuse to accept the line and ask for negotiations. Since the former was improbable, it would choose negotiations, which India would find hard to avoid since Delhi would have been responsible for initiating discussions on the border in the first place. If on the other hand China was left to raise the border issue, India could simply assert, as Nehru already had publicly, that India's boundaries were fixed and there was nothing to discuss. Behind this view, according to Srinath Raghavan, was Panikkar's larger point that instead of becoming embroiled in negotiations, it should turn its attention to shoring up its administration in the borderlands.[5]

Nehru was initially inclined to go with Panikkar's view, but when he saw a Chinese reference to the borders as being a 'scar' of imperialism, he felt it was 'better to be absolutely straight and frank'.[6] Bajpai, retired from the foreign service and now Governor of Bombay State, once again disagreed with Panikkar's soft-pedalling. Writing to his successor in Delhi, he presciently warned that China 'may seek to heal or erase this scar on the basis of frontier rectifications that may not be to our liking'.[7] In the meantime, Panikkar had finished his term in Beijing. Upon his return to Delhi, he persuaded a wavering Nehru that it was not the right time to talk to China about the border. In the end Nehru, after tilting one way and then another, seems to have agreed with Panikkar that India was not ready to negotiate, given its uneven control and administrative reach in the borderlands. He therefore ordered India's diplomats to avoid discussion on the border issue in the negotiations over Tibet.[8]

Clearly, in private, the Indian view was that China would challenge the border as it was then defined. Delhi would have to deal with the matter – sooner or later. The Bajpai–Patel–Menon view was that 'sooner is better', while the Nehru–Panikkar view was that 'later is better'. The sooner school wanted to link a final Tibet agreement to a border settlement, from the beginning; the later school wanted to wait until China raised the border issue. The sooner school assumed it was better to engage Beijing when China was relatively weak and preoccupied with internal consolidation (e.g., in Tibet) and external challenges (in Korea, in Taiwan, and in relation to the US). The later school assumed that notwithstanding China's challenges, India faced perhaps even greater challenges, both internal (e.g., national integration and governance capacity) and external (Pakistan, Cold War pressures). In the end, the later school prevailed. Three months after the two sides signed an agreement in 1954 in which Delhi gave up its rights in Tibet, Nehru decided not to broach the subject of border definition when he met his counterpart Zhou Enlai on 25–28 June 1954.

Both sides in the Indian debate had a plausible view, and neither side was 'idealistic'. Both accepted that eventually differences over the border would arise and would have to be candidly discussed with Beijing. Both recognized that Indian capacities and control in the borderlands had to be expanded: on this Bajpai–Patel–Menon and Panikkar–Nehru were agreed. However, the sooner school thought it was better to know what India was up against early in the relationship, whereas the later school wanted to give China and India time to settle into a relationship, to use diplomacy to build goodwill, and to increase Indian political and military capacities in the borderlands. Given the depth of differences with China that were to appear in the years ahead, the sooner school probably had it right. To be fair, though, the later school had a case, given that India had just come out of a war with Pakistan in 1948, was dealing with the consequences of Partition, and constructing a new constitutional, political, and economic order.

We know much less about Chinese thinking on the border in these early days after the communists took power. This is largely because of the paucity of sources. China did open its archives briefly after the Cold War, but quickly closed them again. Chinese and Western scholars used that opportunity to write about the period, but their focus was elsewhere: China's relations with India were regarded as secondary to engagement with the Soviets and the US. Tellingly, Chinese officials and experts are more likely to use the term 'skirmish' in referring to the 1962 war. If it was a skirmish rather than a full-blown war, why bother to write about it in detail? Western scholars who got access to the archives, too, were occupied with China and its relations principally with the US and paid little attention to archival materials on India.

At any rate, from what we do know, China had a rather similar internal debate in the early years. The Chinese scholar Dai Chaowu, who did access the archives, suggests that China, like

India, was reluctant to broach the territorial issue. In conversation with Panikkar in September 1951, Zhou stated that 'there was no territorial dispute or controversy between India and China' and insisted that the borders could be stabilized through negotiations.[9] This may have been designed to lull Delhi into complacency, but it is quite plausible that the communists were genuinely uncertain of their own claim-lines and were playing for time in order to reach an internal consensus on how to proceed with India. For instance, in 1951, the senior Chinese jurist Zhou Gengsheng in the Ministry of Foreign Affairs delved into the 1914 Simla agreement between British Indian, Chinese, and Tibetan representatives. He concluded that China had accepted the draft convention but had refused to ratify the final version, and the boundary lines drawn, including the McMahon Line, were therefore illegal.[10]

By 1953, China had developed an understanding of its own position, at least in the eastern sector. Chinese officials in Tibet had by then submitted a report which outlined what became Beijing's view. In essence, the report drew attention to the Indian takeover of areas south of the mountain crest line in the North-East Frontier Agency (NEFA). It argued that China had claims south of the McMahon Line and that India should withdraw from those areas. It also argued that the line itself was based on imperial treaties and therefore illegitimate. The report concluded with the suggestion that China should open negotiations with India. This in effect was the Chinese 'sooner' school, which wanted to engage India early.[11]

The Chinese leadership, on the other hand, was the 'later' school. It concluded that China was not ready to deal with the border problem as it was still trying to bring Tibet under control. It recognized among other things that Tibet was highly dependent on 'vital commodities' from India, which was the largest destination for some key Tibetan exports. Beijing was annoyed by what it saw as Indian attempts to manipulate Tibet's economic vulnerability but concluded that, as it moved to integrate the province, a diplomatic row with Delhi was better avoided.[12] China would therefore only 'raise the issue to recover these regions' after it was 'well prepared'.[13] The Chinese central government also had other reasons for refusing to raise the matter with India. Nehru was being helpful at the time in the repatriation of Chinese prisoners in the Korean war, in paving the way for China's participation in the Bandung Afro-Asian Conference of 1955, and in helping set up informal diplomatic talks between China and the US.[14]

Contradictions and inconsistencies

By 1954, the two countries were overcoming their hesitations in raising the border issue but were saying and doing contradictory and inconsistent things, at least in the other side's view. At their first meeting in June 1954, Nehru and Zhou discussed world affairs but apparently did not deal with their territorial concerns. Yet, after the meeting, the Indian leader was worried enough to order India to change its maps to show Aksai Chin and what was then NEFA as part of India. As soon as the maps were published, they would have been available to China. Beijing could very well have seen Delhi's actions as duplicitous: maintaining a silence over the border during the summit and moving immediately thereafter to revise its maps. Chinese behaviour also seemed contradictory. Zhou had failed to mention the border in his meeting with Nehru, but just days later, on 17 July 1954, China protested the presence of Indian troops in Barahoti (in present-day Uttarakhand) – the first signs that Beijing had a clear, firm view of its boundaries and would not be quiescent.

More contradictory behaviour was to follow. After Barahoti,

Nehru decided to tentatively raise the border issue. When he met Zhou in Beijing in October 1954, he asked why Chinese maps showed Indian territory as part of China. India's boundaries, he insisted, were fixed, but he wondered, 'Supposing we publish a map showing Tibet as part of India, how would China feel?' Zhou replied soothingly that communist China had not revised its maps and was using the old Kuomintang maps. Beijing needed 'a little time' to publish its new maps. As for India's new maps, Zhou did not raise an objection to them.[15] However, within days of Nehru's return from Beijing, the Chinese embassy in Delhi produced and handed out yet more old Kuomintang maps that incorporated large portions of Indian territory.[16] The embassy's actions suggested that contrary to Zhou's calming remarks at the summit, China affirmed its old Kuomintang maps and rejected India's new 1954 maps.

A similar train of events was to occur in the period from 1956 to 1958. In December 1956–January 1957, Zhou visited India. At his meeting with Nehru, the Chinese premier referred to the McMahon Line during a discussion on Burma. China, he explained, did not like the McMahon Line (which extended into Burma), as this was a legacy of imperial rule. Nonetheless, it would accept the line as a practical matter. Nehru thus assumed that China would also be pragmatic on India's stretch of the McMahon Line. On the western sector, Zhou was silent, despite the publication of India's new maps.

If all this was reassuring to Delhi, there were worrying contradictory signals. In 1956, China had apparently handed out 'thousands' of old maps showing large parts of India as well as Bhutan, Nepal, and Sikkim as part of Chinese territory.[17] Two years later, the Chinese embassy in London distributed the same map. In Delhi's perception, here was a pattern: Zhou reassuring Nehru in Delhi in October 1954 that existing maps were the work of the predecessor Kuomintang government, followed by the distribution of maps that contradicted what he had said; and Zhou again reassuring Nehru in 1956–57 that China would accept the existing boundaries in the eastern sector, even as it hawked around maps incommensurate with the premier's private remarks. From India's perspective, there were other discrepancies in Chinese behaviour. While Zhou seemed reassuring in both 1954 and 1956–57, China was proceeding with road building in the western sector, possibly in contested ground. Beginning sometime in 1951, China had begun to build a highway from Xinjiang to Tibet through Aksai Chin to move its forces and supplies to the restive province. Indian intelligence may have obtained information on the road as early as that year, but by May 1956 Delhi had clear enough evidence of its existence – in September 1957, China's *People's Daily* published a map showing the road, removing all doubt.[18]

The contradictions and inconsistencies in China's stand were now more or less at an end. When Indian patrols confirmed the existence of the road, India protested to China. As India and China exchanged diplomatic notes on the road, Nehru, aroused by developments in Aksai Chin, wrote to Zhou in December 1958. Focusing on the eastern sector (probably because the diplomats were already in conversation on the western sector), he reminded Zhou that China had said it would recognize the McMahon Line. Zhou's reply in January 1959 was categorical: a properly defined border with India did not exist, and the McMahon Line accepted by Tibetan representatives in 1914 at the Simla conference with British India was improperly drawn. Nevertheless, China would take 'a realistic attitude'. As before, Zhou asked for time to deal with the matter. On the western sector, too, he expressed China's clear disagreement, asking that both sides stick with the status quo pending resolution of their differences.[19] In reply, in March

1959, Nehru accepted that the border had not been altogether delineated between India and China, but he argued that by and large the line went along the watershed. In the western sector, there were nineteenth-century imperial treaties regulating the borderlands, in the middle sector there were traditional norms, and in the eastern sector there was the McMahon Line which had not been challenged until then by Chinese authorities. India agreed in any case to avoid unilateral action.[20]

Although we do not have detailed studies of China's views on Indian policy in this period, a thought-experiment suggests Beijing could well have concluded that Delhi's statements and actions too were marked by contradictions and inconsistencies. For instance, in 1950, in Parliament, Nehru noted that the western sector all the way to Nepal was delineated by 'usage and custom'.[21] Yet, in March 1959 and September 1959, Nehru instead emphasized the 1842 treaty between Tibet and Ladakh (which also had the assent of the 'Emperor of China'). According to the treaty, the two sides agreed not to tamper with Ladakh's boundaries going back to ancient times. Implicitly, here Nehru was invoking international law under which treaties once signed are subject to *pacta sunt servanda* – 'agreements must be kept' – rather than merely relying on usage and custom to argue for the status quo. India's actions on maps also may have confused and annoyed China. British era maps and indeed Indian maps up to 1952 had shown Aksai Chin as being part of an area that was 'undefined'. Yet, in its new 1954 maps, India had clearly defined its territory which included all of Aksai Chin.[22] Reinforcing the message of the new maps, in October 1954 Nehru told Zhou, 'our frontiers are clear' and are 'not a matter for argument'.[23]

Four years later, on 4 September 1958, Nehru was still adamant. Speaking in Parliament, he said about the border, '[it] is not a matter of dispute as far as we are concerned. It is a fixed thing.

There is nothing to talk about . . . [the border] stands defined and does not require further and formal definition'.[24] In contrast, in March 1959, in a reply to Zhou, Nehru admitted that the border was not demarcated everywhere. Then, in August 1959, Nehru's statements in Parliament suggested that India was no longer certain of its claims in the western sector. He noted that the Aksai Chin road, according to India's map, was in Indian territory but admitted that the actual line was not 'marked' – by which he presumably meant properly delineated on maps and on the ground. The western sector was therefore open to discussion, at least parts of it that were 'so very remote and uninhabited'. In any case, the conflict in the west was 'minor', China had strategic reasons for building the road, and India was prepared to enter into discussions.[25]

From here, the contradictions and inconsistences in India's statements and actions waned. Zhou responded to Nehru on 8 September 1959, saying that a settlement should take account of the historical background and 'existing actualities', i.e., the facts on the ground after all the incursions. He repeated China's view that no boundary delimitation existed in the west and the McMahon Line was a legacy of imperialist aggression. Nonetheless, Chinese troops would not challenge the McMahon Line. On 12 September, in Parliament, Nehru agreed that a formal, detailed delimitation of the border in the western sector did not exist but insisted that India's broad claim to Aksai Chin remained.[26] In his letter to Zhou on 26 September, he outlined India's strongest and clearest statement of its stand, rebutting all of Zhou's contentions in detail. In his defence of India's case, he invoked the historical record, as the Chinese premier had done, to arrive at exactly the opposite conclusion: the imperial agreements were valid because they had never been substantially challenged until then.[27]

Tipping points

With Nehru's August 1959 statement in Parliament on being ready to enter into discussions (although in September he rejected talks until the Chinese pulled back in various places along the boundary[28]), with Zhou's offer of a negotiated settlement in September 1959, and with both premiers agreeing that a delimitation of the western boundary was lacking, an accommodation should have been possible. Yet at least four occurrences caused the quarrel to tip over into almost irreversible disagreement.

The first tipping point was the briefing to Nehru in February 1960 by the Indian historian and adviser on the border, Sarvepalli Gopal. Based on his research, Gopal's conclusion was that India had a strong claim in Aksai Chin. If Nehru still harboured any doubts about India's western sector, they apparently evaporated after several hours with Gopal. India's stand now hardened.[29]

The second tipping point was the news in January 1960 that Beijing had struck a deal with Rangoon on the China–Burma border dispute. In the deal, China had recognized a section of the McMahon Line. Burma had accepted in return that the border was not delimited.[30] Nehru had just come round to inviting Zhou to visit Delhi once again – not for thoroughgoing 'negotiations' on the border but rather for 'talks' to help ease military tensions.[31] Delhi expected to be offered a swap deal involving recognition of Chinese claims in the western sector in return for the status quo in the eastern sector. In light of Gopal's evidence and other briefings, as also the growing anger in India on China policy, the Indians decided they would reject the Chinese offer. In a private meeting, Nehru declared, 'If I give them that [the swap] I shall no longer be Prime Minister of India – I will not do it.'[32]

The third tipping point was the summit meeting itself, which turned out to be a diplomatic disaster. Nehru and Zhou talked one-on-one for twenty hours over seven meetings. In addition, Zhou met other Indian leaders. At the end of it, though, both sides had restated well-worn positions, without any breakthroughs. As for the swap, it is unclear how categorically the Chinese made the offer, but at the very least Zhou signalled that the swap was a possible solution – or part of a solution. However, except perhaps for Vice President Sarvepalli Radhakrishnan (incidentally, Gopal's father), no one of standing in India supported a swap.[33]

Why did India reject the swap, which seems such an obvious way to settle the conflict? The record suggests that the Indian side was unsure whether the offer was formal and unequivocal: in Delhi's view, Zhou had changed tack several times on the McMahon Line going back to 1954 and had provided nothing in writing anyway. Also, a swap meant India would relinquish its western claims altogether and in return get to keep its eastern claims. China would therefore come out better. Its forces would advance in the western sector while India's forces would remain where they were in the eastern sector. Beyond this worry was the fear that the swap might be the slippery slope to yet more swaps, leading to further loss of territory all along the border. If India agreed to a swap after a series of military clashes with China, what guarantee was there Beijing would not use the tactic again – clashes followed by a swap offer? As Secretary General of the External Affairs Ministry N.R. Pillai explained to the British High Commissioner: 'If we gave way now on this matter, it would only encourage the Chinese to feel that they [India] were weak and to press even more ambitious claims later on.' Finally, the Indian Supreme Court clarified in March 1960, in the case of the Berubari enclaves in East Pakistan, that any territorial transfers would require an amendment of the Constitution. With growing domestic opposition to Nehru's China policy, enacting constitutional change would be a serious political challenge.[34]

Were these insuperable difficulties though? Could Delhi not have explored the swap further to test Zhou's sincerity? Nehru and his officials probably could and should have done so, but they had gone into the summit determined to reject the swap, and they let the opportunity go. Zhou was pessimistic coming into the summit, yet the Chinese were disappointed at the outcome. In response, China resumed setting up military posts in Aksai Chin.[35]

The fourth tipping point was the post-summit officials' talks in 1960–61 and its aftermath in Beijing in July 1961. The summit had ended in one point of agreement – that Indian and Chinese officials would take discussions forward on establishing the 'facts' about the border. The ensuing talks on the 'historical documents, records, accounts, maps and other relevant materials' achieved little, indeed may have led to further exasperation. The officials met in Beijing, Delhi, and Rangoon from June to December 1960 and produced seven reports of the discussions in early 1961. What was clear in the reports was the enormous gulf between the two sides. They were unable to agree on anything – which was the only thing they agreed on.[36]

Despite the failures of the 1960 summit and the officials' discussions, the two sides held 'unofficial talks' in Beijing in July 1961 (talks that have largely been forgotten). At the talks, the Chinese argued: 'one cannot get tangled up in the details. The relationship between our two countries is too important; we should view from a greater distance, from an elevated height, considering the big picture, and seek resolution.' The Indians agreed saying the 'two sides have sharp differences . . . one method is to place the [officials'] reports to one side and ignore them, while both sides proceed from a political angle to reconsider [the issues]'.

Significantly, the Indian team added: 'But the difficulty lies in swaying popular opinion.'[37] That both countries should be mindful of the strategic–diplomatic 'big picture' had been expressed by the Chinese before. In 1954, in a meeting with Nehru, Mao had said, 'We are a new country. Although we are counted as a large country, our strength is weak. Confronting us is a larger power America . . . therefore we need friends. PM Nehru can feel this. I think India also needs friends.'[38] In a démarche to India in May 1959 over its supposed role in the Tibet uprising (a démarche that was written by Mao personally), the Chinese had urged India to recognize the strategic challenges facing both countries:

> The enemy of the Chinese people lies in the East . . . India is not an opponent but a friend of our country . . . China will not be so foolish to antagonize the US in the East and again to antagonize India in the West. Our Indian friends! What is your mind? Will you be agreeing to our thinking regarding the view that China can only concentrate its main attention eastwards of China but not South-West-ward of China . . . Friends! It seems to us that you too cannot have two fronts . . . Will you please think it over?[39]

In 1959 and then again in 1961, India failed to be persuaded by the strategic argument that China advanced.

Why so? Indian officials in Beijing had hinted at one difficulty: popular opinion at home. Also, as we will see in the next chapter, by 1955–56, Delhi was more comfortable diplomatically with both Moscow and Washington and had concluded that the balance of power internationally favoured it in the emerging rivalry with Beijing. This too, probably, caused India to be cool to the Chinese idea of strategic necessity. Finally, as in 1947–48 on Kashmir, India felt confident – at least by 1960 – that its legal position was strong, indeed unassailable. It should have learned from its experience in the UN – that legalism only went so far and that ultimately the big powers operated on the basis of hard strategic calculations. The apparently unassailable Indian case on Kashmir had failed to persuade the international community to support India against Pakistan. Yet Delhi persisted with its historical–legalistic stance with Beijing. Perhaps this was because Nehru himself was a lawyer, and right through the nationalist struggle the Congress party had used legal–constitutional arguments against British rule even when it relied on Gandhian fasting and mass protests. By contrast, Mao was a strategist, and during the civil war and war with Japan he had constantly made hard choices in the fight against the Kuomintang and the Japanese. For him bargains and compromise more than forensic battles and argumentation were determinative.

After the Beijing 1961 meeting, as tensions boiled up along the border, both sides made a series of last-ditch offers and counter-offers. In June 1962, Delhi proposed to send a ministerial-level delegation to discuss all issues without preconditions (a significant change in its approach). In July 1962, it suggested that once tensions eased the two sides should hold discussions on the 1960–61 Officials' Reports. China rejected both initiatives – Foreign Minister Chen Yi saying that India should 'unequivocally and publicly' withdraw what he called 'all fictitious and false claims on Chinese territory' and that China could not be expected to withdraw from its own territories as a way of reducing tensions.[40] On 13 September, China responded with a three-point proposal which included the offer of talks on the 1960 Officials' Report. India accepted on condition that Chinese forces withdrew from incursions in the western sector. On 3 October, Beijing suggested talks on the entire border be held on 15 October. India accepted on 6 October, again on condition that Chinese intrusions, this time at the McMahon Line, were ended. Clearly, the two sides were quite far apart: India by and large insisting on Chinese withdrawals as a precondition to talks and China insisting on unconditional talks. On the very day that India conditionally accepted China's final invitation, Mao made the decision to go to war. Two weeks later, on 20 October, Chinese forces attacked.[41]

Causes

How can we understand India's and China's reluctance to discuss the border for several years? Why did they adopt seemingly contradictory and inconsistent positions over time? Why in the end did they fail to come to an agreement?

On the reluctance to discuss the border, we have seen that both sides were split between a sooner and a later school. The split related to how ready they were to negotiate. Essentially, both governments were new and were in the process of consolidating their rule at a time of many challenges. Nehru and Panikkar were candid about India's limited capabilities in administering and effectively controlling the outer reaches of the country. Mao and Zhou may well have had the same thoughts about their country, which in land area was two and a half times the size of India. India had just come out of a freedom struggle, a world war, a partition and near civil war (between the Congress party and the Muslim League), and a regional conflict with Pakistan. China too had come out of a civil war, a world war, a partition (the Kuomintang having departed and set up an alternative government in Taiwan), and a regional war in Korea. At the same time, both were entering an unstable international system that was dominated by two opposing superpowers.

India's and China's contradictory and inconsistent statements and actions are also understandable. Neither leadership had negotiated territorial matters. They were not diplomats and had only fledgling foreign services at their disposal. From all accounts, India had only a few historians and cartographers who knew much about the borderlands. Beyond expertise, the documentary and cartographic materials on borders and treaties going back hundreds of years may have been dispersed and damaged in part because of Partition. Some of the materials were in Britain. Nehru only really felt that he had comprehended India's borderlands with China when Gopal briefed him in 1960. Gopal was forced to go to London in order to consult documents and maps that were not even available in India.

Until 1956–57, Beijing was still trying to come to grips with its historical records and maps. The Chinese had produced a report on the border by 1953 but were looking for additional materials. In May 1958, they established a Boundary Committee. Before that, in April 1958, the foreign ministry had instructed the provinces and autonomous regions to furnish relevant materials. Later that year, the leadership noted China's 'limited knowledge about the frontiers, and the lack of historical materials, diplomatic files and accurate maps of the boundary lines'.[42] We should remember that China had been at war from 1937, even before Europe. As Rana Mitter, the Oxford University historian, notes, Chinese civilian and military deaths during this time amounted to 14 million, second only to the 40 million dead in the USSR.[43] In these circumstances, it is quite plausible that Chinese data was fragmented and difficult to pull together – some of it may have been taken away by the Kuomintang to Taiwan as well.

Domestics politics too may have constrained both leaderships and may account for why Delhi and Beijing changed their stances in confounding ways. In the case of Nehru there was opposition within the Congress, within Parliament, in the media, and on the streets. In his history of post-Independence India, Ramachandra Guha recounts the growing domestic opposition to Nehru's

China policy from about 1959 to the outbreak of war in 1962. This included the public quarrel between Defence Minister V.K. Krishna Menon and Chief of Army Staff General K.S. Thimayya which led the latter to hand in his resignation. The civil–military quarrel led to demands in the press for Menon's resignation. Even members of Nehru's Congress party asked for Menon's removal.[44] By late 1959, in the wake of the Longju and Kongka Pass border incidents and with the publication of India's White Paper on the border problem, the press and public opinion were further inflamed. On 4 November 1959, one hundred Congress members of Parliament (MPs) met Nehru to communicate their disquiet over China. Srinath Raghavan notes that though Nehru argued against a hardening of policy, the delegation was 'not satisfied with these explanations'. Erstwhile political colleagues such as C. Rajagopalachari and Jaiprakash Narayan joined in the criticism of Nehru's policies.[45]

Guha quotes an Indian paper as saying Nehru stood 'alone against the rising tide of national resentment against China'.[46] In January 1960, the opposition Jana Sangh asked for 'action to free Indian soil from Chinese aggression'. Just days before Zhou came to Delhi in April 1960 for his last summit with Nehru, protests both private and public broke out. Guha notes that the Himalayan Study Group of the Congress party urged Nehru to stand firm in the summit. The Jana Sangh organized 'a large demonstration outside the prime minister's residence' five days before Zhou's arrival. The non-communist opposition parties held 'a mammoth public meeting in Delhi, where the prime minister was warned that if he struck a deal with the Chinese his "only allies would be the Communists and crypto-Communists"'.[47] J.B. Kripalani, former Congress leader and trenchant Nehru critic, delivered 'perhaps the greatest speech that had been made on the floor of the House since Independence'. He sat down to 'vigorous applause from the opposition benches'. Parliament was frequently in uproar over China policy, with criticism also from Nehru's own party.[48] A foreign diplomat in Delhi concluded that Nehru's almost exclusive hold on foreign policy was 'broken'.[49] The prime minister may have had a massive parliamentary majority, but his room for manoeuvre was considerably narrowed, given the possibility of a revolt within his own party by the late 1950s.

In the case of China, Zhou and Mao were strongly entrenched. However, they had to keep a watchful eye on other centres of power within the CPC. Not all was well, particularly during the period 1958–62 when the so-called Great Leap Forward led to mass famine. Matters were serious enough that Mao briefly had to retreat from day-to-day leadership of the country and hand over to Liu Shaoqi. In his study of the 1962 war, American political scientist John Garver notes, 'It is now pretty well established that Mao's domestic mobilization concerns occasionally helped inspire his preference for confrontational international politics . . . In early 1959 . . . Mao was struggling to push the agricultural collectivization movement to a new high . . . In fall 1962 . . . he was also striving to revive "class struggle" in agricultural policy . . . to reverse the post-Great Leap retreat from collectivized agriculture.'[50]

Between early 1959 and the fall of 1962, China seems to have oscillated between a confrontational and a more cooperative stance in both domestic and foreign policy. On the one hand, Mao and the radicals seemed to favour confrontation coming out of a class-struggle view of politics; on the other hand, Liu Shaoqi and Deng Xiaoping seemed to favour pragmatic accommodation in the interest of economic development. Mao himself wavered. As Garver notes, in early 1959, Mao was confrontational over agricultural policy. In foreign policy, he criticized senior party official and former diplomat Wang Jiaxing's *sanhe yishao* policy of

1961 which had proposed reducing conflict with the big powers and India, as also curtailing aid to revolutionary movements abroad.[51] However, at a party conference in January 1962 Mao supported a more accommodative stance. By the summer of 1962, he had apparently changed his mind again, emphasizing class struggle in agricultural policy and in foreign policy. Eric Hyer's study of China's policies towards its neighbours at this time argues, 'The causes of this change of views [in summer 1962] were rooted in his [Mao's] fears that the success of the pragmatic economic recovery policies, which his fellow leaders Liu Shaoqi and Deng Xiaoping had implemented to alleviate the economic problems that Mao's own brainchild . . . had caused, threatened his political standing within the party and the country.'[52]

Finally, why in the end were India and China so far apart? The answer is that the two leaderships had deep-rooted differences in political values. India under Nehru took a conservative position, arguing that borders inherited from imperial times must be sacrosanct. Legally and from the point of view of international stability, that was vital. Otherwise, the world would be full of newly independent countries all seeking to renegotiate colonial boundaries. China under Mao took a revisionist position, arguing instead that imperially defined borders were illegitimate: they had been forced on China as well as India. Countries could and should come to agreements on boundaries once they had emancipated themselves from the bonds of colonial era treaties and agreements. Perhaps these quite different positions were merely postures lacking substance, when the real issues were strategic gain, honour, and prestige. A less cynical view would be that both perspectives were understandable, in two countries that had just emerged from imperial domination via different historical struggles. Politically, Nehru at his core was an advocate of moderate change in social life, often legalistic and formalistic in his approach; Mao at his core was a champion of radical change and far more strategic and pragmatic. It is hard to ignore these basic ideological differences in understanding their quite opposite approaches to the border negotiations.

Tibet

While conflicts over the border were fundamental to the India–China quarrel, the status of Tibet too was fundamental. As with the border, so also on Tibet, the two sides began with a cooperative attitude. Between 1950 and 1954, Delhi and Beijing came to agree on the status of the province (technically, Autonomous Region). All should have been well, from this positive beginning. Instead, over the next five years, both countries concluded that the other side was failing to honour the understandings worked out on Tibet. Garver's careful archival research on China's decision to go to war in 1962 goes so far as to argue that Tibet was the *casus belli*, the reason for war.[53]

Accommodation

When the communists came to power, they made clear that they would integrate Tibet in China. In 1950, as they consolidated their hold, they moved their troops into the region. Nehru had no great love for the lama system in Tibet, seeing it as feudalistic and oppressive of ordinary Tibetans. At the same time, he was mindful of India's cultural and historical links with the province. Under the British, Delhi had enjoyed a quasi-diplomatic presence there as well. India also traded with Tibet. Indeed, most of Tibet's foodgrains and other consumer products came from India, the transport links to China being difficult over vast distances. Indian public opinion was outraged at China's moves against Tibet in

1950, but the government was realistic. While India provided some arms to the Tibetan government in 1949–50 and protested Chinese actions, there was little else it could do.

Despite India's annoyance over China's actions, its ability to stop Beijing was extremely limited in a material sense, a point that was clearly recognized by Indian decision-makers, civilian and military. Delhi was also keen to engage and partner communist China in emerging Asia and on the larger stage of world politics. This was not idealism. China was widely recognized as a Great Power – President Roosevelt had insisted that it be one of the permanent five in the UN Security Council and the first signatory to the UN Charter. By any standard, it commanded enormous military power after the civil war. India could not match it, even in 1949. By engaging Beijing, Nehru hoped that China would be a stabilizing Great Power, a partner in the international order, and a peaceful neighbour.

Delhi therefore accepted Beijing's takeover of Tibet. Indeed, it was positively helpful. In 1950, when El Salvador sought to move a UN resolution against China's actions in Tibet, India refused to go along and in fact tried to stop the move. Also in 1950, Washington sought Delhi's cooperation in arming the Tibetan resistance. Here too India refused. By 1951, Beijing and Lhasa had signed a seventeen-point agreement on the future of their relationship. In essence, the agreement allowed China to absorb Tibet. In return, the region would have a degree of autonomy: Tibetans would get to keep their political system; the status, functions, and powers of the Dalai Lama and religious freedom would be protected; and the development of Tibet's language and school system would be in local hands as would the process of religious reforms. India then began negotiations with China over its own rights and facilities in Tibet. This resulted in the 1954 'Agreement Between the Republic of India and the

People's Republic of China on Trade and Intercourse Between Tibet Region of China and India'. By signing the agreement, India gave up all its rights and most of its properties in Tibet while retaining its trade agencies as well as access and staying facilities for its religious pilgrims. Most of all, though, the accord underlined Indian acceptance of China's full ownership of Tibet. Once again, Delhi had little choice given Chinese power and India's desire to cultivate China diplomatically for the larger purpose of international and regional stability.

Conflict

From this cooperative beginning on Tibet, trouble set in. The first signs were the Khampa rebellion in 1956 in eastern Tibet against Beijing's reforms and repression. The rebellion did not spread to Lhasa initially, for a variety of reasons including differences between the Lhasa elite and the Kham and Amdo people. However, the Dalai Lama became aware of the situation in the east. His growing unease at Chinese control in Lhasa and perhaps also in the east may have led to his decision to seek refuge in India during a trip to Delhi in 1956. Nehru quickly talked him out of his decision, even as Zhou arrived in India, alarmed by the Dalai Lama's behaviour – the depths of Chinese nervousness can be gauged from the fact that the Chinese premier came to Delhi three times in eight weeks.[54] As Nehru worked on the Dalai Lama, Zhou promised the Indian prime minister that China would deal with Tibetan concerns over autonomy. At the same time, Chinese suspicions about India's role were growing. It is revealing that Chinese accounts of Zhou's trip and of Nehru's role are quite different from the Indian version: they paint a picture of Zhou adroitly intervening with the Dalai Lama even as Nehru threatened China over Beijing's handling of Tibetan autonomy. Revealing too is that when in 1956 the Dalai Lama invited Nehru to visit Lhasa, Beijing intervened to prevent the invitation going out until 1958.[55]

Part of the reason for deepening Chinese suspicions was that from 1956 the rebellion in Tibet was being helped by US intelligence operating from India, a fact that Beijing would have known. Surely, in its view, Delhi was helping the US to stir trouble. In fact, while the US was certainly interfering, it is unclear how much Indian authorities knew and the extent to which they cooperated. Delhi could not be altogether unaware of American activities, but there is no evidence that India actively aided and abetted Tibetan rebels. Instead, it chose to look the other way. Its turning a blind eye was not motivated by a desire to push the Chinese out of Tibet; instead, it arose from a growing view that China was violating the 1954 agreement on Tibet's autonomy. Delhi felt that a degree of pressure on Beijing might act as a check on unbridled Chinese actions.[56]

Whatever Indian motives, officials in Beijing in 1956 would see a picture that was disturbing – a rebellion in eastern Tibet, the Dalai Lama in Delhi seeking political asylum, and American aid to the Khampa resistance. China could be excused for thinking that the three were interrelated. By the summer of 1958, the rebellion in Tibet was gathering force and moving from the eastern part of the province towards Lhasa. Chinese forces were surrounded at Zedong and Dongqing, and these fell to the rebels in early 1959.[57] On 10 March 1959, Lhasa too finally saw the beginnings of rebellion. Beijing decided now to administer the region directly. As Chinese troops massed in strength and threatened the Potala Palace (which housed the Dalai Lama), he slipped out of Lhasa from his summer palace, Norbulinka. On 31 March, he crossed the border into India, where he was given asylum. He was soon joined by thousands of other Tibetans.

India for its part was upset by Beijing's actions which eroded the autonomy that Delhi thought it had secured by its support of the 1951 and 1954 Tibet accords. After the Dalai Lama's arrival in India, Nehru himself, the Indian government, and the aroused public certainly made their feelings known. There were street protests. India banned foodgrain exports to China. Indira Gandhi helped organize an all-party relief committee for Tibetan refugees.[58] Later, India would ban steel products, hand tools, auto parts, fuel, clothing, tea, and sugar to Tibet. The prime minister went to Mussoorie to meet the Dalai Lama, and he edited the Tibetan leader's 18 April 1959 official statement.[59] In a speech in Parliament on 27 April 1959, Nehru made clear that India did not support Tibetan independence but found itself in sympathy with the call to restore Tibet's eroding autonomy. Indian policy, he stated, would be governed by security concerns, by its 'desire to maintain friendly relations with China', and its 'deep sympathy for the people of Tibet'. He added that Tibetan developments had to be seen in the context of 'the wider point of view of the peace of Asia and the world'.[60]

The Chinese view was that India was intimately connected with the origins and continuation of the Tibet rebellion. At a meeting of the CPC in Shanghai on 25 March, Mao pointed to India's role.[61] Under his direction, the Chinese press launched a vitriolic attack on Nehru and India. Garver, in his account of Chinese decision-making, notes that the press was ordered to describe India as expansionist and to criticize the Indian prime minister by name: Nehru had slandered China's actions in Tibet, identified with upper-class Tibetan reactionaries, and exemplified the Indian big bourgeoisie's expansionism which sought to reduce Tibet to a 'buffer zone'. Talking to a group of socialist representatives from various parts of the world, Zhou repeated the message and added that India's Tibet ambitions were 'the centre of the Sino-

Indian conflict'.[62] In Mao's conversation with Soviet leader Nikita Khrushchev in October 1959, he said, 'The Hindus [sic] acted in Tibet as if it belonged to them.' Also in 1959, General Lei Yingfu of the PLA presented an analysis of Indian policy to Mao. He argued that India had worked with the Dalai Lama to try to split Tibet from China. Mao agreed. Years later, Mao told Nepalese visitors that the Indian government thought 'Tibet is theirs'.[63]

Apart from accusing bourgeois India of instigating the revolt, China had a long list of complaints about Delhi's behaviour. These included having the Indian consul general in Tibet meet Tibetan protesters; granting the Dalai Lama and his followers asylum; interacting officially with the Dalai Lama and accepting his references to a Tibet government-in-exile; settling the Tibetan refugees near the Chinese border and allowing political activities by them; restricting trade with Tibet; allowing and/or encouraging the Indian press and protesters to criticize China; and permitting parliamentary speeches and discussions of Tibet. In Beijing's view, Delhi's actions violated the 1954 Panchsheel agreement on peaceful coexistence which India and China had signed in October 1954 during Nehru's trip to Beijing. The five principles were mutual respect for each other's territorial integrity and sovereignty; mutual non-aggression; mutual non-interference; equality and mutual benefit; and peaceful coexistence. India was accused of violating the third principle, mutual non-interference.[64]

Was India subverting Tibet's integration?

Was China justified in its campaign against India and Nehru? Garver's careful assessment is that China got it mostly wrong. Delhi did, as we saw earlier, allow the Dalai Lama and Tibetan refugees to live in India, and it did provide some encouragement to the Dalai Lama and his followers in their resistance. It is true also that India did tacitly cooperate with the US. It was likely aware of US links to the Tibetans in India, especially in Kalimpong, where a command centre of the Tibetan rebels was based.[65] However, much of the US activity in Tibet was conducted from Nepal and Pakistan, not India, as Delhi was thought to be opposed to overt American operations from its soil.[66]

As against this record of aiding and abetting the Tibetan resistance, Garver argues, there was India's helpfulness to China on Tibet. This included rejecting moves in the UN to discuss Tibet and a US call in 1960 for Tibetan 'self-determination'. Indeed, Nehru took the opposite view from the US, repeatedly saying in public that Tibet was part of China. In addition, in 1956, as noted earlier, he persuaded the Dalai Lama to withdraw his appeal for political asylum and to go back to Tibet. In 1959–60, he discouraged Tibetan authorities from approaching the UN (they did anyway – and India abstained on the vote). Beijing berated Nehru for giving the Dalai Lama asylum, but Nehru had had little choice. Domestic and international opinion would have turned massively against him. Interestingly, Nehru thought that China had signalled it would accept the Dalai Lama's stay in India – in remarks that Zhou had made to him as early as 1950 and repeated in 1954 and 1960.[67]

More importantly, Garver argues that China simply did not understand Nehru's motives on Tibet. At the core of his approach was that Tibetan autonomy was a vital Indian interest. This was not just because India had cultural and historical links with Tibetan civilization. Nor was it simply that the Indian leadership felt a moral obligation to try to uphold the agreement. Garver suggests instead that Delhi's calculations were twofold: first, in an autonomous Tibet, the Chinese military presence would be limited and hence India would be safer; and second, the continuation of Tibetan autonomy would demonstrate that India and China could cooperate, which would be a powerful basis for a partnership in Asia and beyond. Indian pressures on China, in the form of support for the Tibetan cause and its tacit backing of US covert activities, were not intended to unravel Chinese communist rule in Tibet. Rather they aimed to push Beijing to honour the original promise of regional autonomy.[68]

Military Actions and the 1962 War

As the conflict over the border and Tibet sharpened, Indian and Chinese forces found themselves increasingly confronting each other, particularly after 1954. The two sides could never agree on who was the aggressor in terms of incursions across the border and who had fired the first shot – with two exceptions, when China admitted its troops had attacked at Longju in August 1959 and when India admitted in September 1959 that its units had crossed the McMahon Line in Tamaden. Yet, both sides did attempt to stabilize military relations and prevent a spiral into outright hostilities. It is tempting to see their actions to head off war as being deceitful and half-hearted. In fact, the record shows otherwise. India's 'Forward Policy' was defensive and not designed to subvert Tibet or grab Chinese territory. And China's military moves were tempered more by a desire to avoid a fight, at least until late September 1962, just days before Beijing finally decided to do battle.

Military moves and stabilization measures, 1954–1959

For eight years leading up to war in 1962, India and China poked and prodded each other at the boundary. Beijing had accused India in 1954 of violating the border at Barahoti in the middle sector; in 1955, Delhi returned the compliment by accusing

Chinese troops of entering Indian territory in the area. A series of minor incursions followed in Barahoti, leading to four years of intermittent discussions between Delhi and Beijing. By 1959, all three sectors – Aksai Chin in the west, NEFA in the east, and the middle sector – were the site of confrontations. One reason for this was that Chinese troops were pushing forward as they dealt with the Tibetan uprising. At any rate, tit-for-tat accusations of intrusions and provocations intensified in the ensuing three years.

Thus, in June 1959, China accused India of intruding at Migyitun and further to the north-east in the eastern sector. Delhi eventually accepted that its forces had mistakenly moved north of the McMahon Line to Tamaden, and it pulled them back. On 28 July, India protested the detention of an Indian patrol in Ladakh. On 7 August, Delhi claimed a fracas occurred at Khinzemane in the eastern sector. This was followed by the most serious clash, at Longju in the eastern sector on 25 August. In a conversation with Khrushchev some weeks later, Mao accepted that China had fired first at Longju but insisted that Chinese actions there were ordered by local commanders. Beijing claimed too that the incident was related to India's prior aggression at Migyitun. In September 1961, there was trouble at Chip Chap in the western sector when Chinese troops tried to capture a post. This was followed by fighting at Kongka, again in the western sector, on 20–21 October: India accused China of ambushing a patrol; China claimed India had started it by more aggressive patrolling. Beijing warned Delhi that if Indian patrols continued to intrude in Ladakh, Chinese troops might do the same in the eastern sector.

With domestic pressure building on the Indian government to respond to China's incursions, Nehru announced the Forward Policy in November 1961 – the advance of Indian troops and the setting up of posts to exert control over territories that India claimed. Whatever China may have thought, it is hard to see that these moves were intended to dislodge Tibet from China or to settle the territorial disputes with China by Indian land-grabs. Nevertheless, Beijing clearly saw matters differently. In response to the Forward Policy, Chinese patrolling grew even more aggressive in Ladakh. Indian and Chinese posts were engaged in a higgledy-piggledy set of deployments – side by side, facing each other, threatening lines of communication. The Chinese advanced on Indian posts in Chip Chap and Galwan but then withdrew in May and June 1962. Fighting broke out in various places in the western sector, and the Indian Army was authorized to fire if Chinese troops got too close. When on 8 September the Chinese occupied the Dhola-Thagla ridge in the eastern sector, a decision was made to evict them. Before Indian troops could do so, the Chinese started a firefight on 20 September. On 10 October, India was caught off guard when the Chinese launched an attack in the Thagla area at Tseng Jong – some eight hundred Chinese troops against just fifty Indian defenders. Just before he left for a trip to Ceylon (now Sri Lanka), Nehru stated publicly that he had ordered the army to recover Indian territory lost in the eastern sector. Even as the Indians planned their next move in the Thagla area, China went to full-scale war on 20 October.

A mainstream Indian view is that China was determined to attack and humiliate India. Going by the fateful meeting of the Chinese leadership on 6 October, that is correct: Mao wanted India to be hit hard and hit where it hurt most, that is, the eastern sector where the Indian Army was strongest, so that it would be clear that India had been taught a lesson. Before that, however, both sides had advanced a series of proposals to stabilize the situation.

In September 1959, at an internal meeting Mao proposed that both sides withdraw twenty kilometres from their confrontational positions at the time. If India rejected this, he told his decision-making team, China should withdraw anyway and stop forward patrolling.[69] After Longju, as noted earlier, India withdrew its troops from Tamaden. When China publicly suggested in November 1959 that both sides withdraw twenty kilometres from their respective control lines and stop forward patrolling, India agreed that the latter was a positive step. However, a symmetric pullback, as suggested by Beijing, would in fact be asymmetric since it was harder for India to move forward if and when necessary given terrain difficulties on its side. Delhi suggested instead that if China withdrew from Longju, India would then not invest it with its forces; further, in Ladakh, the Chinese should withdraw eastwards from the 1956 line while India would withdraw westwards of the line. The seemingly symmetric proposal for Ladakh also was asymmetric since the Chinese, having advanced further, would have to give up more territory. Zhou suggested the two prime ministers meet; Nehru thought this premature. Zhou then came back with roughly parallel arguments about asymmetry that India had made, and so it went: the two sides exchanging notes, letters, and memoranda for most of 1959.[70]

Despite the disagreements and the asymmetric offers on both sides, the Chinese restraint measures of January 1960 on target practice, food gathering, and military exercises in advanced areas did bring some calm, and border incidents reduced. After the 1960 summit, China began to stiffen its response, but even then, it aimed for restraint and negotiations. In response to India's Forward Policy in November 1961, Mao convened another meeting of his senior-most advisers. China decided to resume patrolling and road building, but with the proviso that only Mao could authorize the PLA to fire. As the encirclement and counter-encirclement of posts occurred in early 1962, Mao ordered the PLA to stand firm but not to fire the first shot. He called this posture 'armed coexistence'.[71] In July 1962, Zhou told Chinese

Foreign Minister Chen Yi to meet Indian Defence Minister Krishna Menon during the Geneva conference on Laos. Menon blandly told Chen Yi there was no border problem, that China simply had to withdraw, and that Indian troops were on their own territory. When Chen suggested a joint communique, Menon said he would get back to him on it but never did (by the time Delhi replied, Chen had returned to China).[72] Also in July 1962, Chinese troops were told to hold positions, to warn off advancing Indian troops, and only to fire if Indian units got to within fifty metres and the Chinese felt endangered.[73] All in all, this suggests quite a different picture from the caricatures which portray China as being determined to attack and humiliate India after 1959.

The decision for war

From all accounts, China finally took a decision to go to war on 6 October. They attacked in strength in both the eastern and western sectors two weeks later. Four days into the war, Zhou offered Nehru a deal: in the western sector, both armies would pull back twenty kilometres from the Line of Actual Control as on 7 November 1959. China would then return to its positions north of the McMahon Line. This would be followed by a meeting of the two prime ministers. When Delhi rejected the proposal, China resumed operations on 16 November. With Indian defences crumbling, China abruptly stopped its advance on 21 November and started to pull back to positions north of the McMahon Line. The war, of eleven days of actual fighting, was over. It remains India's shortest war.

Why in the end did China attack? The best account of Chinese decision-making is Garver's, which is based on China's official histories, informed accounts by former officials, and academic writings. In it, he argues that Mao and his senior advisers were convinced that India was destabilizing Tibet and wanted to turn it into an independent buffer zone; that India in the end did not want to negotiate any or all parts of the border sincerely and was not open to a political resolution (that is, the swap); and that the Forward Policy was militarily provocative and dangerous for China. While there may have been other motives as well – and Garver suggests that Chinese discourse on the necessity of war also refers to relations with Moscow and Washington – Tibet, the border stalemate, and the Forward Policy were central.

At the heart of it all was not territory itself. Rather, it was the significance of territory, particularly in the western sector, for Chinese control over Tibet. Given Beijing's assessment of Indian behaviour on Tibet, the border negotiations, and Indian military moves, it decided that Delhi needed to be administered a painful shock. A limited Chinese attack would be fruitless: defeating a weak Indian force in the west would fail to make the strategic point. Mao insisted on a large-scale attack all along the border but aimed particularly at India's military strength, which was in the eastern sector. It was also the case that in border negotiations India had been most adamant in refusing to discuss the McMahon Line. On 6 October, when China received India's rejection of Beijing's 3 October proposal for talks on the entire border, the decision for war was more or less made. The military was told, 'If Indian forces attack us, you should hit back fiercely . . . not only repel them, but hit them fiercely and make them hurt.' Marshal Liu Bocheng, who headed the Central Military Commission (CMC), insisted that Chinese forces could not use limited tactics but rather had to 'kill, wound, and capture the enemy'.[74]

China was helped in its war decision-making by American and Soviet diplomacy. Beijing's relations with both powers were tense, but ironically their messaging reassured China in respect of war with India. In May 1962, Zhou asked the Chinese diplomat

Wang Bingnan to meet his US counterpart in Warsaw. Since 1955, in the absence of formal diplomatic ties, China and the US had convened a dialogue in Poland to deal with bilateral matters (which, in a further irony, India had helped organize). In 1962, Wang's mission was to assess the US response to a possible Taiwanese invasion of the mainland. Beijing feared that the US might allow the Taiwanese, who were threatening to invade, to mount an attack into southern China from Laos. If so, China would have been at war in the west with India and in the south with Taiwanese forces. In June, to Beijing's relief, the US told Wang that Washington would not support a Taiwanese attack. By July, an international peace agreement had been signed, committing the US not to deploy its troops in Laos, further suggesting that China's southern flank was secure. The US may therefore have unwittingly contributed to China's decision to go to war with India.[75]

The Soviet role was less unwitting. Moscow and Beijing had been drifting apart ideologically and strategically since the late 1950s, but in October 1962 as the Cuban missile crisis loomed, the Soviets shifted ground in the India–China quarrel. In 1959, Khrushchev had had some harsh words for Mao and Zhou on their handling of Tibet and India. But by October 1962, knowing that the emplacement of nuclear weapons in Cuba was likely to develop into a crisis with Washington, Moscow wanted to firm up support in the socialist world. China was vital in this regard. On 14 October, just six days before China attacked India, Moscow conveyed to Beijing that it would 'stand together with China' in the event of an India–China war. Garver suggests in addition that the Soviets may even have indicated the dates of the impending missile crisis, namely, late October to mid-November when US congressional elections were due. This time frame coincided nicely with Beijing's eventual plans to go to war with India.[76]

India's mistakes

China was also helped by India's failure to sufficiently prepare for a large-scale attack. After the collapse of the 1960 Nehru–Zhou summit, Mao approved the setting up of forward posts in Ladakh.[77] Indian intelligence noted, however, that when the Chinese encountered Indian units, they would avoid challenging them: in September 1961, the Intelligence Bureau (IB) reported that 'when even a dozen of our men are present, the Chinese have kept away'.[78] This suggested that the Chinese were reluctant to escalate. The Indians concluded that part of the reason for Chinese restraint was geography. The Himalaya posed serious logistical challenges even for the PLA: if the Chinese advanced too far into Indian territory their supply lines would stretch longer and longer back into Tibet.[79] India therefore could push its forces ahead to check the Chinese and even encircle them by means of its Forward Policy.

What Nehru and his key advisers failed to understand was that China's aim was not to mount an invasion. It was to capture key areas near the border and then dig in. As Steve Hoffmann in his detailed reconstruction of Indian thinking notes: 'given his [Nehru's] personal lack of military experience or inclination, the prime minister was unable to imagine that a Chinese military move in NEFA or Ladakh could be something less than an invasion but more than another border incident. He did not speculate on the range of options open to Chinese ground forces, options that might preclude great-power intervention.'[80] The Forward Policy might have dealt with relatively minor 'border incidents'; it was inadequate for dealing with anything larger than that.

Beyond the stopping power of the Himalaya, the basic Indian calculation was that the 'correlation of forces' – the balance of power – would deter China: Soviet, US, and British power plus global opinion would hold back Beijing's hand. In Nehru's view, Beijing would be aware that the US and Soviets might become involved in a wider war: 'the Chinese are unlikely to invade India because they know that this would start a world war, which the Chinese cannot want'.[81] Nehru also thought that Moscow would restrain Beijing due to its own growing rivalry with China.[82] Delhi's view of the correlation of forces turned out to be wrong. India forgot that China had demonstrated an ability to take calculated risks and to defy both the US and Soviets. In 1950, only a year after the communists had seized power in the mainland, they had launched a massive military attack against the US-led UN forces in Korea, fought them at hight cost for three years, and pushed them back down the peninsula. In 1954–55, mainland China had shelled Taiwan despite the risk that Washington would get involved. In the 1950s, India was also among the first to sense that China was standing up to the Soviets ideologically and diplomatically within the global communist movement. Clearly, then, China was far more 'risk-acceptant' than India estimated.

India's confidence that China would avoid a full-scale war was broadcast publicly and underlined by the casual stance of the leadership in the months and weeks leading up to hostilities. For instance, on 5 December 1961, in Parliament Nehru discounted the possibility of war with China.[83] More than Indian statements, though, were the actions of its leadership, in the closing days before the fight. On 17 September 1962, Defence Minister Krishna Menon left for a UN meeting and only returned on 30 September. Nehru went to the Commonwealth meeting in London as well as to Paris, Lagos, and Accra on 8 September and returned only on 2 October. He then left India again, to visit Ceylon on 12 October and returned on 16 October, four days before China attacked. General Kaul, Chief of the General Staff, was away on holiday until 2 October and the Director General of Military Operations was on a cruise on an Indian aircraft carrier.[84]

Why, though, did India lose the war so categorically? Indian military preparations and responses to China's attack have been widely analysed and criticized. When the official military inquiry into the 1962 debacle, the Henderson-Brooks report, is finally released, it will give us an even fuller account of Delhi's thoughts and actions. However, it is clear enough that Indian forces were not numerically inferior in overall terms. Getting precise figures is difficult, at least in part because of the 'accounting system' of the two armies: the size of corps, divisions, brigades, and other units, in terms of which most histories of the war are rendered, are not equivalent. An American estimate, by Larry M. Wortzel of the US Army War College, is that at the start of the war India had about 16,000 troops while the Chinese had about 10,000 troops in the east. In the west, the two sides were about level in terms of numbers: India had about 6000 troops while China had about 6300 troops. By the second half of the war, from 14 November onward, India had 22,000 troops whereas the Chinese had 25,000 troops in the east. In the west, India had increased its forces to 15,000 troops. Wortzel does not provide a final figure for Chinese deployments in the western sector – we can assume that, as in the east, the two forces were roughly in balance numerically.[85]

In the Indian popular imagination, there is a view of its forces being overrun by hordes of Chinese troops. When Indian deployments were overrun it was not because of the overall balance of military forces in the two sectors. It was because the Chinese had concentrated forces and achieved local dominance. Where India statically defended border posts, the Chinese were highly mobile and chose where and when to fight – which they had mastered in the civil war and against the Japanese. Tactics mattered too. The Chinese laid down barrages of fire to pin the Indian forces and soften up positions, attacked the flanks, and initiated battle at night if necessary. They also had better reconnaissance and ground intelligence, robust infrastructure leading to the front, and superior equipment including high-altitude winter clothing (while Indian troops often wore flimsy summer outfits, were poorly shod, and shouldered one-shot bolt-action rifles). Finally, the Chinese used battle-hardened veterans of the Korean war whereas the last time Indian forces had truly fought a war was in 1947–48 against Pakistan. Few of those Indian troops would have been in the military in 1962.

~

The war ended on 21 November 1962 when China declared a unilateral ceasefire. The terms on which it ended were outlined by the Chinese on 24 October in their original ceasefire proposal (repeated on 21 November). Essentially, the Chinese proposed that the dispute be settled by negotiation and that, pending a settlement, both sides respect the Line of Actual Control and disengage forces by withdrawing to a point twenty kilometres behind the LAC as it existed on 7 November 1959. In the eastern sector, this meant the McMahon Line and in the western and middle sectors it meant the traditional customary line which the Chinese had insisted on in their claims. India's acceptance of China's proposal was de facto in the sense that the Indian Army refrained from crossing the 1962 line in the eastern sector and the 1959 line in the western sector.

The Border, Tibet, and Military Relations, 1963–Present

After the war, the two sides gradually normalized relations, eventually returned to border negotiations, largely avoided quarrelling over Tibet, and instituted a series of confidence-building measures that contributed to military stability. Yet in the end they failed to resolve the border quarrel, found themselves periodically at odds over Tibet, and from 2013 were involved in a series of military confrontations. The climax to this period of failed cooperation was less spectacular than in 1962. The melee at Galwan in June 2020 did not escalate to outright hostilities, but the threat of real fighting loomed large. We see here a repeat of the period between 1949 and 1962 – the gradual ratcheting up of the quarrel, the attempts to cooperate, and increasing military tensions.

Border Negotiations Resumed

For several years after the war, China–India diplomatic intercourse was low key and minimal. Intermittently, there were tensions too. In 1963, Pakistan ceded the Shaksgam area of Pakistan-occupied Kashmir to China as part of a border agreement, to which India strenuously objected. In 1965, during the India–Pakistan war, it seemed that China might open a second front against India to divert Indian forces; in the event, it chose not to do so. In June 1967, diplomats from both countries were expelled from their respective embassies for spying. From 11 to 14 September 1967, India and China fought in the eastern sector, at Nathu La in Sikkim: India's estimates put the Indian toll at eighty-eight dead and the Chinese toll at 300 dead. China's estimates are sixty-five and thirty-two, respectively.[86] On 1 October, they had another short duel at Cho La, about seven kilometres from Nathu La. For a brief time after 1968, China lent some support to the Naxalites, the Indian Maoist group. Until the mid-1970s, China also helped separatists in the Indian North-East including the Nagas and Mizos. In November 1970, Beijing accused Delhi of continuing to support both Tibetan rebels and the government of Taiwan, an accusation it continued to make periodically. When Sikkim was integrated into the Indian Union in 1974, the Chinese press ran critical commentary. Four Indian soldiers were killed in Arunachal Pradesh on 20 October 1975.[87]

The thaw

It is forgotten that this was also a period marked by calls for negotiation and by diplomatic warming. In September 1964, two years after the war, India's Ministry of External Affairs stated that Delhi would be happy to restart border negotiations if Chinese forces withdrew from seven posts in Ladakh. Beijing rejected the proposal. In January 1969, in another attempt to break the status quo, Prime Minister Indira Gandhi announced India was ready to deal with all bilateral issues without preconditions. Disregarding diplomatic protocol, Mao then greeted the Indian Charge d'Affaires Brajesh Mishra at a reception line in Beijing in May 1970. Just days before the outbreak of war between India and Pakistan in 1971, Mrs Gandhi and Zhou exchanged friendly messages. Mrs Gandhi felicitated China on finally taking its place at the UN, and China thanked India for its support. Finally, the two countries restored diplomatic ties to the ambassadorial level in 1976.

With full diplomatic normalization, the two countries moved to repair the relationship and to settle the border. In February 1979, Minister of External Affairs Atal Bihari Vajpayee visited China to meet Premier Hua Guofeng, Vice Premier Deng Xiaoping, and Foreign Minister Huang Hua. The visit was marred by China's attack on Vietnam, but this was the first official meeting of Chinese and Indian leaders since the early 1960s. During the visit, the Chinese offered to settle the border in a swap as they had done in 1960. In June 1980, in an interview with an Indian journalist, Deng Xiaoping repeated the offer.[88] The Chinese foreign minister for the first time since 1962 attended the Indian embassy Republic Day reception. Mrs Gandhi met her Chinese counterpart at the funeral of the Yugoslavian leader Josip Broz Tito in May 1980. In November 1980, China's Deputy Foreign Minister Han Nialong suggested that the border dispute with India could be solved through negotiations. He also sought to allay Indian fears over Chinese arms sales to Pakistan. Vice Premier and Foreign Minister Huang Hua returned Vajpayee's visit in June 1981.

In 1982–83, China once again offered India a swap – first in a meeting between Deng and Mrs Gandhi's trusted adviser and former ambassador to China G. Parthasarathi in 1982, and then again in 1983. At the 1982 meeting, the two sides reportedly agreed to the swap. Parthasarathi's son, Ashok Parthasarathi, in his biography of his father, suggests that the two sides exchanged letters confirming the deal, leaving details to be worked out. He also claims that there were five rounds of negotiations on the deal and that the talks were eventually sabotaged by a senior Indian diplomat posted in Beijing who, on his own authority, suddenly conveyed to the Chinese that the deal was off the table.[89] In 1983, according to former foreign secretary Shyam Saran, India proposed a modification of the swap by proposing a deal in which 'India would retain the territory it claimed in the eastern sector while China would concede some additional territory in the western sector'. China showed interest but contingent on Mrs Gandhi visiting China. Mrs Gandhi apparently 'wanted to wait until after the general elections in 1985' before taking a final decision. With her death on 31 October 1984, the high-level swap initiative ended.[90]

What led to this thaw between 1979 and 1983? Delhi and

Beijing were on opposite sides of the Cold War, and relations might have spiralled negatively. In fact, even though the basic alignments of India, China, the Soviets, and the US stayed in place until 1989, Delhi and Beijing tried to reduce their differences. As we will see in a later chapter, Delhi was preparing to reach out to Washington for economic reasons and a desire to avoid being too dependent on Moscow, especially after the Soviet invasion of Afghanistan in December 1979. Improving relations with Beijing was a parallel track: Delhi needed a peaceful regional environment to deal with its internal economic and political problems (for example, separatism). Beijing made a similar calculation. It sought stability on its borders with the Soviets and wanted greater bargaining room with the US. Mending fences with Delhi would stabilize its western border and allow it to concentrate on its economy.

The first phase of border negotiations, 1981–1988

The thaw in relations led to eight rounds of border talks between 1981 and 1989 – talks that are often unfairly disparaged. These were the first set of serious negotiations on the border in twenty years, after the Nehru–Zhou summit of 1960 and the Officials' Report of 1961. While they failed to produce a breakthrough, they did bring greater clarity to the emerging views of the two sides – views that have largely endured. In this sense, they were something of a success: at the end of the eight rounds, neither side was left with illusions about the other's stand. The reason for their relative success is that they were held away from the public gaze: unlike in 1960, when the Nehru government and then China made the mistake of publishing the bilateral correspondence, the substance of the dialogue was kept relatively secret.[91]

What was achieved? First of all, India was able to abandon its insistence that a settlement of the border must precede the full normalization of relations. After 1962, India had insisted that it would not resume normal relations with China until the border was settled. New Delhi finally agreed to separate the resumption of economic and other interactions from progress on the border. This volte face became public during Prime Minister Rajiv Gandhi's December 1988 visit to Beijing. Secondly, the two sides agreed that they would adopt the view that 'until everything is agreed, nothing is agreed'. This meant India and China would have to agree sector by sector and then further agree that all the sectoral agreements were acceptable in order for any sector to be finally settled. Thirdly, and most importantly, both sides finally abandoned the idea of the swap. Since 1962, Delhi had assumed that China's claims south of the McMahon Line were limited and the main claims were in the western sector. The swap offers right up to 1983 lent weight to the interpretation that above all Beijing wanted to ensure the security of its road from Xinjiang to Tibet. At the sixth round of the talks, China changed its stand completely, arguing that the eastern sector was more important than the western sector and that India would have to make concessions in the east if it wanted a settlement in the west.

Why did China abandon the idea of a swap, and why did it change its view of the relative importance of the two sectors? It is hard to know exactly, but Beijing must have concluded that it was wasting its time on the swap. After the first round of the negotiations, India's Foreign Minister P.V. Narasimha Rao had categorically rejected the swap in his statement in Parliament: 'The government of India has never accepted the premise on which it is based, namely, that the Chinese side is making a concession in the eastern sector by giving up of territory which they allege is illegally incorporated into India.'[92] The Chinese had nonetheless persisted with the idea until the fourth round. By then, it was clear that, despite the defeat of 1962 and the passage of nearly two decades, Delhi continued to reject the swap. India insisted on the sector-by-sector, all-or-nothing approach – perhaps there was more to be gained for China by going along. As Garver notes, 'if concessions in one area were no longer to be linked to gains in some other area [as in the swap], it made the most sense to push for the maximum in all sectors'.[93]

Garver also suggests that since Rao had rejected the notion that China was making a concession in the east, Beijing may well have concluded that Delhi needed reminding that China still maintained a strong claim in the eastern sector. Whatever India might think, in Chinese thinking giving up its claims in the eastern sector *was* a concession. Yet another possibility, according to Garver, is that the Chinese negotiators responded to a growing view that China should adopt a harder position in the discussions.[94] China was no longer weak as it had been in 1960, the region south of the McMahon Line was rich in timber, hydroelectricity, and minerals (one-third of the resources 'of all of Tibet') and had prime agricultural land. The eastern claim was therefore more important than Aksai Chin, which had no natural resources and was no longer logistically that important (since Tibet had been brought under control and was serviced by alternative routes).[95]

Finally, the Indian diplomat Ranjit Singh Kalha suggests that the Chinese may have concluded that if they conceded in the eastern sector, India would press even harder in the west. They may have decided therefore to scuttle the talks on the border and turn discussion to other issues such as normalization. In any case, they may have calculated that Rajiv Gandhi did not have the political strength at home to come to a final settlement.[96]

India's rejection of the swap clearly played a role in China's abandoning the idea and hardening its stand on the border.

Garver reconstructs Chinese thinking after both the 1960 and 1980 offers were rejected:

> It is difficult to overstate the impact on informed Chinese opinion of India's two-fold rejection [1960 and 1980] of China's east-west swap proposal . . . By rejecting China's reasonable proposal, India demonstrated once again, its arrogant attitude: what's mine is mine, and what's yours is mine . . . the same sort of arrogance India demonstrates repeatedly towards its other neighbours . . . The Indian leaders were students and heirs of British imperialists . . .[97]

The Singapore diplomat Kishore Mahbubani was told by a senior Chinese official, who was personally involved in Sino-Indian negotiations, that there was always a standard conversation between the Chinese and Indian sides in the border negotiations. The Indian side would begin the negotiations by observing that senior Chinese leaders, including Zhou and Deng Xiaoping, had proposed on at least three occasions that both sides reach a final settlement of the border issue based on the existing line of control with no major adjustments in territory. The Indian side then would ask, 'Why doesn't China table this proposal again?' The Chinese official said that the response to this question would be, 'Why didn't you accept it when China proposed it?' and that's where the conversation would end.[98]

In 2020, a more recent perspective emerged on why a border settlement, and indeed a larger rapprochement, appears so remote. Sun Yun, Senior Fellow of the Stimson Center in Washington, DC, a perceptive China scholar, suggested that Beijing is unwilling to accommodate Delhi, including on the border, in the belief that Delhi will not make meaningful reciprocal concessions: 'For China, key concessions such as the border settlement are irreversible hard commitments, while all that India can deliver in return, such as its neutrality between China and the US, is ephemeral and can be easily reversed.'[99] If China truly holds to this position, then virtually any border settlement and larger diplomatic accommodation becomes untenable.

The second phase of border negotiations, 1989–2005

Almost coincident with the petering out of the border negotiations was the military confrontation in June 1986 between the two militaries at Sumdorong Chu in Arunachal Pradesh. India accused China of coming south of the mountain slopes in the state. China insisted that its forces were north of the line. Both sides quickly amassed large forces, and hostilities looked possible. In the end, the danger was averted through some timely diplomacy, but seeing how close the two had come to a confrontation despite seven years of border talks, Rajiv Gandhi decided to visit China in 1988 – the first Indian prime minister since 1954 to land in Beijing.

In Beijing, the two sides agreed that, along with normalization, they would continue with border negotiations but now in the form of a dedicated Joint Working Group (JWG). The JWG met fifteen times from 1989 to 2005. The focus of the group was not so much on finding a settlement of the border quarrel; rather, it focused on military stability along the LAC. The results of this more limited aim were the agreements in 1993 and 1996 on confidence building measures and an exchange of maps on the alignment of the LAC in the middle sector. When the two delegations followed up with an exchange of maps on the western sector, their claims were so far apart that they decided to stop the process of further map exchanges so as not to jeopardize the JWG negotiations. This is why China has continued to reject a delineation of the LAC: the delineation efforts made relations more contentious, and it is therefore better to stop trying – reminiscent of Beijing's view in the 1950s and 1960s that it is more fructuous to focus on the strategic 'big picture' in order to find a settlement rather than get immersed in historical and cartographic minutiae. As Huang Xilin, a Chinese official, said to Indian journalists years later in 2015: 'If we find that a clarification of the LAC is a building block, then of course we should go ahead. But if we find that it could become a stumbling block, it could complicate further the situation, then, we have to be careful.'[100]

The third phase of border negotiations and the 2005 agreement

The border negotiations entered a third phase, in 2003, when Delhi and Beijing decided to raise negotiations to the level of Special Representatives who would report directly to the political leaderships. The result of these discussions was an agreement in 2005 titled 'Political Parameters and Guiding Principles for the Settlement of the India–China Boundary Question'. The agreement featured six key principles:

1. the two sides would seek a 'political settlement'
2. they should make 'adjustments . . . so as to arrive at a package settlement to the boundary question. The boundary settlement must be final, covering all sectors of the India–China boundary.'
3. they would give 'due consideration to each other's strategic and reasonable interests'
4. in reaching a settlement, they would rely on 'historical evidence, national sentiments, practical difficulties and reasonable concerns and sensitivities of both sides, and the actual state of the border'

5. the final boundary should be 'along well-defined and easily identifiable natural geographical features'
6. they would 'safeguard due interests of their settled populations in the border areas'

This is the most explicit statement regarding the nature of a settlement, and though it has not resolved the conflict, it did prepare the ground. The six points made clear that the two governments had given themselves plenty of room for manoeuvre in relation to their publics – virtually any criticism of a future settlement could be deflected by citing one or more of the six principles.

The 2005 agreement is notable for several things but broadly two elements stand out. The first is that there is a balance between India's preference for history, geography, and national 'sentiment' to play a part in determining the boundary lines and China's preference for politics, strategic interests, and the facts on the ground ('the actual state of the border') to play a part. India wanted a sector-by-sector approach and China wanted a deal that covered the entire border in a package, all-or-nothing stipulation, and the agreement reconciles the two positions. The second notable aspect of the agreement is that despite the use of the term 'package', it does not endorse the old swap idea. A package settlement in the 2005 accord implies that the two sides will agree to adjustments in each sector and that neither side will get everything it wants in any sector. Until they are agreed on all three sectors, they do not have an overall settlement. India and China cannot, for example, settle the relatively easy middle sector in a separate agreement and then proceed to the other sectors. They must settle all three sectors in one comprehensive agreement.

From 2003 to 2019, the Special Representatives met twenty-two times. After the early breakthrough in the 2005 agreement, stalemate and discord once again set in. Conflict, as in the past, began to replace cooperation. In 2006, as we will see shortly, China suddenly laid claim to all of Arunachal Pradesh. It also indicated its unhappiness over Clause VI of the 2005 accord which had suggested that any agreement would 'safeguard due interests of their settled populations in the border areas' – India took this to mean that only minor adjustments in the eastern sector would be necessary. By 2008, India was recording growing Chinese incursions. Outright military confrontations occurred in 2013, 2014, 2015, and 2017.

After the 2014 confrontation, India changed tack on the border, in two respects. Since 1988, it had gone along with the view that normalization would lead to military stability and eventually a border settlement. Delhi now reversed the causal logic. A border settlement and military stability were essential for further normalization. Up to 2005, India and China had also seemingly agreed that a border settlement was central to their negotiations. Delhi replaced this with the contention that the delineation of the LAC was more urgent than a final border settlement. At a press conference with Xi, during his official visit to India in 2014, even as Indian and Chinese troops were eyeball to eyeball in Chumar in Ladakh, Prime Minister Narendra Modi gestured at both changes in the Indian approach: 'peace and stability in our relations and along our borders are essential for us to realize the enormous potential in our relations [i.e. normalization] . . . [and] clarification of Line of Actual Control would greatly contribute to our efforts to maintain peace and tranquility'.[101]

When Beijing failed to respond positively, Modi repeated his suggestion on the LAC at a press conference in China the following year.[102] During the same visit in a speech at Tsinghua University he summarized India's emerging position:

> In recent years, we have deepened our political engagement. We have kept our borders peaceful . . . Yet, if we have to realise the extraordinary potential of our partnership, we must also address the issues that lead to hesitation and doubts . . . we must try to settle the boundary question quickly . . . But, a shadow of uncertainty always hangs over the sensitive areas of the border region . . . It is because neither side knows where the Line of Actual Control is in these areas . . . That is why I have proposed resuming the process of clarifying it. We can do this without prejudice to our position on the boundary question.[103]

China remained unmoved. All that the joint statement could say was: 'The two sides affirmed that an early settlement of the boundary question serves the basic interests of the two countries and should be pursued as a strategic objective by the two governments.'[104] Despite Modi's very public pitch, Beijing refused to commit to a delineation of the LAC. Two years later, the two militaries squared off at Doklam, near the trijunction of India, Bhutan, and China. With the Doklam crisis, Rajiv Gandhi's 1988 policy of normalization leading to a border settlement had crumbled. It was being replaced by the view that a border settlement or at least a delineation of the LAC was a precondition for normalization – the position that Delhi had adopted after the 1962 war and abandoned in 1988.

To recap, in the period from 1981 to 2019 the two countries had forty-five rounds of border negotiations, which is an average of more than one round of talks a year over nearly forty years. The negotiations made it possible for India to abandon the corner in which it found itself after 1962, namely, that relations with China could not be normalized until a boundary settlement was reached. Also, there was much greater clarity on the concerns and preferences of the two sides. The old swap/barter deal was finally abandoned. It was replaced by the idea of a package settlement – settling the border sector by sector, with concessions to be made in all three sectors. The progress on clarifying each other's positions and agreeing to a broad set of protocols notwithstanding, negotiations achieved little after 2005. Indian frustration grew and Chinese obstinacy increased, climaxing in a series of military confrontations between 2013 and 2017. The confrontations caused Indian policy to shift back towards the older stand which tied normalization to a border settlement. The 2020 crisis in Ladakh threatened war. Between 1949 and 1961, India–China relations went from cooperation to conflict and war. The period from 1963 to 2020 was marked by a rather similar pattern drawn out over nearly six decades – cooperation descending into conflict and climaxing in the threat of full-scale war.

Tibet Again

India and China have gone through a cooperation to conflict phase in Tibet as well. Immediately after the 1962 war, Delhi hardened its approach to Tibetan affairs. Gradually, though, it softened its stand and avoided provoking Beijing unduly. By the early 2000s, it had recognized almost fully Tibet's integration in China. However, in 2006, India's Tibet policy changed in response to China's policy on Arunachal Pradesh. Conflict over Tibet is a possibility especially in the post–Dalai Lama future.

Towards cooperation

After the 1962 war, Delhi's involvement with Tibet was initially focused on dealing with the exiles in India and occasionally poking Beijing in the eye. In 1963, Delhi set up the Special Frontier Force, which consisted of Tibetan refugees in India.

The force was designed to be used in high-altitude warfare in the western and eastern sectors in the event of hostilities with China. It fought for India in the Bangladesh war of 1971, at Siachen in the 1990s, and was used in Galwan in 2020 (with one highly publicized fatality).[105] Beyond this, also in 1963, Delhi helped the Dalai Lama write a constitution for Tibet.[106] Garver claims that in addition in the 1960s India set up a communications station in Odisha to maintain contact with Tibetan insurgents, coordinated with the CIA on the insurgency in the province, and organized former Indian Air Force personnel to air-drop supplies to resistance fighters.[107] In December 1965, after Beijing's belligerent statements and actions during the India–Pakistan war, Delhi for the first time supported a UN resolution on Tibet. By 1966, it seemed to be on the verge of recognizing the Tibetan government-in-exile, but Prime Minister Lal Bahadur Shastri's death at the summit in Tashkent stopped further action (it has still not recognized the so-called Central Tibetan Administration, as the government-in-exile came to be called).

Despite these signs of obstreperousness over Tibet just after the 1962 war, Delhi maintained a dual and ambivalent stance towards the Dalai Lama. He was, by and large, restricted to Dharamshala, to manage religious and community affairs. On the other hand, over time, as he attracted greater international attention, India issued a special document to enable him to travel. He made his first trip to the West in 1973 and to the US in 1979. From 1987, he travelled abroad at least once a year, and between 1954 and 2000 he made 183 trips to 57 countries.[108] Whatever India's concerns about his actions and China's annoyance at his increasing international popularity, legally and morally Delhi had little choice. Also, his increasing following in the West made it difficult to curb his movements. China remained sensitive to the Dalai Lama's presence in India and his international activities. It repeatedly asked India to curb him. In 1978, it also established direct contact with the Tibetan leader. The Dalai Lama responded by sending delegations to Tibet from 1979 to 1982.[109] In September 1993, he clarified that he looked to a 'solution [with Beijing] which does not ask for independence of Tibet'.[110]

Delhi's response to Beijing's nervousness and outreach to the Dalai Lama was to support China's ownership of Tibet, beginning with the joint press communiqué of 23 December 1988 at the conclusion of Rajiv Gandhi's visit to China. A series of reassuring Indian statements followed: the final communiqué at the conclusion of Premier Li Peng's visit in 2001, the Declaration on Principles for Relations and Comprehensive Co-operation signed on 23 June 2003, the joint statement of 11 April 2005, and the joint declaration signed during Hu Jintao's visit to India on 21 November 2006. All these statements refer to China's ownership of Tibet. In 1988, when Rajiv Gandhi had visited China, the joint communiqué had said that India recognized Tibet as 'an autonomous region of China'. By 2003, when Vajpayee visited China, India went even further. The communiqué stated that 'the Tibet Autonomous Region is part of the territory of the People's Republic of China'. This formulation was repeated in the 2003, 2005, and 2006 statements signed by the two sides.

Towards conflict

However, in 2008, Indian policy abruptly shifted. The joint document issued on 14 January 2008 during Prime Minister Manmohan Singh's visit to Beijing and the joint communiqué issued at the end of Premier Wen Jiabao's visit to New Delhi in 2010 omitted any reference to Tibet, even as it repeated India's adherence to the one-China policy.[111] The 2010 communique went further, dropping reference to both Tibet and the one-China policy while endorsing the 'basic principles and consensus' on bilateral relations set out in 2003, 2005, 2006, and 2008.[112] What caused the change? In all probability, India's reluctance to endorse its earlier statements on Tibet was related to its unhappiness over a series of Chinese actions on Arunachal Pradesh.[113]

Beginning in 2006, India concluded that China had hardened its position on Arunachal Pradesh. In November 2006, the Chinese ambassador in India stated, 'In our position [sic], the whole of the state of Arunachal Pradesh is Chinese territory. And Tawang is only one of the places in it. We are claiming all of that. That is our position'.[114] Then, in June 2007, Chinese Foreign Minister Yang Jiechi told Indian External Affairs Minister Pranab Mukherjee that the 'mere presence of populated areas in Arunachal Pradesh would not affect Chinese claims on the boundary' – this seemed to repudiate Article VI of the 2005 agreement on the nature of a final settlement.[115] Also in June 2007, an Indian official from Arunachal Pradesh was denied a Chinese visa. These moves were followed in November 2008 by Chinese objections to Pranab Mukherjee's visit to Tawang and in October 2009 to Prime Minister Manmohan Singh's visit to the state.

The reasons for China's tougher position on Arunachal Pradesh from 2006 onward are still something of a mystery. According to Prem Shankar Jha, the veteran journalist, Beijing's new stance was related to developments within Tibet and to Chinese perception of a change in India's handling of Tibetan issues. The increasing influence of Tibetans abroad may have caused protests within Tibet that subsequently led to riots in March 2008. Also in 2008, in talks with Beijing, the Dalai Lama insisted on autonomy not just for the Tibet Autonomous Region but also 'Greater Tibet' which includes large parts of other provinces. Before and during the Beijing Olympics, China saw evidence of an overseas Tibetan attempt to embarrass it in front of the world. Before this, China had noticed a change in Delhi's handling of Tibet. In 2005, India upgraded formal contacts with the Tibetan exile community, including having the Foreign Secretary meet the Dalai Lama. Jha notes that China may have been particularly sensitive to these upgraded contacts since they occurred just after Premier Wen Jiabao had visited India, had signed the 2005 deal on the basic principles of a border settlement, and had announced China's recognition of Sikkim as part of India.[116]

Mohan Malik, a specialist on India–China relations, offers an alternative set of perspectives based on his reading of Chinese sources between 2006 and 2009. One view among Chinese experts was that Arunachal Pradesh is simply too large to give up completely, 'equivalent to two and a half Taiwans and as large as Jiangsu province'. A second view was that the Chinese leadership at the time had no one of the stature of Mao or Deng. Making concessions to India would be virtually impossible for their less powerful successors. A third view was that Arunachal Pradesh was a resource-rich region and could not therefore be given away. Fourth, China was outstripping India in terms of comprehensive national power: why then should it concede anything? A final perspective was that a harder stand on Arunachal Pradesh could exert pressure on India to give up Tawang, which is a vital centre of Tibetan Buddhism.[117]

At any rate, whatever the reasons for Beijing's hardening stand from 2006 onward, India and China once again drifted apart on Tibet to the point that, as shown earlier, Delhi stopped affirming its recognition of Chinese sovereignty over the province. No joint statement since then has mentioned Tibet. From May 2014, with Modi's coming to power, differences over Tibet deepened. At his inauguration, the prime minister invited Lobsang Sangay, the sikyong (or president) of the Tibet government-in-exile, to attend. A group of Chinese dissidents was allowed to hold a conference in Dharamsala in April 2016. In December 2016, the Dalai Lama was invited to an event at Rashtrapati Bhavan and had a meeting with President Pranab Mukherjee. The Dalai Lama was later given permission to visit Taiwan. In March 2017, he was also allowed to visit Tawang accompanied by Minister of State for Home Affairs Kiren Rijiju, and in July of that year, during the Doklam stand-off, Sangay was allowed to unfurl the Tibetan flag at Pangong Tso. In preparation for the informal summit in Wuhan in April 2018, India dialled back this tougher policy – for instance, discouraging official participation in Tibetan activities in India – but by then Delhi had shown its teeth on Tibet. Those teeth were to show again in Ladakh in 2020 when the Indian military used the Special Frontier Force manned by Tibetan refugees. The death of one of the fighters during the deployment was marked by a highly publicized official funeral attended by a leading functionary of the Bharatiya Janata Party.

Military Relations

After the 1986–87 confrontation at Sumdorong Chu, Delhi and Beijing recognized the need to stabilize military relations. In 1993 and 1996, they signed two major confidence-building agreements. Both agreements were regarded as successes – and indeed, they seemed to promise a period of never-ending peace at the border. Yet by 2008, the Indian military was recording an increasing number of incursions by China (the Chinese side does not publicly report Indian incursions). After Xi Jinping's rise to power in 2012, the two militaries squared off almost annually – at Depsang in 2013, at Chumar in 2014, at Burtse in 2015, at Doklam in 2017, and in a broad swathe in Ladakh in 2020, despite another series of confidence-building measures. We see here too a 'repeat' of the 1950s and early 1960s before the war:

India and China negotiating on a border settlement and Tibet, trying to stabilize military relations in the borderlands, and yet finding themselves increasingly heading towards confrontation.

Confidence-building and incursions

In 1993, India and China agreed to keep border forces to a minimum level 'compatible with friendly and good neighbourly relations' and eventually to reduce force levels. The agreement prohibited military exercises in zones along the LAC and provided for prior notification of exercises. The agreement also asked both sides to ensure that air intrusions did not occur. In any case, there were to be verification measures to determine force levels at the border. A 1996 agreement was even more detailed. It reaffirmed the reduction of forces along the border. It also aimed to reduce combat tanks, infantry combat vehicles, artillery, and missiles. Both militaries would exchange data on forces and armaments and establish arms limitations at the LAC. Large military exercises in advanced areas were to be avoided. Air flights near the LAC were banned, and if needed, they were to be notified. There was to be no firing within two kilometres of the LAC, and demolitions were to be communicated in advance. Flag and other meetings were to be held regularly, and communication between medium- and high-level border authorities was to be strengthened. Finally, early clarification of the LAC, especially where they had differences, and an exchange of maps based on their respective perceptions of the LAC was to happen 'as soon as possible'.

As confidence-building measures go, the 1993 and 1996 initiatives were thorough and very much in line with the kind of measures that NATO and the Warsaw Pact had negotiated during the Cold War; indeed, they were inspired by them. At the heart of the various measures were restraints on the use of force at the

LAC, commitments by the two sides to withdraw if challenged, and the holding of consultations locally and/or at higher military–bureaucratic levels in the event of stand-offs between the two forces. Each has some specifics that were different. During the 2020 Ladakh crisis, Indian analysts argued that China had fooled India into accepting the term 'Line of Actual Control' in these agreements. Since the LAC was subsequently never defined – apparently because Beijing refused, arguing that the process would only cause more contention – Chinese troops could continue to press forward. The LAC would then be defined, at any given moment, by wherever China chose to stop its troops.[118] In hindsight this may have turned out to be the case, but at the time India's strategic community was very positive on the two agreements, at least in public.

Unfortunately, the confidence-building measures failed to build enough confidence. By 2008, India was claiming that the Chinese military was increasingly intruding into areas that they had so far left alone. When asked about the growing incidence of intrusions, General V.K. Singh, Chief of the Indian Army, attempted to defuse the stir in the media by suggesting that both sides were to blame and that it was all fairly routine:

> I think at times things get unnecessarily blown up. There are no intrusions. There are transgressions. Transgressions are in areas where a certain alignment is disputed between the two countries. You [India] feel that the alignment should be at a particular place and you go up to that place. They [China] feel that the alignment should be at a particular place, so he comes up to that place ... There is nothing very alarming about it.[119]

Assuming that both militaries were indeed to blame, why suddenly was there an increase in incursions? General Singh blamed the fuzzy nature of the border and the unwitting actions of patrols. Another possibility is that the incursions were probes designed to test the other side's reconnaissance capabilities, alacrity of response, and willpower. Straying across the LAC may also have been part of a tacit system used by the two militaries to signal their respective claims – in other words, they were reminders. Finally, the intrusions that became confrontations may have occurred as a result of the improvements in infrastructure on both sides of the border. Owing to these improvements, Indian and Chinese troops were able to patrol further and longer than before, taking them into regions where they came face to face for more extended periods of time. Where they once used to patrol intermittently, they were now in a position to visit more frequently. With better intelligence, communications, and infrastructure, they were able to respond to each other's patrols more quickly and in larger numbers as well.

This last interpretation is favoured by M. Taylor Fravel, professor of political science at the Massachusetts Institute of Technology (MIT), an expert on China's territorial quarrels including with India. In an analysis of China's view of the border incursions and confrontations over the past twenty years, he argues that a perceptible increase occurred after 2010 and that 'the general increase in Chinese activity' is due to 'China . . . responding to several changes along the border'. He identifies three changes, from Beijing's perspective: 'substantial improvement of India's border infrastructure'; 'modification of the Indian military's force structure directed at China'; and 'an increase in the frequency of Indian patrols along the LAC'. He attributes the confrontation in Daulat Beg Oldie in Depsang in April 2013 and in Chumar in September 2014 to patrolling and the building or modernization of existing infrastructure in the area.[120]

To his list, we could add the conflict in Burtse in September 2015, which the Indian media seems to have forgotten but which also occurred when the two militaries objected to the other's infrastructure activities in Ladakh. These three incidents in Ladakh were followed by a seventy-three-day stand-off in Doklam (Donglang) near the trijunction of India, China, and Bhutan in 2017. The stand-off occurred in Bhutanese territory when the Indian Army, with Bhutan's knowledge, crossed over to Doklam to confront a Chinese road-building crew that was extending an old road. Here again, it was border infrastructure activity that led to a confrontation.

At any rate, with growing intrusions after 2008, it was necessary for Delhi and Beijing to sit down to put in place further understandings on peace and stability along the LAC. In 2012, they agreed on a Working Mechanism for Consultations and Coordination on matters related to the border. Mid-level officers in the two foreign ministries were charged with increasing cooperation between the militaries especially at the border, discussing tensions that might arise there, and holding regular consultations once or twice a year. In effect, the two sides felt the need for the two foreign ministries to be involved parallel to the militaries to ensure stability. The agreement may have been forged out of a worry that local commanders and forces were too close to the action and could lose sight of the bigger strategic picture. Cooler heads in Delhi and Beijing were needed to supplement local efforts at peacemaking.

Unfortunately, the working mechanism didn't work, just as the confidence-building measures didn't build much confidence. In 2013, six months after the three-week stand-off in the Daulat Beg Oldie/Depsang area, India and China signed the Border Defence Cooperation Agreement (BDCA). The BDCA endorsed earlier mechanisms. The two sides were also to cooperate on a slew of other challenges at the border such as the smuggling of arms, wildlife, and contraband as also to work together on natural disasters and infectious diseases. The agreement endorsed meetings between local border units, regional commands, the defence ministries, and the working mechanism of the foreign ministries. At the border it recommended institutionalizing meetings in all sectors, improvements in local telecommunications, and the start of a hotline between the military headquarters. It suggested that front-line troops should meet to celebrate together in various ways and even consider joint training exercises. More to the point, and less ethereally, they were to avoid tailing each other's patrols, particularly in areas where they disagreed on the alignment of the LAC.

Growing confrontation

Less than a year after the signing of the BDCA, the two sides were back to confronting each other. The journalist Srijan Shukla provides an insightful summary of the 2014 and other confrontations. In September 2014, even as President Xi Jinping sat on a swing with Prime Minister Modi in Gujarat during their summit, Indian and Chinese troops glowered at each other in Ladakh after Indian forces had tried to stop the Chinese extending a road from Chepzi to Chumar. The PLA also pushed their civilians into Indian areas of Demchok to stop India building a canal. India had to rush two battalions of troops to reinforce its position, before the crisis simmered down. China eventually agreed to stop the road-building, and India agreed to dismantle an observation tower and bunkers. In 2015, at Burtse, Indian troops demolished a Chinese surveillance structure, leading to another stand-off. The PLA called up reinforcements as did the Indian Army. The matter was resolved locally after a week of negotiations. The two armies capped the resolution of the confrontation by a twelve-day joint training exercise.

Then on 16 June 2017, the Indian Army, with Bhutan's permission, stopped a Chinese unit from extending a road in Doklam. Following intense high-level negotiations, the stand-off ended with both sides returning to pre–16 June positions. Nevertheless, a few months later China had built even more infrastructure including a helipad on its side of the line and installed a much larger and more permanent troop presence.[121] August 2017 featured another confrontation that has receded from memory. Just as Doklam was being resolved, a melee occurred between Indian and Chinese troops at Pangong Tso – the same lake which featured so prominently in the 2020 crisis – where the two sides fought with sticks, stones, and rods. This may have been provoked by India's allowing Lobsang Sangay to unfurl the Tibetan flag there in July 2017 in the midst of the Doklam crisis.

Finally, from April–May 2020 onward Indian and Chinese troops once again faced off in Ladakh, this time in a broad area from Depsang in the north down to Pangong Tso, with several intermediate areas included among the flashpoints. While there is intense speculation on the reasons for the 2020 confrontation, a growing Indian view backed by Chinese public statements is that infrastructure building, this time by India, seems to have sparked the row. As India's new road from Leh to Daulat Beg Oldie (which terminates just short of the Karakoram Pass in China) neared completion, Chinese troops moved into Galwan in areas the Indian Army has patrolled without incident since 1962. On 15 June, twenty Indian soldiers and an unconfirmed number of Chinese soldiers died in a brutal melee that lasted several hours in subzero temperatures at over 4000 metres – the first casualties between India and China since the border incident in 1975.

Conclusion

Over seventy years, India and China have not been able to agree on very much – on the delineation of the border, on the status of Tibet, and on appropriate military actions and behaviours. In the 1950s, both saw the other as insincere and stubborn in the border discussions. They concluded that the other had failed to honour commitments on Tibet. And they came to regard the other as militarily aggressive and themselves as militarily defensive. Having said that, now and then their differences on the border did narrow, they agreed on the status of Tibet (in 1950/51 and 1954), and they tried to avoid escalatory military actions. In the end, though, the points of convergence faded away. Both sides were at fault for letting slip the opportunities for striking a deal and avoiding war, and probably the best period was between their first encounters in 1949 when the communists came to power in China and 1954 when Nehru went to Beijing to meet Mao and Zhou.

In the decades after 1962, they normalized relations, negotiated on the border for nearly forty years, reaffirmed Chinese sovereignty in Tibet (with China reciprocating on Indian sovereignty in Sikkim), and instituted a series of military confidence-building measures. In 2005, it looked as if they had made a breakthrough on the border settlement. Within a year, that positive moment was gone, to be replaced by Chinese territorial claims that were even more extensive. In 2013, 2014, 2015, 2017, and finally in 2020, Indian and Chinese troops faced off in the biggest military confrontations since 1967. In January 2021, reports suggested that China had built a village four to five kilometres beyond the McMahon Line into Indian territory, south of Migyutin, where in 1959 China had accused India of intruding. This suggested that the western and eastern sectors of the border could become flashpoints simultaneously.

Why after seven decades can India and China not agree on anything vital relating to their perimeters? One answer is that they still do not trust what the other is saying and doing: India and China do not accept each other's historical claims to territory, do not believe their commitments on Tibet, and do not see the other side's military moves as defensive. Their interpretations of past agreements, of the significance of their policies and responses to each other at critical moments, and the chronology of events are gulfs apart. If they do not trust each other, part of the reason is that the two societies lack a rich diplomatic history with each other. As we saw in the previous chapter, they rarely dealt with each other from their centres of power, from great imperial capital to great imperial capital. Rather, contact was largely through monks, pilgrims, traders, borderland populations, and, for a time, between China's imperial court and regional kingdoms in southern and eastern India. In more modern times, as we will see in the next chapter, they have never been strategic allies except briefly against imperial Japan during the Second World War. As a result, they do not have a long diplomatic past on which to draw to reassure themselves about the motives and behaviours of the other. They cannot turn to a series of positive mutual interactions to illustrate the possibilities of trust building and cooperation.

Over the past two decades, their top leaderships have met regularly, to overcome the legacy of history. At the level of heads of government – prime minister of India and president of China – they have visited each other's country fourteen times in the period 2000 to 2019, sometimes on a state visit and sometimes for multilateral meetings. In addition, they have met at the BRICS summits, the Russia–India–China summits, the G-20 summits, and the East Asia summits, among others. Their foreign ministers, too, have met regularly, and now and then the Indian president goes to China and the Chinese prime minister comes to India. Yet despite scores of meetings intended to build communication and trust, the rising arc of tensions in the past two decades suggests that the levels of miscommunication and mistrust have risen not fallen with the increase in high-level meetings.

A second answer to their continuing disagreements is that India and China have a zero-sum view of security. Neither country seems to be able to accept that a compromise or concession could make both parties more secure. Any ceding of ground in a negotiation is resisted because it implies a loss of security to one side and a corresponding gain to the other side. To be fair, both leaderships did at times countenance what they considered a compromise or concession. In China's view, the swap was a compromise/concession even if India did not see it that way. India did contemplate a creative compromise/concession as well: in 1959, given the strategic importance of the Aksai Chin road for Beijing, Nehru proposed privately to his colleagues that China could be allowed to use it. Opposition within his own team caused him to water down the proposal and to offer the road for civilian use only.[122] The problem, particularly in India, is public opinion, which is more prone than the leadership to associate compromise and concession with appeasement and weakness.

A third answer to why India and China are mired in disagreement is that both sides have what psychologists call 'cognitive dissonance'. More often than not, information from the other side is assimilated to pre-existing and unshakeable views. The other side's actions are regarded cynically: its statements and actions are seen as Trojan horses intended to deceive. Only an unbending stance can therefore bring security. Cognitive dissonance is not peculiar to India and China. Individuals and entire political systems are prone to discounting discrepant information, and they try to overcome it by what one might call 'triangulation' – by getting a variety of views and constant cross-checking. The problem in India and China was that in Nehru and Mao they had two enormous and forceful personalities who tended to be fed information and ideas that reinforced rather than challenged their views. Nehru and Mao are long gone, but neither system is notable for academic and policy expertise on the other country, expertise that might provide alternative views. With Modi and Xi at the helm, India and China are once again governed by rather magisterial personalities not known for reaching out to those with other viewpoints.

A final answer to why India and China have been unable to agree on anything related to their perimeters with each other is that neither political leadership, at least since Nehru and Mao, has had the ability and courage to handle nationalist domestic opinion. Lack of trust, a zero-sum view of security, and a discounting of uncomfortable evidence could be overcome by a leadership which makes the case that cooperation is possible, that security is not always necessarily zero-sum, and that prevailing views must change in light of new information. However, Indian leaders have to deal with factions within their own political parties, with opposition parties that could challenge them in elections, and with the media and public protests. Chinese leaders are to a greater degree insulated from these pressures, but they face rivals within the CPC. While they do not need to worry about an opposition party or traditional media, they must keep an eye on social media platforms which even Beijing cannot altogether control. And China has a history of street protests, even if these go unreported in its media. The differences in the two political systems suggest that the constraining effect of domestic politics is more severe in India, but even as dominant a leader as Xi in contemporary China will find it difficult to give away what ordinary Chinese regard as their territory.

What does the future hold? The lack of trust and effective

communication, the zero-sum view of security, the persistence of cognitive dissonance, and weak leadership that marked an earlier era are still very much in evidence. The rising number of confrontations including in Ladakh in 2020 have done little to increase trust between India and China. Nor have the many summits and high-level meetings improved communication and belief in the other's word. Modi and Xi held two informal summits (2018, 2019). Yet Indian and Chinese forces came to blows in Galwan in 2020. A zero-sum view of security has meant that months after the 2020 incident, neither side has been willing to give up an inch of territory. As far as we know, Delhi and Beijing hold firmly to their overall claims across the entire border. It was again clear that the two sides are far apart on everything connected with border incidents – who encroached, when the encroachments happened and to what extent, how many casualties were incurred, what was agreed in the disengagement negotiations, who provoked the flare-ups, and so on. No amount of information exchanged between the two governments seems to have overcome the cognitive dissonance in both capitals: neither side has changed its views, going by their public reactions and responses. Modi's podium-thumping references to resisting outdated eighteenth-century 'expansionism' and Xi's fist-shaking insistence that China will protect its territorial integrity no matter what the challenges indicate that the two supreme leaders have both stoked nationalist fervour rather than dampened it.

Another confrontation along the border is therefore quite possible. Until the mid-1980s, China had signalled that it was principally concerned about the eastern sector. After 1985, it made clear that it regards both sectors as important, with perhaps the western sector somewhat more important. The Doklam crisis and the confrontation at Naku La in Sikkim in May 2020 suggest that the Sikkim area too is brittle. Only the middle sector has been incident-free in the past several years. However, as we saw, the first military incidents between India and China were in Barahoti in 1954 in this central part of the disputed border, and so nothing is certain even there. In 2020, reports emerged of Beijing's actions in Tibet to disperse rural Tibetans and move towards re-education camps for them on the model of the Uighurs in Xinjiang. China remains nervous about Tibet's future, and that means serious disturbances in the province will affect military behaviour along the India–China boundary. A post–Dalai Lama Tibet could become unstable, which could lead to tensions along the border.

Will India and China fight now or in the foreseeable future? As we will see in our discussion of the India–China power balance, full-scale war is unlikely. While the Chinese military is certainly superior, geography mitigates the imbalance. Neither side has the ability to strike deep into the other's territory and sustain its advance. Provided that the Indian military gets its deployments and tactics right, that it is able to move supplies efficiently, and that morale remains high among the officers and troops, it will be able to deter a Chinese attack. If an attack nevertheless occurs, Indian forces should be able to hold, particularly in a short war. The great uncertainty is whether China's military reforms, featuring integrated commands and the development of high-technology weaponry, have gone far enough to give it a decisive edge. The other uncertainty is the role of nuclear weapons in a war. As we will see later, they will probably not come into play, at least in part because India's ability to use nuclear weapons in a fight with China is still very limited.

If India and China do once again fight a war over their borderlands in Ladakh and Arunachal Pradesh, a lot of the world will wonder why. Only three countries – Pakistan, India, and China – have thought it sensible to fight at the impossible heights that are contested in some stretches of territory. Pakistan and India have subjected their soldiers to a fearful life on the Siachen glacier at elevations of 5400 metres above sea level. Temperatures there can fall to minus 50 degrees Celsius. India and China have fought at similar elevations and could do so again, in similar temperatures. The air in these places is so thin that sustained activity can cause pulmonary oedema leading to death – you drown in the water that collects in the pouches in your lungs. Indian and Chinese soldiers could die trying to fight rather than die in an actual fight.

Yet, strategists constantly tell us that there are real military objectives in these places. Some seem sensible and some seem phantasmagorical. Here are the phantasmagorical: that if Pakistan controls the Siachen glacier it could seriously threaten India's security in Kashmir; that if India controls the glacier it could bear down meaningfully on the China–Pakistan Karakoram Highway; that if China controls the heights above the Daulet Beg Oldie road it can threaten Indian military moves all the way to China's Karakoram Pass and could eventually link up with Pakistan at – or near – the Siachen glacier and push India off its perch there. Here are the sensible objectives. It is comprehensible that China would want to preserve and protect its road from Xinjiang to Tibet. Aksai Chin therefore becomes strategically important. India by contrast has no great need for control of Aksai Chin. It is comprehensible that India wants control over the southern slopes of the mountains in Arunachal Pradesh since that could be the gateway to the entire North-East. Defending its claims to the McMahon Line is strategically important. China by contrast has no crying need to plant its flag on the southern slopes.

Is this another way of saying that the swap is the correct answer to the border quarrel? The swap deal is probably dead forever: it has got a bad name on both sides of the boundary, and few will dare talk about it publicly. Saying that there are sensible strategic and military objectives is a way of saying that both societies need to ask themselves, much more than they do, what they should care about in the borderlands and why. As things stand both peoples know they care about their claims, but few know exactly what those claims are and why they are important.

With Indian academics and officials, I am careful in raising the subject of what is sensible and what is phantasmagorical in the borderlands, fearing accusations of being a 'liberal' and perhaps even a 'panda hugging' China-appeaser. Few even among India's strategists or small tribe of 'China hands' want to ask too many questions about the real importance of the various territorial claims. The experts all have thoughts on what is to be done with China in the here and now, but the origins and unfolding of the quarrel over time are hazy and complicated, and not even those who have seen the files on it are terribly clear. Understandably, for decision-makers, the border areas in contention are important because they are important – the question is how to resolve or, even more so, manage the dispute.

One year, at a conference in Shanghai, I fell into step with a Chinese colleague and realized that it is much the same in China – the hazy knowledge of complicated interactions and lack of clarity about why the two countries had quarrelled so bitterly. As we walked out of the seminar room, he and I talked about our memories of 1962. I was seven years old, in London, and I remembered the strained silence at home during the four weeks of the war, as India faced defeat. The winter of 1962 was one of the coldest in London's history. The pipes in our home froze. My father was at the embassy a lot; my mother was unwell. I was telling my Chinese colleague rather disjointedly about those days. He remembered much less. He could not even be sure if he had any recall of the war – perhaps what he had was a 'phantom memory', one that had lodged in his mind from others who had talked or written about the war.

What was so important about the territories in question between India and China, I asked my Chinese companion? Without waiting for his answer, I followed up with another question: why had China solved all its land-border disputes except with India? I should probably not have asked the second question. He stopped and looked down at the floor: 'You know, Arunachal Pradesh is 89,000 square kilometres in area. That is bigger than Taiwan.' He stopped and smiled at me, staring into my eyes. The stare told me that he had had enough of the subject. It sounded, for a moment, like he had the answer to why China had failed with India. On reflection, I was not so sure. Over various trips to China, I have had rather similar Chinese reactions: an unbending sense that the border is a problem because it is a problem and best not to ask too many questions.

3

Partnerships: From Entente to Rivalry to Cold War

China's and India's policies towards each other are driven not just by negative perceptions of each other and the quarrel over perimeters but also by their partnerships with the USSR/Russia and the US. To be clear, partnerships – sometimes called strategic partnerships – are different from alliances. Alliances are formal obligations to come to the aid of another against an enemy, usually clearly identified. Strategic partnerships – or partnerships for short – are much looser and refer to a broad set of understandings to consult and cooperate. The objectives of partnerships can vary, from exchanges of ideas and information, to coordinated actions against a common threat, to building up each other's capabilities. Partners may therefore collaborate diplomatically, share intelligence, and transfer weaponry among themselves. They may give each other preferential economic treatment and share technology as a way of growing their strength. They may even invest in building broader capabilities in each other's societies including in education or research. Deepening people-to-people ties through tourism, culture, and sports may also be part of the partnership toolkit. Strategic partnerships do not necessarily entail an obligation to fight alongside each other.

The relationship between India, China, the USSR/Russia, and the US can be described in two broad periods. The first period is from 1949 to 1988, when India and China moved from a brief entente against the US to open rivalry with each other by 1959. The entente was not a strategic partnership, but rather a convergence of interests in opposing 'neo-imperialism' and fostering a sense of solidarity with Asian and African countries. With the end of their entente, India partnered primarily the Soviets against China, though the US was briefly an ally in the 1962 war. By 1969, India and China found themselves more firmly embedded on opposite sides of the Cold War, a situation that was to last until 1988. The second period, the post–Cold War, goes from 1989 to the present. It began, as in the Cold War, with an India–China entente against American hegemony. By 1999, however, India had come together increasingly with the US against China. And by 2009, India and China were more firmly on opposite sides of a new global Cold War, this time between the US and China.

At least three conclusions stand out across these two periods. First, India and China have both partnered the USSR/Russia and the US. The idea that China is a shrewd operator in international politics and that it cleverly combines with others is a widely shared view, one that garners admiration all round. India by contrast is seen as a strategic innocent and is routinely derided for its supposed aversion to partnerships. In fact, though, it has a continuous history of opportunistic partnering in the interest of its security.

Second, the main target of India's partnerships has been China. Its principal big-power partner against China was the USSR, but briefly in the 1960s and increasingly after 1999 it has relied on the US to balance Chinese power. On the other hand, China's partnerships with the Soviets, the US, and later Russia have not been directed against India, primarily because the Chinese feel they can deal with India more or less on their own (with some help from Pakistan).

Third, except for two brief periods of entente when they feared and resented the US, India and China have always been on opposite sides in terms of their partnerships. This has meant that they must deal with an added layer of suspicion and competition in their relationship. It has also meant that they have no history of working closely together, of building a stock of strategic knowledge and trust between them. With such a stock, they might have dealt with mutual conflicts differently.

The story of these two periods is not exclusively about India–China relations. Developments that had nothing to do with India or China, or that did not necessarily impinge immediately and directly on India–China interactions, had a 'conditioning' effect – setting a context within which Delhi's and Beijing's dealings with each other occurred. In other words, India's and China's partnerships and their bilateral relations have to be understood as part of what academic historians call 'global history' – a larger history not entirely of their making. What is clear in this history is that contrary to their triumphalist narratives about themselves as being sturdily unaligned, neither has stood altogether alone. Whether their partnerships have served their interests is debatable, but that they have repeatedly chosen to partner either the USSR/Russia or the US is undeniable.

1949–1988: From Entente to Rivalry to Cold War Rivalry

During the Second World War, India, China, the USSR, and the US had been allies against the Japanese, with Indian forces fighting under British command. After its independence in 1947, India might have been expected to be closer to the US (given its Anglo-American political values and institutions) and China to the USSR (given the ideological convergence). In fact, non-aligned Delhi soon became resentful of the US, and aligned Beijing started to fall out with the Soviets. For a brief time, from 1954 to 1958, India and China (with the USSR) were in a tacit entente against the US. By the late 1950s, though, Moscow and Delhi were partnering against Beijing, and by 1969 China and the US were close to cementing a quasi-alliance against the Soviets. From then until 1988, India and China were Cold War rivals, on opposite sides of global politics, though from 1981–82 they began a détente of their own.

Entente, 1949–1958

In 1947, India was determined to be non-aligned between the US and USSR in the emerging Cold War. It admired both societies for different reasons and wanted good relations with the two superpowers even as it was wary of them. With the civil war behind it, communist China was closer to the USSR and suspicious of the US. By the mid-1950s, India and China were closer to the USSR and convergent in their worries about the US.

Non-aligned India Between the US and the USSR

Delhi's relations with Washington immediately after independence were complicated by differences over Pakistan, India's perceptions of the Cold War, and US views of non-alignment. Delhi was convinced that the US had followed the UK's lead in favouring the Pakistani position on Kashmir. Cold War considerations rather than the merit of India's and Pakistan's respective arguments on

Kashmiri accession had determined the Anglo-American position. This reinforced India's worry that the Anglo-American powers had an overly alarmist view of communism and were pursuing the wrong strategy in dealing with it. Another global war might result from their ill-judged policies, resulting in the use of nuclear weapons, with disastrous consequences for the world at large. Nehru insisted that India wanted to be friends with everyone and did reach out to Washington for diplomatic, military, and economic reasons, but he also deplored Washington's Manichean view of international politics and its ridiculing of non-alignment.

By 1950, whatever its view of non-alignment, the US was increasingly worried that India would tilt towards the Soviets or even go communist. Even though Nehru had his own brand of anti-communism and had assured the US that India would side with the Anglo-American powers in a 'third world war', Washington was afraid that Delhi would eventually align with the Soviets. Worse, if India failed to deliver on economic development, good governance, and democracy, it might fall to communism – abetted by Moscow through the Communist Party of India. Finally, in the US view, China did not have the attractions of the USSR or its resources, but its economic success might swing the developing countries, including India, towards socialism and the communist bloc.

It was against this possibility that by the mid-1950s President Dwight Eisenhower and Senator (later President) John F. Kennedy came to see India as pivotal in the fight against communism despite its irksome non-alignment. Eisenhower, unlike his predecessor Harry Truman, hit it off with Nehru, and paid a successful visit to India in 1959 just as relations between Delhi and Beijing were becoming acrimonious and violent. Nehru, setting aside his snobbishness over American materialism and brashness, had been to Washington three years earlier. He had been received warmly by Eisenhower in 1956 – an American news clip shows Nehru bounding up the White House steps to meet the US President, and the two leaders seemed to genuinely enjoy each other's company. The newsreel shows a rather happily grinning Vice President Richard Nixon on the steps of the White House – the same Nixon who would be so anti-India later (and so racist). In the same year, Kennedy famously articulated a growing view that there was a competition between India and China and that Washington should weigh in: 'No struggle in the world today deserves more of our time and attention than that which now grips the attention of all Asia . . . And that is the struggle between India and China for leadership of the East . . . We want India to win that race.'[1]

Delhi's relations with Moscow had been frosty in the initial years, but in 1953, with the death of Stalin, the Indian ambassador Sarvepalli Radhakrishnan started to get time with the Soviet leadership. Stalin's successor, Khrushchev, quickly toned down the hostility to Nehru, India's democracy, and non-alignment. Nehru visited Moscow in July 1955, and Khrushchev returned the visit in November of the same year. During his visit, Khrushchev supported India's view on the liberation of Goa from Portuguese rule and Kashmir's future status. Soviet aid to India followed, including the setting up of the Bhilai steel plant, the first time Moscow had aided a non-communist country. Bilateral trade increased sevenfold between 1955 and 1957.[2] More importantly from the perspective of relations with China, the Soviets agreed to Indian arms purchases.

By the mid-1950s, then, non-aligned India, after an initial period of hesitation and awkwardness, was developing friendlier ties with both the US and the USSR. The two powers in turn, after their initial scepticism over Nehru's foreign policy, had come to appreciate that India was worth cultivating.

China allies with the USSR

Communist China began its journey in international politics as a brother-state to the USSR. In fact, its partnership with the Soviets went back further, to the pre-communist days of Chiang Kai-shek and the KMT. From the 1920s to 1941, Moscow was often only grudgingly supportive of the CPC. When the KMT entered its death spiral against the CPC on the mainland, Moscow finally changed sides. As a result, in 1949, Mao went to Moscow to see Josef Stalin. Despite being kept humiliatingly waiting for several weeks, he went on to sign the Sino-Soviet Treaty of Friendship, Alliance, and Mutual Assistance in 1950. Under treaty terms, the USSR returned Chinese territories it had acquired from Japan after defeating it in the Second World War. It also provided Beijing with economic assistance, military factories, and nuclear plants. When Chinese troops were flung against the US-led United Nations troops in Korea in 1950, the Soviets, after initial hesitations, helped China with air cover.

By 1956, in the aftermath of Stalin's death, China and the Soviets were heading for a collision. Khrushchev's de-Stalinization programme and his 'peaceful coexistence' policy towards the West alarmed Mao, who denounced Moscow for being 'Marxist revisionist'. Moscow in turn thought that Beijing was geopolitically adventurist. Mao's aggressive stance on Taiwan in the mid-1950s alarmed the Soviets, as did China's insouciance over a possible nuclear war with the US. As the name-calling climaxed, Khrushchev withdrew Soviet advisers in China and terminated nuclear cooperation, including the promised transfer of nuclear weapons.

China's relationship with the US, too, is a tangled history. In the late 1890s, the US had protected Chinese unity. As the European colonial powers and Japan eyed China for their commercial purposes, Washington insisted on a policy that kept the mainland open to trade and investment, preventing any single power from carving out a sphere of influence within it. American interests were selfish – Washington wanted to ensure that it would have unfettered access not only for its businesses but also for its Christian missionaries. Selfish or not, US policy helped preserve China's unity when the Europeans and Japanese were spoiling to divide it. When in 1937 the Japanese invaded Manchuria in northern China, Washington once again moved to protect Chinese unity. It condemned Tokyo's action and provided the Chinese with military and economic aid. In the Pacific war against Japan from December 1941 onward, Chiang Kai-shek was an ally. The US later recognized the special relationship by insisting that China be made a Permanent Member of the UN Security Council despite opposition from the UK. Indeed, Washington ensured that the first country to sign the UN Charter was Chiang's China, arguing that it had played a vital part in the war against Germany, Italy, and Japan.

Washington's closeness to Chiang Kai-shek and dislike of communism did not stop it from developing relations with Mao and the CPC. Joe Stillwell, the American general of Second World War fame, went so far as to argue that the CPC was a better political and military force than the corrupt KMT. Various US military envoys tried to broker cooperation between the CPC and the KMT. While US President Truman strove to keep the door to the communists open, developments in Korea led to its closing for the next two decades. In late November 1950, as UN troops under US leadership pushed the invading North Korean forces all the way back to the border with China, Beijing acted. It threw millions of troops at the UN forces, causing them to retreat down the peninsula. Relations with the US worsened even further when China shelled Taiwan across the straits in 1954–55.

The US Navy sailed into the straits to end the mounting conflict, and Eisenhower threatened to use nuclear weapons against the mainland.

In sum, by the mid-1950s, just as India was growing closer to the two superpowers, China was in conflict with both of them. The split with the USSR was not altogether public, but it was gathering strength. With the US, China had nearly once again come to the point of war, this time over Taiwan.

The India–China–USSR entente

Washington and Moscow may not have liked non-alignment, but the posture allowed India to develop relatively friendly ties with both the US and the USSR. Until 1956, when the first reports of Chinese road-building in Aksai Chin surfaced, Delhi was close to Beijing as well. On balance, India was more comfortable with the Soviets and China during this period than with America. US anti-communism and its support for Pakistan made life awkward for India and translated into at least two key problems. The first was Delhi's struggles with getting the US to provide developmental aid and invest in India's industrialization. Washington was reluctant to commit funds to a planned socialist economy and remained fairly deaf to Indian requests. The second problem was Delhi's inability to buy American weaponry. Washington's refusal to sell advanced military systems arose from its concerns over US alliance commitments to Pakistan.[3] Relations were further complicated by India's attempts to persuade the Anglo-American powers to accommodate the communist powers in the interests of international stability. Delhi's equivocations on the Soviet intervention in the Hungarian revolt in 1956 and support for mainland China to replace Taiwan as a permanent member of the UN Security Council added to America's unhappiness. In 1955, despite uneasiness in the US (and UK), Delhi helped organize a summit in Bandung to which China as well as several Asian and African countries were invited. Nehru was keen to build Afro-Asian solidarity and hoped that China would be part of an effort to stop the spread of the Cold War.

China was initially hostile to Nehru's India, seeing it as a bourgeois junior partner of the Western imperial powers, and the commentary on Indian politics and policies was often critical, even contemptuous. The Korean war of 1950 began to change Beijing's view. India refused to join the US-led UN combat force in Korea and attempted to mediate between China and the US. Delhi's championing of China's membership of the UN and its steady criticism of the Western powers was helpful to Beijing and was an indication that Nehru was more independent of the West than the Chinese leadership had originally thought. The Afro-Asian meeting in Bandung turned out to be more of a triumph for Beijing than for Delhi – several Asian countries turned on India including Ceylon and Pakistan, and Zhou was the star of the show. India had introduced China to the newly independent countries only too well, to Beijing's advantage. The following year Delhi mounted a diplomatic attack on the Anglo-French intervention against Egyptian nationalization of the Suez Canal. This too would have impressed the Chinese.

To say that India and China were in an entente is to somewhat exaggerate the relationship. Both converged in their fear of US power, military and economic. They also converged in worrying that Asia might once again succumb to imperialism, with the American-led alliance system extending into the continent. Both therefore were critical of US policies, and both resisted – India diplomatically, particularly in multilateral organizations; and China militarily in Korea and, in time, in Vietnam. If there was an entente-like quality to their relationship, it was largely due to India's efforts – in Korea, in championing China's UN membership, in criticizing Western policies generally, and in promoting Beijing's entrée into Afro-Asian affairs.

Rivalry, 1959–1968

By the late 1950s, both Moscow and Washington regarded Beijing as provocative and destabilizing to the international system. The two superpowers had gradually begun to construct Cold War norms and limits between the two blocs. China on the other hand had a more radical view: it wanted to challenge the US and Western powers in the name of socialism. The USSR and the US were warming to India at the same time. By the early 1960s, however, there were signs of a huge geopolitical shift, with India coming closer to the Soviets, and the Chinese and Americans reaching out to each other.

The USSR tilts to India

As China's relations with India deteriorated in the late 1950s, peaking in the Longju clash in August 1959, it wanted a clear sign from the Soviets that they sided politically and diplomatically with their communist ally in the border quarrel. It did not expect or want Moscow's military backing. It had repelled the US-led UN force in Korea with very little help from Moscow, and Indian military power was hardly in the same league as the international coalition. China did, however, expect the communist world to stand politically together against a bourgeois-minded India.

Responding to Beijing, Moscow urged compromise and moderation with Delhi. Then, in September 1959, the Soviets suddenly and very publicly declared neutrality in the India–China conflict. Where Stalin had been supportive of China, even urging

Mao to deal with the Tibetan problem by settling Han Chinese populations in the region, Khrushchev expressed unhappiness.[4] At a seven-hour meeting with Mao in October 1959, he did some plain-speaking on the intensifying India–China conflict. Khrushchev defended Nehru, blamed China for the flight of the Dalai Lama to India earlier that year (Beijing's repression, in his view, being the cause), and criticized the attack on Indian troops at Longju. China's replies were defensive, rejecting Khrushchev's finger-pointing over Tibet and the Longju incident. The latter, Mao claimed, had occurred without permission of the central government. In any case, he mollifyingly replied, 'The border conflict with India – this is only a marginal border issue, not a clash between the two governments.'[5]

By 1960, India had received more Soviet aid than China. In March 1961, Delhi bought eight Antonov-12 military transport airplanes. In May 1962, five months before the war with China, news surfaced of India's likely purchase of the MiG-21 fighter, an aircraft Moscow had refused to sell to China. Under pressure from the US and the UK over the purchase of the MiGs, Nehru confided to a senior British diplomat that the military value of the fighters was less important than the sale's negative impact on Sino-Soviet relations.[6] In August 1962, just weeks before the outbreak of war, India signed the MiG deal as also an agreement for more Antonov airplanes. After the war, between 1964 and 1968, India bought tanks (in the hundreds), combat aircraft (primarily, four MiG squadrons), and artillery.[7]

When the war of words between Delhi and Beijing worsened further, Moscow found itself embroiled in the nail-biting Cuban missile crisis with Washington. As late as 18 October, two days before the Chinese attack on India, it urged both India and China to avoid violence. When war broke out, the Soviets abruptly sided with China in an effort to rally the socialist world against the US, but as soon as the crisis with Washington ended, Moscow turned critical of Beijing again. The Soviet newspaper *Pravda* sniffed that 'Aspirations for war is foreign to the nature of a socialist state'.[8] Not surprisingly, Sino-Soviet relations worsened, despite the ouster of Mao's bugbear, Khrushchev, in 1964. When Soviet tanks rolled into Czechoslovakia in 1968 to put down an anti-communist rebellion, Beijing was harshly critical of Moscow – its stand paralleling that of the West.

The US backs India against China

From the 1940s, despite its differences with the US, India had received a growing amount of American aid. Initially, these were food shipments. Later, the aid was more broadly developmental. The amounts grew substantially, from $400 million in 1957 to $822 million in 1960, in addition to a four-year food deal worth $1.276 billion. The US also footed half the bill for the Indus rivers projects that were agreed with Pakistan under the aegis of the World Bank.[9] As relations with Washington warmed, Eisenhower made the first US presidential visit to India in December 1959, just months after the Longju incident.

While the Soviets briefly turned pro-China during the 1962 war, the US almost as briefly turned into India's military partner. Late in October, during the fighting with China, Washington endorsed India's view on the McMahon Line as the legitimate border in the eastern sector.[10] When India found itself in trouble in the war, it urgently requested military aid. The US and the UK responded by flying in arms and ammunition and carrying out supply missions from Calcutta to India's airbases near the front. In the second phase of the Chinese offensive in November, Delhi dramatically (and secretly) requested air transport. More importantly, Nehru asked for direct US involvement in providing radar facilities and defending Indian cities while the Indian Air Force attacked Chinese communications and supply lines. He also urgently asked the US to make available two squadrons of B-47 aircraft to be manned by the Indian Air Force which would carry out bombing-runs into Tibet.[11]

In the event, the US decided on a more moderate response – increasing supplies and transport as also sending the USS *Enterprise* aircraft carrier towards the region (the same carrier that in 1971 would be sent *against* India in the Bangladesh war). Before the US could become more directly involved, China halted offensive operations. Bruce Riedel, a former CIA officer, in his book on the US's role in the 1962 war, concludes that if hostilities had continued, Kennedy would have responded to 'Nehru's desperate appeal for Americans to start flying combat missions to fight the Chinese and defend India . . . Almost certainly Kennedy would have responded positively . . . we can be reasonably certain that America, India, and probably Great Britain would have been at war together against China.'[12]

From this high point in India–US strategic relations, the level of engagement and cooperation quickly declined. India and the US had drawn closer during the India–China war, with plans for further military cooperation. In the event, the American military pipeline soon dried up. The Anglo-American insistence in 1963 that India negotiate with Pakistan reignited Delhi's resentment of London's and Washington's role in South Asia. Also, India wanted to refurbish its non-aligned credentials and put some distance between itself and the US. The death of Kennedy in November 1963 and Nehru a few months later in 1964 brought leadership change in both countries and a less positive view of the bilateral relationship. In 1965, the US began to send its combat troops into Vietnam, which led to years of Indian criticism. During the September 1965 war with Pakistan, Washington stopped all military aid to both South Asian countries – the halt in aid suggested it was not a reliable partner. Stung by Delhi's criticism of his Vietnam policy and annoyed by Mrs Gandhi's socialistic policies, Kennedy's successor, Lyndon Johnson, insisted that India devalue its currency and carry out agricultural reforms in order to qualify for development assistance. When India urgently needed US grains to deal with its food shortages, Johnson instituted a 'short-tether' policy of releasing tranches of foodgrains conditional on Indian economic reforms.

The China–US détente

Even as Delhi's relations with Moscow deepened and its relations with Washington deteriorated, China and the US were eyeing a détente. While Nixon is correctly credited with the diplomatic opening to China, Kennedy had been contemplating a change of policy as early as 1963.[13] In 1965, under Johnson, the US lifted the travel ban to China, and in February 1965, it announced that Chinese journalists could visit the US. Johnson publicly declared that reconciliation with China was inevitable.[14] America's growing involvement in the Vietnam war caused Beijing to recoil. Also, back at home, Mao was preoccupied with internal reform and his own grip on power. The Great Leap Forward from 1958 to 1962 had backfired, and his leadership was under challenge within the communist party. In 1966, China was in the throes of the Cultural Revolution, and once again Mao was preoccupied with domestic politics.

The drift towards a détente and a subsequent partnership against the Soviets soon resumed. Thanks to America's involvement in the Vietnam war, the US presidential election of November 1968 brought Richard Nixon to power. A confirmed Cold War hawk, Nixon had made known his by-then dovish views on China. Writing in the American journal *Foreign Affairs* in 1967, he argued that the US must engage the communist Chinese leadership:

> Taking the long view, we simply cannot afford to leave China forever outside the family of nations . . . China, within three to five years, will have a significant deliverable nuclear capability . . . For the short run, then, this means a policy of firm restraint . . . designed to persuade Peking that its interests can be served only by accepting the basic rules of international civility. For the long run, it means pulling China back into the world community . . .[15]

Nixon's intent was not just integrating China into the international system more fully. It was also to take advantage of the Sino-Soviet split and turn Beijing more decisively against Moscow so as to tilt the balance of power in favour of the US. In China, Mao read Nixon's article and perspicaciously concluded that if the Republican aspirant came to power the US would be looking to engage diplomatically with Beijing.[16]

The Nixon opening to China was matched by a Mao opening to the US. The Chinese, picking up on cues from the mid-1960s and the Nixon article, played their America card. On 26 November 1968, just days after the US presidential elections brought Nixon to power, it nudged Washington. It proposed that the ambassadorial talks with the US, which had been held intermittently since 1955, be reconvened (the same talks India had played a role in encouraging after the Korean war). Beijing's message was duly received in Washington. Before Nixon was inaugurated as president in January 1969, he and his advisers were already chalking out a response.[17]

Cold War Rivalry, 1969–1988

International politics was turned upside down between 1969 and 1988. In 1969, China and the USSR fought a brief but fierce war. This led to a quasi-alliance between Beijing and Washington. And in 1978, the Saur revolution in Afghanistan overthrew the post-monarchy republican government. A year later, Soviet troops intervened in Afghanistan to restore order in the face of growing instability. The 1970s ended with a deepening of rival alignments that were already a possibility in 1968: India with the USSR, and China with the US. Those alignments persisted to the end of the Cold War, even though by 1982 Delhi and Beijing were edging away from Moscow and Washington, respectively. By the time the USSR unravelled in the late 1980s, India and China had arrived at a détente, underlined by Rajiv Gandhi's trip to China in 1988.

China and the US align

Between March and September 1969, Chinese and Soviet forces fought a series of military battles along their contested border. Responding to the conflict, Moscow tried to rally global communist support against Beijing. Crucially, it also reached out to the US. In the early 1960s, Washington had proposed to Moscow that the two powers combine to stop the Chinese nuclear programme in a joint military strike.[18] In 1969, it was Moscow's turn to explore interest in a combined attack. The Nixon administration, already on its way to normalizing relations with China, made clear it would not be a bystander if the Soviets acted.[19] In the meantime, Washington sent out a series of diplomatic feelers to Beijing. On 31 July 1969, Nixon set off on an international tour, visiting India and then Pakistan, among other countries. The India visit was almost certainly a cover for his main destination, Pakistan, where he had real business. In Islamabad, he asked his host, President Yahya Khan, to intercede with China. On his way home, Nixon stopped in Romania on a similar mission. Washington also turned to Poland and France to mediate with Beijing.

China simultaneously was coming round to the view that the US was less dangerous than the Soviets: the Americans, Mao reasoned, had never occupied Chinese territory. In 1969, fearing war and Soviet military power, a high-ranking PLA generals' committee recommended that it was time to 'play the American card'.[20] In August of that year, when threats of Soviet nuclear strikes against China were rife, Beijing reached out to Washington. The China–US entente climaxed on 9–11 July 1971, in the middle of the East Pakistan crisis. US National Security Advisor (NSA) Henry Kissinger travelled to Pakistan. From there he made his way surreptitiously to China to lay the groundwork for Nixon's famous trip to Beijing in 1972.

India and the USSR align

The trip to China changed the US's stance towards India in one crucial respect. Despite Delhi's difficulties with Washington after 1962, it had always counted on the US as a deterrent against China. After Kissinger's trip to Beijing, it was clear that American strategic interests had pushed it into neutrality in the India–China conflict. Neutrality in effect meant a tilt to China.

Just before the trip, on 6 July, Kissinger had hinted to P.N. Haksar, adviser to Mrs Gandhi, that the US would find itself in an uncomfortable spot if China intervened in an India–Pakistan conflict over the Bangladesh crisis. He also told Jagjivan Ram, India's defence minister, that Washington would 'take a grave view of any Chinese move against India'.[21] However, when he met the Indian ambassador to the US on 17 July, just days after his return from Beijing, he communicated entirely the opposite view, saying categorically, 'we [the US] would be unable to help you against China'.[22] What had changed? In his meetings with Zhou, Kissinger became convinced that China was carefully testing the US commitment to Pakistan: if the US did not stand by Pakistan, would it ever stand by China? Standing by Pakistan meant stopping India from going to war over East Pakistan. Threatening US inaction in case China intervened in a South Asian war was Kissinger's way of telling Mrs Gandhi that Washington would no longer protect India against its northern neighbour – the hope was that this would deter Delhi.

Washington's China opening galvanized Delhi into action. It immediately dusted off a 1969 proposal from Moscow on Asian collective security and turned it into a twenty-five-year treaty of peace, friendship, and cooperation. The treaty included clauses that read like an alliance: both sides were to consult each other in case of a threat to their security and to take appropriate action; and neither side would assist an enemy third party. In the end, the importance of the treaty was probably more symbolic and psychological than material. Given the stopping power of the Himalaya, the logistical challenges Chinese forces would have faced if they intervened in an India–Pakistan war, and Beijing's worries about security along the Sino-Soviet border, China was unlikely to attack India.

However, the treaty did boost Indian morale at a time when the country found itself ranged against China, Pakistan, and the US. It was also pivotal in sealing Delhi's gradual embrace of Moscow that had begun in the late 1950s. Economic relations were quite robust by this time: financial and technical assistance from the Soviets was playing a significant role in developing India's heavy industry sector.[23] More importantly, India's key weapon systems between 1969 and 1978 were imported from the Soviets. These included tanks, submarines, frigates, patrol boats, landing craft, combat aircraft, armoured personnel carriers, helicopters, and surface-to-air missiles (SAMs).[24]

The Soviet intervention in Afghanistan

The polarization between India and the Soviets, on one side, and China and the US, on the other, might have been halted by the warming of ties between Delhi and Washington after Nixon and then Kissinger left the stage. With Jimmy Carter in the White House, American foreign policy took a more cosmopolitan turn. Carter was attentive to the issue of human rights, and relations with China soon came under strain (even though, as a naval officer in the Second World War, he had 'fallen in love with the country and with its people'[25]). The new president was also upset with the rather cringing US attitude to China during the Nixon–Kissinger period. With India, after Mrs Gandhi's electoral defeat in 1977, there was the prospect of a new relationship.

In fact, however, Washington's relationship with Beijing strengthened rather than weakened. From 1972, leveraging on the new relationship with the Chinese, the US had brought the Soviets to the negotiating table on arms control and a wider political understanding that climaxed in the signing of the Helsinki Accords (1975). The détente with Moscow spectacularly collapsed four years later. In 1978, Afghanistan, far from the centre of Cold War geopolitics, was plunged into internal crisis due to the struggle between rival factions in the new revolutionary government. By December 1979, Moscow had sent in its forces to ensure the survival of its preferred communist faction. The US reaction to the intervention was to team first with Pakistan and then with China to recruit Islamist radicals to fight the Soviets in Afghanistan. Carter quickly saw that the US would have to release American high-technology and weaponry to China in order to persuade it to join the fight. Sensing the opportunity to hurt the USSR and enlist the US in its military and economic revival, Deng Xiaoping told visiting US Secretary of Defence Harold Brown: 'We must turn Afghanistan into a quagmire in which the Soviet Union is bogged down for a long time in guerrilla warfare.'[26] Beijing would go on to provide economic aid, but more importantly, arms and training to the insurgents.

The strategic partnership between the US and China deepened under Ronald Reagan in the 1980s. Reagan authorized an economic opening as well as the transfer of technology and weapons to China. He also granted Beijing Most Favoured Nation (MFN) status, made available credits and facilities by which China could import US technology, and persuaded Western allies to loosen Cold War rules that constrained high-tech exports to communist countries. In 1985, Washington allowed General Electric to sell gas turbine engines for Chinese destroyers and helped with the modernization of munitions and artillery as well as advanced avionics for China's F-8 aircraft. In 1986, the first US ships with nuclear weapons capabilities visited Chinese ports. It was not all strategic interaction. People-to-people links also increased rapidly: in 1982, 100,000 Americans visited China, and 10,000 Chinese students were in the US. By 1986, American visitors to China had increased threefold, and by 1987 Chinese students in the US had increased by a factor of ten.[27]

Détentes

Despite India's misgiving about the Soviets in Afghanistan, India too deepened its partnership. It opposed the Soviet presence but refused to criticize Moscow too publicly. More importantly, it continued to buy Soviet weaponry, often on concessional terms. Between 1980 and 1985, India may have bought Soviet arms worth up to $13 billion.[28] By late 1981, though, Delhi was looking to mend relations with Washington. The geopolitical environment around India in South Asia had worsened due to the Soviet intervention in Afghanistan: as a front-line state against the Soviets, Pakistan was receiving massive economic and military assistance; the Pakistani nuclear programme was advancing thanks to the US and China; and India confronted a China–Pakistan–US coalition. At the same time, the Indian economy was in the doldrums, and it needed technology and investment from the West.

The key to India's geopolitical and economic challenges was improving ties with the US. The US responded positively to India's outreach. Its principal motive was to draw India away from the Soviets, and in 1981 Reagan met Mrs Gandhi at Cancun. The following year Mrs Gandhi made her first visit to America in a decade. Her assassination in 1984 brought Rajiv Gandhi to power, and his 1985 and 1987 visits to Washington attempted to build on his mother's opening to the US. However, when his economic reforms at home stalled due to domestic opposition, so largely did the diplomatic opening to America.

The year 1982 also produced new thinking in Beijing and Moscow. China's relations with the US had become difficult over American support to Taiwan. Washington had also slowed the transfer of advanced technologies. It was a good time for a measure of reconciliation with the Soviets: an opening to Moscow would increase Beijing's bargaining room with Washington. Beijing also wanted to reduce the tensions around its borders so that it could focus more on economic reforms at home. For its part, Moscow, confronted by a gung-ho America under Reagan, a China that was in partnership with the US and making strides economically after its 1979 reforms, and a military stalemate in Afghanistan, saw the chance to drive a wedge between China and the US. In addition, Moscow, like Beijing, wanted to focus more on economic development, and easing tensions along the Sino-Soviet border would allow it to concentrate on matters at home.

Over four years, China and the Soviets held nine rounds of talks. Between 1981 and 1986, their bilateral trade grew ten times.[29] In 1985, with the coming to power of Mikhail Gorbachev, the pace of reconciliation increased. Moscow reduced its troops along the boundaries with China and finally accepted that border negotiations were necessary. The two sides moved to normalize diplomatic relations and to stop their ideological name-calling. The Soviets renounced the Brezhnev Doctrine (which justified Soviet intervention in communist countries). In 1986–87, Gorbachev announced that Soviet troops would withdraw from Afghanistan, and by 1989 the last units had pulled out. With this, and the collapse of communism in Eastern Europe, the Cold War ended.

India and China started out the last decade of the Cold War on opposite sides of global politics. Both used the partnerships with powerful protectors to advantage. They would remain geopolitical rivals until the end of the Cold War in 1989, but by 1982 they sensed that the costs of doing so were rising. Before the Soviets and the US wound down the Cold War, India and China had already begun a détente process of their own. As we saw in the previous chapter, the two leaderships now met for the first time since the 1960s. Mrs Gandhi and Chinese Premier Hua Guofeng encountered each other at Marshal Tito's funeral in 1980. The following year, the Chinese foreign minister Huang Hua came to Delhi. This led to the resumption of border negotiations for the first time in twenty years and eventually to Rajiv Gandhi's seminal trip to Beijing in 1988.

1989–Present: From Entente to Rivalry to Cold War Rivalry . . . Again

The Cold War lasted forty years. The post–Cold War is already thirty years old. In this no-name period, India's and China's relations with Russia and the US have gone through three decade-long shifts. In the first decade, India and China, along with Russia, held rather similar negative perceptions of a triumphant America and took steps to resist US hegemony. This entente was succeeded by a decade in which India and the US saw a rapidly rising China as a rival. Russia, after hoping it would find a dignified place in the new US-led world order, turned to its great Asian neighbour for succour but kept to a middle position between Delhi and Beijing. The third decade after the end of the Cold War was witness to China's continuing rise and new assertiveness, especially after the global financial crisis of 2008. India–US relations continued to deepen in reaction to China's growing power. Russia partnered China more explicitly while still maintaining a diplomatic and arms relationship with India. In sum, over thirty years, India and China moved from a period of entente-like relations in the shadow of US hegemony to an era in which India increasingly tilted towards the US against China and finally to an outright rivalry, with India partnering the US in a new Cold War. This repeated the cycle of the period 1949–89 in which India and China went from entente partners to Cold War rivals.

1989–1998: Entente

For Delhi and Beijing, the immediate post–Cold War era was reminiscent of the 1950s. India and China soon found themselves ranged against the US and were joined by Russia. All three powers cooperated with the US, which dominated world politics, but for the first time since the mid-1950s, they also found themselves in a loose entente against America.

Tiananmen Square and China–US tensions

As the Cold War ended, a new era began, with a Chinese thunderclap. With a decade of transformative economic growth and social change in China, pressures for a political opening had built up. The Soviet reforms under Gorbachev and the collapse of communism in Eastern Europe undoubtedly also had an effect on a generation of young Chinese who wanted a loosening of government control over their lives. The pro-democracy movement was at its strongest in Beijing. Beginning in April 1989, a wave of protests washed over the capital city and spread to scores of other parts of the mainland. The movement peaked in the June Fourth Incident in Beijing's iconic Tiananmen Square when the CPC leadership sent the military armed with tanks into the square to clear the protests. Estimates vary on the numbers killed and injured, but the heavy hand of repression led to international criticism including in the US, China's erstwhile ally.

While Washington condemned Beijing's actions, it continued to do business with China. Ordinary Americans and the human rights community in the US were shocked, but President George Bush 'took a conciliatory approach . . . he deplored the loss of life, but he did not criticize individual party leaders' in order to stay engaged. US arms sales to China were suspended, but the president sent his NSA and deputy secretary of state to meet Deng Xiaoping. He wrote Deng three letters. In one extraordinary passage, he wrote almost like a supplicant: 'Please do not be angry with me if I have crossed the invisible threshold lying between constructive suggestion and "internal interference"'. A few months later, his NSA would shake Deng's hand and gush, 'My president wants you to know he is your friend forever.' The messaging was that the president had been forced by US public opinion to act against China, but the anti-Chinese measures were temporary and limited. In Congress, Bush made sure that 'dual use technology' with both civilian and military application continued to flow, including the sale of US satellites. Over the next two years, the World Bank, controlled by the US, sanctioned $4 billion worth of loans to China: no other country received as much. When the US needed China to support a UN resolution against Saddam Hussein in September 1990, Washington resumed high-level contacts (in the event the Chinese only abstained from voting). On human rights, missile and nuclear proliferation, and US support for China's entry to GATT, Beijing stuck to its positions, and on each issue Washington caved.[30]

Nevertheless, China–US relations were fraying. Beijing now moved to a more equidistant posture between Washington and Moscow. Gorbachev was in Beijing even as the Tiananmen protests were unfolding, but he avoided commenting on the situation. Despite the new democratic spirit of perestroika and glasnost in the USSR, Moscow's comments on the protests and subsequent repressive actions were subdued. When despite Bush's conciliatory stand the flow of US arms was stopped, Beijing turned to Moscow for weapons. Most importantly, the Soviets' border negotiations with China, which had been in progress since 1987, came to a head, and in 1991 the two sides came to an agreement on the border dispute.

Even as US–China economic relations flowered after the Tiananmen incident and China dramatically opened up to US goods and investment in the 1990s, trouble loomed. Anti-Western and particularly anti-US feelings were encouraged in China: the Chinese had been 'humiliated' by the West (and Japan) for a century, and a 'China that can say no' must now stand up. In the

US, with Bill Clinton in the White House, human rights concerns in China again formed part of American policy. A growing view was that with the disappearance of the USSR, China was the principal threat to US supremacy and values. In 1995–96, when the Taiwanese president received a US visa to speak at his alma mater, Cornell University, Beijing's relations with Washington further deteriorated. In July 1995, China began to lob missiles over Taiwan. A Chinese general warned the US that China was nuclear-armed and ready: 'So you [the US] are not going to threaten us again because you care a lot more about Los Angeles than Taipei.'[31] The US responded by sending two aircraft carrier battle-groups to the Taiwan Strait.

India's nuclear tests and India–US tensions

The end of the Cold War had vindicated the Indian view that the rivalry between the Soviet and American blocs was not immutable and statesmanship could end it. Having said that, India, allied to the Soviets, had come out on the losing side of the Cold War. On the other hand, China and Pakistan had come out on the winning side as partners of triumphant America. Worse, the post–Cold War period brought India's human rights record in Kashmir, Punjab, and Assam into full international view. Its closed economy was an anomaly in a world where the market increasingly ruled, and in 1991 its foreign exchange reserves fell so low it almost defaulted on its external bills. Finally, its nuclear programme was under scrutiny and pressure from the US and other non-proliferation crusaders as never before. For its part, Delhi was uncomfortable with the Comprehensive Test Ban Treaty (CTBT) despite having co-sponsored the negotiations in the UN. It was annoyed at Washington's insistence that the Nuclear Non-Proliferation Treaty (NPT) should be permanently extended. And it resented the US attempts to put it and Islamabad in the category of irresponsible nuclear states.

India's nuclear tests, followed by Pakistan's, led to a rough patch with Washington. According to US law, sanctions, an aid cut-off, and the termination of military supplies were mandatory American responses to nuclear proliferation. The US also piloted a unanimous UN Security Council resolution condemning the tests and asking India and Pakistan to stop their nuclear weapons programmes. The resolution urged them to join the NPT and the CTBT, to act with restraint, and, in a sting for India, to address the 'root causes' of their tensions, including Kashmir. As with China after Tiananmen, so also with India after the nuclear tests the White House soon stepped back from a serious diplomatic break. Within weeks, after Delhi promised to honour a moratorium on testing, India's Minister for External Affairs Jaswant Singh and Deputy Secretary of State Strobe Talbott were in intensive discussions on strategic and nuclear issues which lasted two years and fourteen rounds of negotiations. In the end the talks failed, but they laid the foundation for the nuclear deal with America that was eventually signed in 2005.

Entente against the US

As a result of the Tiananmen Square actions of the Chinese government and Indian nuclear policies climaxing in its nuclear tests, Delhi and Beijing often found themselves in opposition to Washington. With the US firmly ensconced as the hegemon, the two Asian powers (with others) came together to urge 'multipolarity', a democratization of the international order, and resistance to initiatives which might impinge on their sovereignty. Moscow held similar oppositional views, and in December 1998 Yevgeny Primakov, the Russian foreign minister, proposed a

Russia–India–China strategic partnership. Despite its coyness on the subject of the US, the grouping was clearly an attempt to 'soft balance' against American power. Delhi and Beijing rejected Moscow's proposal formally, but the mote of an idea had appeared and would grow. Global history had seemingly come full circle from the 1950s when the three powers in varying degrees had opposed the US.

In fact, the three powers were all hedging: coexisting and cooperating with the US but trying to improve their bargaining power with Washington by signalling they could 'defect' to an oppositional coalition. In response, the US, by the late 1990s, was beginning to see India as a check against a dramatically rising China and hoped to pull Delhi to its side: with a population projected to surpass China's, a new economic philosophy after its 1991 reforms, a commitment to democracy, and the English language, it was the only power that could compete with China demographically, economically, politically, and culturally over the long term. China's rise, America's search for partners against the Chinese behemoth, and India's growing worry about the relentlessly increasing power gap with its northern neighbour would cause the entente between India and China to erode.

Rivalry, 1999–2008

The terrorist strikes on the twin towers of the World Trade Center in New York on 11 September 2001 have come to define our understanding of the international politics of the ensuing decade. The period stands out for the US's 'global war on terrorism', the support it received in varying degrees from India, China, and Russia, and the worries of the four powers about Islamist terrorism. In fact, though, fissures were growing, principally between the US and China. Delhi sided increasingly with Washington by the end of this period, and Beijing was increasingly alienated from Washington and more in sympathy with Moscow. From their entente, India and China were drifting into international rivalry.

Growing China–US conflict

China–US relations were mixed but increasingly tended towards conflict. Two events typified the widening gulf. In May 1999, the US Air Force mistakenly bombed the Chinese embassy in Belgrade during its campaign against the Federal Republic of Yugoslavia under Slobodan Milosevic. China accused the US of a deliberate attack, and street protests including attacks on American diplomatic missions on the mainland followed. Washington apologized several times for the attack and paid compensation for the death of three Chinese journalists as also damage to the embassy. Then, in April 2001, a US signals-intelligence aircraft hit a Chinese fighter in mid-air, leading to the death of a Chinese airman. The damaged US aircraft landed on China's Hainan island. Washington later issued letters of 'sorrow and regret'. Again, Beijing protested US actions, accusing it of straying into Chinese airspace and attacking its fighter plane.

At the same time, US economic engagement, public and private, with China dramatically increased. When trade and copyright tensions between the two countries escalated, Washington proposed that in return for Chinese compliance with international trading and intellectual property norms, it would support China's membership in the World Trade Organization (WTO). A trade deal with Beijing in 1999 led to China's eventual membership in the WTO in December 2001. At the private level, US investment firms led by Goldman Sachs advised Beijing on how US investors could help fund financially strapped Chinese state-owned enterprises (SOEs). It was not just economic engagement. After the Al Qaeda attacks in the US, China was the first country to phone President Bush and express its sympathy and support. Beijing went on to vote for the UN resolution authorizing the use of force in Afghanistan. When the extent of the North Korean nuclear programme became clear, Bush asked for and got Chinese help to bring Pyongyang to the negotiating table.

Even as US–China relations oscillated between conflict and cooperation, Beijing and Moscow drew closer. In 2001, they signed a Treaty of Good-Neighbourliness and Friendly Cooperation and increasingly supported each other on global issues. With a group of Central Asian republics, they also formed the Shanghai Cooperation Organization (SCO) that year. In 2004, they settled their disputes in the eastern part of their borderlands. Economic interactions grew dramatically. Bilateral trade in 2001 was nearly $11 billion but by 2008 had grown to $57 billion.[32] When Russia was hit by a financial crisis in 2008, Moscow turned to Beijing for loans. China's energy imports from Russia's far east became a major element of their relationship. The Chinese military bought Russian defence equipment to the tune of $2 billion per year from 1999 to 2005, consisting largely of naval equipment and the Su-30 aircraft. They agreed on co-production, licensed production in China, and joint R&D. Two thousand Russian scientists worked in Chinese defence establishments. They exchanged military personnel, attended each other's training academies, and the two General Staffs met regularly.[33]

India and the US as 'natural allies'

As the differences between China and the US sharpened and the power gap between them shrank, India and the US looked to build a strategic partnership. In September 1998, hoping to repair ties with the US after the nuclear tests, Prime Minister Atal Bihari

Vajpayee publicly averred that 'India and the United States are natural allies in the quest for a better future for the world in the 21st century' – the first time an Indian leader had used the word 'ally' in the same breath as 'India and the United States'.[34]

Pakistan's military ingress into Kargil May–July 1999 only served to bring Delhi and Washington closer. Given the possibility of the conflict escalating to the nuclear level, Washington intervened to get Pakistani troops to withdraw. Terrorists attacked the Kashmir legislature in October 2001, just weeks after the events of 9/11, and then followed with an attack on India's Parliament in December 2001. In response, India mobilized its forces, threatening to go to war against Pakistan. Again, and for similar reasons, Washington stepped in, leaning on President Pervez Musharraf to rein in terrorist groups operating in Pakistan. Musharraf's televised address to his country mollified India enough for Vajpayee to call off Operation Parakram, the full-scale military mobilization on the India–Pakistan border.

When President Clinton addressed the Indian Parliament in March 2000, he endorsed Vajpayee's words on the strategic affinity between India and the US. The phrase passed into the lexicon of India–US diplomacy, and with variations – natural friends, strategic partners, critical allies – it has stayed there. The word 'natural' suggested that the two countries were not allies in the formal sense, obliged to come to each other's defence against a common enemy. Being 'natural' allies, they were bonded by something deeper, almost metaphysical, by common values or a shared worldview.

In fact, though, they almost became allies in the formal sense when in the wake of 9/11, within hours of the attack, India offered the US 'everything', as American forces prepared to intervene in Afghanistan. Everything included overflight rights, logistics, and basing.[35] Where China had helped the US after 9/11 diplomatically and with some intelligence sharing, India had offered actual alliance-like military cooperation. In the event, Islamabad's support for the Afghanistan invasion was vital, and so Washington politely refused Delhi's offer. However, in February–March 2003, it was the US that came calling, asking for Indian troops to operate in Iraq alongside coalition forces in case of war with Saddam Hussein. Despite uneasiness over US actions there, and a parliamentary resolution deploring it, Delhi gave serious thought to putting 'boots on the ground', before eventually saying no.[36]

While India and the US did not ally on Afghanistan and Iraq, there remained US interest in cultivating Delhi for the long term. In 2000, Condoleezza Rice, the Stanford professor who would go on to be George W. Bush's NSA, wrote in the journal *Foreign Affairs*: 'India is an element in China's calculation, and it should be in America's, too. India is not a great power yet, but it has the potential to emerge as one.'[37] Five years later, this line of thinking produced a declaration that the two countries would aim for 'full civilian nuclear cooperation', at the heart of which was an agreement that India would identify its civilian nuclear reactors, separate them from the military ones, and open them to international regulation. The separation of reactors would pave the way for the resumption of nuclear collaboration, which had been stopped after India's 1974 nuclear tests. India, for its part, accepted a continued moratorium on testing and other standard non-proliferation norms and practices. In 2008, the two sides unveiled and signed the final accord which would get US congressional and international approval. The deal in essence gave India access once again to advanced nuclear technology and scientific interactions and yet protected its military reactors and programme. It also formed the basis for greater diplomatic trust between India and the US. India's nuclear programme had divided the two countries diplomatically since 1974; it now brought them together.

Delhi's growing friendship with Washington could have alienated Moscow as US–Russia relations grew more fractious. In fact, the relationship held, though without much warmth. India and Russia were preoccupied with domestic economic and political challenges, and for Moscow, more than Delhi, the relationship no longer held the same importance. What Delhi did with Washington was no great worry for Moscow. Bilateral trade with India had collapsed after the Cold War, particularly after the suspension of the rupee–rouble payment system. In 1999–2000, two-way Indo-Russian trade stood at a mere $1.57 billion; by 2005–06, it had risen to just $2.7 billion.[38] This was minuscule compared to the volumes of Sino-Russian trade.

What remained significant was the arms relationship, despite Moscow's deepening links with China. Under a 1997 accord, and the strategic partnership agreement of 2000, India bought Russian equipment and cooperated in military R&D. The two began to jointly develop the BrahMoS supersonic cruise missile. In 2002, India received its first Su-30 MKI fighters and then proceeded to manufacture them domestically. In 2007, the two sides began to cooperate on designing a fifth generation fighter aircraft (FGFA). Other purchases included battle tanks and the *Admiral Gorshkov* aircraft carrier. India also leased a nuclear-powered submarine from Russia.

Entente unravelling

India–China bilateral relations during this period were marked largely by pragmatism, but China's rise would push India into the US corner. In 2004, Nathu La, where in 1967 the two sides had briefly fought, was opened for border trade. When Wen Jiabao visited India in the same year, he visited Bangalore and suggested that the two countries could cooperate in IT. In 2005, the two sides agreed on the basic parameters and guidelines that would guide a final border settlement. In 2006, they agreed to put in joint bids for oil exploration in third countries. Bilateral trade boomed, going from $2.75 billion in 2000 to $42 billion in 2008.[39] When Pakistan and the smaller South Asian states proposed that China be admitted as an observer member of SAARC, India acquiesced. Yet, particularly in retrospect, the emerging alignments between India and the US on one side and China and Russia on the other presaged trouble for the India–China relationship. The alignments were both cause and effect. Delhi drifted closer to Washington to balance Beijing; Beijing and Moscow converged in their suspicion and resentment of Washington; and Washington began to leverage Delhi against the alliance of China and Russia and particularly against the 'senior partner' in that alliance, China.

In the summer of 2008, a series of bankruptcies in the US financial sector brought about the biggest slowdown in the US and Western economies since the Great Depression. There were knock-on effects all round the world, including in India and China. Indian and Chinese fiscal responses stemmed the damage, though, and their economies grew while the developed countries floundered. Out of the ashes of the global financial crisis, it was China that emerged the most impressively. Rising Chinese power and declining American power had been anticipated for almost a decade. Suddenly, the power transition was in motion in 'real time'. China's dramatic ascent would have an impact on the relationship of India, China, Russia, and the US and on India–China relations over the next decade.

Cold War Rivalry, 2009–Present

China's rise after 2008 pushed India and the US together. It also drew Russia further into the Chinese orbit. As the India–US partnership took shape against China, Moscow was poised between Delhi and Beijing but increasingly opposed to Washington. A new Cold War was taking shape.

An India–US partnership

China's rise has defined the last decade more than anything else. It is worth rehearsing some economic comparisons to see just how dramatic the shift has been. From 2009 to 2019, China's economy grew at an average of 7.84 per cent while India's economy grew at an average of 6.84 per cent. In the same period, the US grew at an average of just 1.84 per cent. In 2009, China's GDP was $5.1 trillion, India's was $1.24 trillion, and the US's was $14.44 trillion. By 2019, China stood at $14.34 trillion, India at $2.87 trillion, and the US at $21.42 trillion. In eleven years, China added $9.24 trillion, India added $1.53 trillion, and the US added $7.98 trillion to their GDPs. In 2009, China was roughly $9 trillion smaller than the US economy; in 2019, it had reduced the gap to $7 trillion. For India, in 2009, the gap with China was $3.76 trillion; by 2019, it had grown to a gargantuan $11.47 trillion. In sum, the gap between China and the US reduced, but the gap between China and India grew massively. India was within shooting distance of China in 2009; by 2019, China was out of sight. Russia, meanwhile, went from a GDP of $1.45 trillion in 2009 to just $1.76 trillion in 2019, which made it slightly bigger than South Korea.[40]

Not surprisingly, India and the US grew their partnership during this period. The pace of summits increased, with the top leaderships meeting almost every year until Trump came to office. A raft of dialogues began – economic, military, cybersecurity, and the so-called '2 plus 2' (defence and foreign policy). In 2010, President Obama endorsed India's claim to permanent membership of the UN Security Council – which left only China among the P-5 refusing to go along. By 2016, Washington had designated India as a major defence partner so that it would enjoy access to US defence technology reserved for treaty allies. Between 2002 and 2020, India signed four so-called foundational defence agreements with the US to enhance information, communication, intelligence, and logistics cooperation. American arms sales increased steadily, with India buying cargo and transport aircraft, attack helicopters, missiles, artillery, and torpedoes since 2008. In 2020, the US authorized total defence trade of $20 billion, in that year alone.[41] India–US trade overall boomed, rising from $37 billion in 2009 to $92 billion in 2019 (the comparable figures for India–China trade are $41 billion and $84 billion in 2019).[42]

Most importantly, India engaged the US in a range of diplomatic initiatives. With Washington, it issued a statement on protecting maritime access in the South China Sea. It also brandished a 'US-India Joint Strategic Vision for the Asia-Pacific and Indian Ocean Region'. When the Americans proposed a Free and Open Indo-Pacific (FOIP) in 2017 to counter China's growing influence in Asia, India became a member of the group along with Australia and Japan. It joined the Quadrilateral Security Dialogue – or 'Quad' – in November 2017 which includes Australia, Japan, and the US. The Quad is the military–defence counterpart of the FOIP. In 2020, India and the US signed a Global Comprehensive Strategic Partnership which was largely a restatement of many of the ideas and initiatives that had brought them together over the past several years. Though they coyly refused to name it in these various initiatives, China was the object of their common concern.

India and Russia charted a different course in the shadow of Chinese power: largely transactional–commercial to strengthen India's military and energy access. Russia was above all a source of arms: air defence systems, helicopters, fighter aircraft, tanks, and a range of naval vessels including nuclear-powered submarines. India increasingly insisted on transfer of technology, modernization of existing equipment, purchase of cutting-edge weaponry, and joint R&D. While Russia's share of arms exports to India dropped, it still supplied roughly 60 per cent of its weapons.[43] India also turned to Russia for energy. After the India–US nuclear deal in 2005, which resumed international cooperation with the Indian civilian nuclear programme, it was Moscow that signed most of the contracts. In addition, India bought Russian natural gas and invested in oil and gas fields in Russia. While the relationship was largely transactional, India was also attempting to diversify Russia's foreign policy options away from China. As part of weaning Moscow from Beijing, India held a growing number of military exercises, dialogues between service chiefs, and high-level meetings with Russian officials.

A new Cold War

China's relations were the reverse of India's relations with the US during this period. As Chinese power grew, Washington pivoted to Asia to restore American influence. In 2016, it helped launch the Trans-Pacific Partnership with eleven other Pacific Rim countries. Economic tensions, primarily over Chinese intellectual property theft and over China's huge trade surpluses with the US, continued to damage relations. Chinese military facilities on reefs and atolls in the South China Sea rang alarm bells in the region and in Washington. In 2017, the US National Security Report pointed to China (along with Russia) as the main threats to the US. In 2018, Washington announced a series of tariffs on Chinese goods which led Beijing to retaliate. The arrest of the Chinese computer giant Huawei's chief financial officer, Meng Wenzhou, in Canada at American instigation led to a further deterioration in relations. Despite the 'phase one' China–US trade deal in January 2020, relations worsened over US accusations that China was a currency manipulator, Washington's support of the pro-democracy movement in Hong Kong, and Beijing's initial response to the Covid-19 pandemic.

China–Russia relations, like India–Russia relations, were built around military and energy sales. Despite unauthorized Chinese copying of Russian arms, Moscow continued to pursue an alliance-like relationship, selling the S-400 missile system, infantry vehicles, and helicopters, and cooperating in the development of space capabilities and China's FGFA. In 2019, it agreed to work with China on an anti-missile warning system that would provide information on a possible US attack. As Chinese technology improved, the cooperation was increasingly a two-way street. The two militaries exercised extensively on sea and on land, laying the foundation for greater interoperability. Hundreds of Chinese officers were trained in Russia. At the diplomatic level, Beijing and Moscow were largely in agreement on global issues and cast several joint vetoes in the UN. Bilateral trade went from $57 billion in 2008 to $84 billion in 2017.[44] Energy cooperation expanded, with sales and joint construction of pipelines from Russia to China leading to a virtual energy alliance. Indeed, China and Russia increasingly functioned like all-round strategic allies, with annual summits.

By 2018–19, then, the US and China were heading towards a Cold War, with India and Russia lining up with their preferred partners. Once again, Delhi and Beijing found themselves on opposite sides in global politics. In a dynamic that marked earlier periods, Delhi came to side with a bigger power principally because it feared China; and Beijing aligned with a partner not because it feared India, but rather to balance US power.

Conclusion

Situating India–China relations in a global history shows that India and China have never truly been on the same side except during the Second World War. Even then, Indians worked largely with the Kuomintang and not the communists in the fight against Japan. In terms of their partnerships, Delhi and Beijing had parallel and compatible interests in only two brief periods – in the early 1950s and in the decade after the Cold War, for a total of perhaps fifteen years in a seventy-year history. Crucially, despite these two brief ententes against the US, they have never been allies or true strategic partners against either the Soviets/Russians or the Americans. As allies or partners, India and China would have developed a history of give and take. Their leaderships, officials, and militaries would have got to know and trust each other more. Shared memories of collaboration could have helped tide over or even pre-empt conflict in other periods.

Instead, for much of the period from 1949 to the present, a supposedly non-aligned India, in varying degrees of intensity, partnered with the Soviets and the Americans in order to deter or balance China: in the 1960s, primarily with the Soviets and very briefly with the US; from 1971 to 1989, with the Soviets exclusively; and from about 2001 onward, with the US. On the other hand, China partnered both the Soviets and the US, but not because it needed to deter or balance India: it initially aligned with the USSR against the US, later with the US against the USSR, and finally, after the Cold War, with Russia against the US.

The history of India's and China's relations with the USSR/Russia and the US also shows that while India and China sought partnerships with those powers for their own security, they were used in turn by Moscow and Washington for their own purposes. During the Cold War, the USSR and the US each wooed China to side with them against the other. Both powers tried to recruit India against each other and against China. If India and China ended up on opposite sides in global history, it was often because the almost inexorable logic of power balancing (and ideology preferences) in the India–China–US–USSR quadrilateral shaped Indian and Chinese choices. To some extent, then, India and China have come to look at each other warily for reasons beyond their bilateral quarrels.

Finally, our global history of India, China, the USSR/Russia, and the US shows that change is the only constant. Sometimes, change was endogenous, resulting from one party or more making decisions about who their friends and enemies were; and sometimes it was exogenous, being the consequence of developments outside the four-power system. The Czech revolt of 1968 sparked a Soviet intervention that further antagonized and alienated Beijing from Moscow. The East Pakistani turmoil in 1970–71 ended in the creation of Bangladesh, but at the geopolitical level it gave the US an opportunity to woo China and it pushed India into the arms of the USSR. Developments in Afghanistan in the late 1970s that led to the Soviet invasion, and in turn to a deeper partnership between China and the US, was another exogenously induced shift. The 9/11 attacks on the US is yet another instance which for a decade brought India,

China, and Russia into a degree of alignment with the US against Islamic extremism.

What this suggests is that while the present partnership of India with the US and of China with Russia seems durable, endogenous and exogenous developments could alter the strategic landscape. With Joe Biden in the White House, the US could rethink the relationship with China and decide to work with rather than against it. A crisis in mainland China–Taiwan relations or between the two Koreas could have profound consequences for India, China, Russia, and the US. The coronavirus pandemic may have quite unpredictable geopolitical consequences over time, which are yet to be apparent.

4

Power: From Parity to Asymmetry

The differences between India and China on their mutual perceptions and worldviews, their perimeters, and their strategic partners might not matter if the power balance between them was more symmetric. In fact, the power gap between the two countries has grown relentlessly since about 1990. The consequence of this power gap is that China, given its superior position, is often assertive and insensitive towards India, and India, conscious of the gap, is increasingly desperate to be recognized as an equal and determined to stand firm in the face of Chinese challenges. Neither country is disposed to be accommodative. From a position of strength, China does not see the need to accommodate, while from a position of weakness, India feels it cannot afford to do so and risk further loss of standing and strategic autonomy.

Measuring a power gap is complicated. Fortunately, social scientists have given us some leads on the components and measures of power that allow us to make an estimate of the India–China gap. The Harvard political scientist Joseph S. Nye famously distinguishes between hard power and soft power. Hard power is the ability to get others to do what you want by force or coercion, usually through economic and military means; soft power is the ability to get others to do what you want by means of persuasion, usually by means of playing on their attraction to or regard for one's values, institutions, and achievements.[1] Based on these distinctions, India's and China's power balance is asymmetric, but with some surprises. From a relatively symmetric position in 1949, the power equation has shifted decisively in China's favour economically – this is well known, though the huge size of the gap is worth underlining. In military terms, China holds a lead, but after accounting for geography and possible Indian strategic responses the gap appears quite modest. This flies in the face of a general perception that the Chinese military will be rampant in a conflict. As for soft power, contrary to the generally held view, China betters India. The economic, military, and cultural elements of power are synergistic: they each magnify the other, so unfortunately for India, the power gap becomes even more formidable. If you have more economic and military power, there is a good chance that others will be 'persuaded' to do what you want. If you have cultural or soft power, you can conserve the use of hard power for when you really need it and not fritter it away over every disagreement.

~

In 1998, I was in Singapore for an international conference on the newly formed ASEAN Regional Forum (ARF). The main ARF countries were all represented – the ten countries of the Association of Southeast Asian Nations (ASEAN) and the ten ASEAN Dialogue Partners. The Dialogue Partners included Australia, China, the European Union, India, Japan, and the US. My memory is that the biggest delegations were from China and the US and that their teams were of equal strength. Today, this would not surprise – it would be a considerable diplomatic error if either had more delegates than the other. In 1998, the China–US parity made you think. At the same time, the India–China gap was quite apparent: I think there were only two of us representing India.

It was a stimulating conference for what was said but just as interesting for what was not said – the seemingly innocuous performances and actions which in fact turned out to be rather significant. For one thing, the Chinese delegates were unlike any academics and officials from the mainland that I had previously encountered. The men and women delegates were young, dressed in tight black business suits, and all over the floor during the breaks, busily engaging delegates from the other countries. They looked cosmopolitan and assured – gone was the dour manner, the shabby attire. I was accosted too (eventually), and a pleasant discussion ensued, which the Chinese steered good-humouredly to the question of how to deal with entitled Westerners. Another surprise: my interlocutors all spoke effortless American English. Several had probably studied in the US. They were friendly, light, nimble. Where had humourless, stentorian, obstreperous China gone, I remember thinking.

Perhaps the most telling moments came during the conference sessions. We had been ordered to stick to ten minutes of prepared remarks – the chairs insisting they would cut us off mid-sentence if we violated the time limit. Yet, when the Chinese delegates spoke, the injunction evaporated. I slyly and then more obviously looked at my watch during my session as the Chinese presenter sailed past the ten-minute mark, with no finger-wagging from the chair. And so it went, session after session. 'The Chinese are not comfortable with English, *lah*,' one of my Southeast Asian colleagues explained, 'so they need a little more time.' I looked around the hall, wondering about the English fluency of our Cambodian, Japanese, Korean, and Vietnamese colleagues.

Our hosts were not deliberately giving the Chinese more time. It was simply that China's power had 'arrived'. It was not just the hosts. Unthinkingly, most of us in the conference room were simply acknowledging the new reality by indulging the Chinese delegation – as we would have the American not so long before. Even in 1998, China was a behemoth – I knew the raw figures as well as anyone. Here, though, was a personal, direct, live, real-time experience of Chinese power and the opening moments in the scripting of a new world order. To use the title of former US secretary of state Dean Acheson's autobiography, I was – in a very small way – 'present at the creation'.

Economic Power

Estimations of economic power are many, and an India–China comparison could fill an entire book. Here we confine ourselves to an overall comparison of economic vitality (GDP, financial reserves, technological innovation, and market leadership), infrastructure and energy, and quality of population in terms of productivity.

Economic Vitality

According to World Bank figures, in 1962, the year that India and China fought, India's GDP (in current US dollars) was $42 billion. China's GDP was $47 billion. The gap was a mere $5 billion – virtually nothing. In 2019, India's GDP was $2.875 trillion, and China's was $14.343 trillion. The GDP gap was $11.468 trillion (it is over $14 trillion if you go by purchasing power parity figures). From a position of rough equality in 1962, India's economy is now one-fifth of China's, and India's per capita GDP is one-fourth of China's.

Between 1962 and 2019, there is not a single year when India equalled China's GDP. In terms of GDP growth rates, in the fifty-six years between 1961 and 2019, India surpassed China only thirteen times, despite the fact that from 1949 to 1980 China's was a centralized, communist economy and India's was a mixed economy with a robust private sector. The economic historian Angus Maddison's 2010 data set shows that the last time India beat China in overall GDP terms was in 1700 – when the Mughals were at their peak.[2]

A country's total reserves (for example, hard currency, gold) is another indicator of economic strength. In 1980, India's total reserves are estimated to have been $12.01 billion. China was just embarking on its economic reforms in that year and had $10.09 billion. The gap was in India's favour by $2 billion. The figures today are astonishingly different for both countries, and the gap is massively in China's favour. In 2019, India's total reserves were estimated at $463.47 billion while China's were $3.222 trillion. China had roughly seven times India's total reserves, and the gap was $2.759 trillion.

In the long run, a key element of sustained economic growth is technological innovation. Measuring innovation is a complex matter, but one crude index is the number of scientific–technological patents that a country's nationals file. According to WIPO's Patent Cooperation Treaty System (PCT), from 2014 to 2019 India filed 10,012 patents in total, for an average of 1668 per year. In the same period, China filed 259,716 patents in total, for an average of 43,286 per year. Put differently, Chinese inventors filed roughly twenty-five times the number of patents that their Indian counterparts filed.[3]

Another measure of economic vitality is the number of market leaders that a country has – in essence, Fortune 500 companies. The US and China dominate, with China close to surpassing the

Americans in terms of the total number. In 2019, India had seven out of 500 whereas China had 112 (the US had 121).[4] Clearly, India is nowhere in the league tables of the world's biggest companies. Nor can India match China in terms of the super-rich. In 2020, Mukesh Ambani was the richest person in Asia, but in the list of the 50 richest people in the world, India has only Ambani while China has nine magnates.[5] If we are looking at market leadership, in terms of companies and individuals, India fares very poorly compared to China – indeed there is no real comparison.

Transportation and Energy

Economic growth and development depend on infrastructure – transportation and energy. How do the two countries fare in terms of access to railways, highways, civilian aviation, and shipping as well as energy?

The total number of rail miles in India and China is about the same. In 2019, India had 123,542 kilometres, and in 2018 China had 131,651 kilometres. The total road network in India in 2017 was 5.897 million kilometres and in China in 2019 it was 5.012 million kilometres. India's national highways amounted to 114,158 kilometres in 2017 while China had 149,600 kilometres in 2018.[6] These figures for rail and road connectivity suggest the two countries are roughly equal – which is a bit of a surprise given the image of China as an infrastructure leader. In fact, given the much larger land area of China, it should have a more extensive set of railways and highways. The figures are not the whole story though. They omit the frequency of trains and how many lanes typically feature on Indian and Chinese highways: clearly, any estimate of the volume of traffic on trains and highways must be multiplied by train frequency and the number of lanes, respectively.

More importantly, the figures say nothing about the quality of rail and road travel and traveller experience. In 2012, I was in Beijing and Shanghai to conduct interviews with Chinese officials, academics, and think tank experts on the state of India–China relations. After a round of interactions in Beijing, I decided to take the Jinghu high-speed railway to Shanghai. The train had begun operations only a few months earlier in 2011, and I was curious. It was also the quickest way to get to my Shanghai hotel, given that the train takes you from downtown Beijing to downtown Shanghai and you avoid the drive to and from suburban airports.

Drawing on memories of Indian railway journeys, I expected a noisome building and heaving/shoving fellow passengers as we boarded the train. Instead, the station was like an international airport – high-domed, all chrome and crystalline, serviced by smartly attired personnel, and easy to navigate all the way to the compartment. I had paid to travel executive class, which I innocently expected might be equivalent to the highest class on the Indian Shatabdi trains. In fact, I stepped into an interior that resembled business-class air travel and was shown to my seat by an elegant steward. The journey of 1300 kilometres took roughly four hours – the Beijing–Shanghai high-speed train is widely acknowledged to be the fastest intercity train in the world. The countryside flew by my window, with a gentle thrumming and swaying against air resistance. Leaning back, I thought of my train rides from Delhi to Mumbai: the same distance, covered in sixteen rattling hours. Indian railway journeys have their joys; but speed, comfort, and graciousness of service are not among them.

Leaving such refinements aside, the really telling difference between India and China in the transportation sector is in aviation and shipping. Here the disparities are enormous. In 2019, the Indian civil aviation fleet was a mere 669 aircraft. The corresponding number in China was 3772 aircraft, roughly five and a half times India's.[7] India's total air passenger traffic in 2018–19 was 316.51 million while China's was 1.35 billion. In 2019, India had 137 airports while China had 237 airports.[8] With respect to shipping, the disparities are gargantuan. One way of seeing this is to look at the total number of containers that ports handle. In 2018, Indian ports handled roughly 16.4 million containers. China by contrast handled 225.8 million, approximately fourteen times India's numbers. To get a sense of the scale of China's port operations, it handles two and a half times the volume of India, Japan, and the US combined.[9]

Beyond transportation, energy supplies are crucial for economic power. Here the imbalance between the two countries is huge. Aggregating across non-renewable and renewable sources, in 2018, India's electricity supply was 1,593,709 GWh and China's was 7,519,344 GWh.[10] In other words, China generates about five times the amount of electricity that India generates. Note that the Chinese economy is also roughly five times India's. While the mix of hydrocarbons and renewables in India and China is the same – roughly 85 per cent hydrocarbons – China's massive energy use is far more environmentally damaging if not unsustainable in a time of deepening climate change. To grow, India must increase its energy use, but to emulate China-like consumption would be catastrophic for climate change unless other countries reduced their consumption substantially. It is therefore unclear if India can ever match China's rates of energy consumption and explosive economic growth: at the present stage of technology, it is simply not possible to substitute renewables for non-renewables at levels that would put India on a high-growth path.

Size and Quality of Population

Economic power depends not just on the size of a country's population but also on the quality of its population, particularly its labour force – looking ahead this may turn out to be the most important factor.

India's population will surpass China's by 2027, according to the UN. By 2050, India's population is expected to be 1.5 billion whereas China's population is expected to have shrunk to 1.1 billion – a gap of 400 million people.[11] The overall numbers could count in India's favour. India also has a potential demographic dividend, that is, a lot of young, physically able people who can power economic production. China by contrast is already facing a future in which its younger population is declining relative to older people. In 2050, India may have 220 million more working-age people between the age of twenty-five and sixty-four.[12] Crucial here is labour force productivity. India's demographic lead will be a plus if its labour force is highly productive. The trends show otherwise, comparatively speaking. China's labour productivity in 1970 was estimated to be one-third India's, but by 2002 the two countries were on a par. In 2016, India's labour productivity had fallen to two-thirds of China's.[13]

Labour productivity in turn depends on a variety of factors but most fundamentally on education and health. A worker must be literate, perhaps up to the eighth grade, and must be physically strong enough to operate machines and other devices in the fields and factories during a normal workday. India's record here suffers in comparison to China's. According to the World Bank, in 2018, India's adult (over fifteen years of age) literacy rate was 74 per cent, a figure that China passed in the late 1980s, nearly forty years earlier. By 2018, China's adult literacy figure was nearly 97 per cent.[14] How many children persist to the end of their primary school education, that is, until the end of the sixth grade? In 2018, the figure for India was 86 per cent. China achieved that figure in 1990. In 1997, the last year that China reported the figure, it was nearly 94 per cent, eight points higher than India's in 2018. The worrying fact about India's record is the steady *worsening*: in 2014, 93 per cent of Indian children had persisted to the end of primary school.[15] At the other end of the education continuum, at the tertiary level, India has an even longer way to go. India's gross enrollment ratio – the proportion of Indians between the age of eighteen and twenty-three who go to college – is only 27 per cent. The figure for China is 49 per cent.[16]

When they get to college, Indians will find the quality of their education compares badly with that of their Chinese counterparts. The Times Higher Education (THE) rankings of the top 100 universities in the world indicates that in 2019 India had no universities and China had three in the elite group. In the Quacquarelli Symonds (QS) rankings of top universities in 2019, India had none while China had six in the top 100. Between 2014 and 2019, India remained at none; China on the other hand went from three to six universities. A more refined search of the QS rankings that focuses on the top 300 world universities shows that in 2019 India had six and China had twelve universities. Among the top 300 Asian universities, India improved to a count of thirty-nine whereas China had seventy-three.[17] In the QS 2021 rankings, India's highest ranked university was the Indian Institute of Technology Bombay, which came in 172nd. China's highest ranked university was Tsinghua University, which came in at 15th.[18]

What about India's and China's health profiles? Three indicators are key from the point of view of the number of able adults who can work more or less efficiently and whose cognitive abilities have developed normally: the extent of undernourishment; the extent of stunting; and the extent of wasting (acute malnutrition). A comparison between India and China shows once again that India does badly. In terms of the percentage of the population that is undernourished, the most recent figures (2017–19) indicate that India had 14 per cent and China had less than 2.5 per cent. The prevalence of wasting among Indian children below the age of five in 2015–19 was 17.3 per cent whereas among Chinese children it was 2 per cent. As for the prevalence of stunting among Indian children below the age of five in 2015–19, it was 34.7 per cent for India and 5.5 per cent for China.[19]

Speaking to a group of Indian administrators, I once made the point that Indians were among the shortest people on average in the world and had one of the highest rates of stunting. In terms of average height, Indian men ranked 180th out of 200 countries and Indian women ranked 182nd out of 200 (Chinese men and women ranked 65th and 54th in the world, respectively, and were the tallest in Asia).[20] More importantly, I mentioned that India had one of the highest rates of stunting in the world and the largest absolute number of stunted individuals. Several officers shrugged, annoyed at my 'negative comment on India', and insisted that height did not matter. After all, as one officer huffily put it, Napoleon was short, as was Nehru. The point though is that stunting is not so much about height; what matters are the cognitive implications of stunting, namely, the impairment of normal development. Moreover, there is evidence that the mental effects cannot be reversed if malnutrition persists after age two to five. If so, India will have tens of millions of adults, perhaps as many as 400 million, who did not recover from early childhood stunting and will live a life with impaired cognition. This would mean several hundred million people with low numeracy–literacy and deficient problem-solving skills, with its consequences for workplace productivity, especially in a modern industrial and service economy. If so, India's demographic dividend could turn into a demographic nightmare.

~

Any Indian who has travelled in China will have experienced the greater productivity – or efficiency – of Chinese workers and will undoubtedly have their favourite rueful story. My story is from 1998, when I was in Shanghai for a conference. One afternoon after lunch, the Indian Sinologist Giri Deshingkar and I ventured out to encash our travellers' cheques. Walking along, we marvelled at the gleaming skyscrapers and clean streets around us, at the orderly hustle and bustle of the city, as we sought out a bank. At the bank, Deshingkar said to me in the tone of Sherlock Holmes to Watson: 'Just observe.' I observed that the bank had only one employee present at the time. I also observed several other foreign and Chinese customers in line and urged Deshingkar to leave our transactions to another day: or we would be late for the conference. Deshingkar shook his wise head and kept us in the queue. In twenty minutes, the bank clerk had dealt with all of us including helping the foreigners fill out various forms – and all this with cool courtesy. I left thinking about my bank back at Jawaharlal Nehru University. The little Shanghai bank was clean, subdued, and air-conditioned. My equally little Indian bank, populated by six or seven clerks and a chaiwalla boy, was paan-spattered, boisterous with bank officials and customers, and cooled by whirring ceiling fans. The banking modes and experiences were worlds apart.

Military Power

Military power is the second component of hard power. For most analysts of international security issues, it is the most important component, the 'sharp end of the stick'. Economic power is the basis in the long run for military power. That is why it is important to begin a relative power assessment with economic capacity. However, when the chips are down, military power counts. Compared to the enormous disparities in economic strength, India and China are not as far apart in military strength. Indeed, given the stopping power of the Himalaya and the maritime distances, the imbalance is less daunting. Having said that, relying on a strict numerical assessment and geography is misleading. Strategy – or how you deploy and use your forces – counts for a lot.

Ground Forces and Air Balance

Since the primary theatre of active military confrontation between India and China is the border, it is best to begin with the army and air balance. At last count, in 2020, according to the International Institute of Strategic Studies (IISS) in London, India's armed forces personnel numbered roughly 1.4 million as against China's 2 million. Of these, their armies accounted for 1.237 million and 975,000, respectively, the Chinese having downsized dramatically in a modernization drive. Backing up the troops will be artillery and, to a lesser extent, armour (primarily tanks). In 2020, India had 10,913 artillery pieces where China had 9196. In the case of tanks, the imbalance was reversed: India had 3565 tanks while China had 5850 tanks. In 1962, neither India nor China used their combat aircraft. That kind of restraint is unlikely in the future. As for air power, in 2020, India was outnumbered by a factor of three: 850 aircraft against 2921 aircraft.[21]

What do these numbers tell us about the ground and air balance between the two militaries? India has slightly more ground forces and artillery pieces but is behind in the number of tanks. This suggests that quantitatively the two forces are in rough balance along the border. However, not all troops serve on the India–China border. India deploys large numbers against Pakistan and on internal security in counter-insurgency missions as well. China has fourteen land neighbours (along with Russia, the largest number of neighbours in the world), and it cannot therefore devote them all to the border with India. It too needs forces for internal security. No easy conclusion about the balance in ground forces can be derived from the numbers, though the disparity in tanks is glaring. The air balance is distinctly lopsided, and since aircraft can be moved around quickly in case of war, the gap in numbers is significant. Admittedly, this is pure 'bean counting' – just going by the numbers of weapons and not their quality – but it gives us a snapshot of the military relationship.

If the quality of weapons on both sides as well as the quality of manpower, leadership, and fighting spirit on both sides are more or less equivalent, the crucial factors in case of actual combat will be strategy and logistics. The word strategy has many connotations, but here it simply refers to the application of force at various levels against an opponent, from basic decisions about whether to go on offence or emphasize defence, to more tactical decisions about how to fight on the battlefield. Logistics refers to the supply of warfighting and other materials to the military, as well as the ability to move units in and out of battle and within battles.

In the Second World War, the German military was outgunned by French and British forces in every major weapon system. However, its blitzkrieg strategy in 1940 decimated Allied forces in six weeks. The key elements of German strategy were the concentration of highly mobile forces led by tanks, the use of surprise, and the massive use of dive-bombers in support of ground forces that broke through French and British lines and raced towards Paris causing a collapse of Allied defences. Crucially, the Germans delivered supplies efficiently in the field to sustain their advances. In sum, strategy and logistics proved decisive against superior numbers.

For a variety of reasons, war between India and China will be quite different. Terrain will not permit a blitzkrieg: the Himalaya are not the plains of France. Yet the broad principles of modern warfare cannot be ignored: the ability to concentrate forces, to support ground forces with devastating air attacks, to achieve surprise, to advance rapidly towards command-and-control centres, to interrupt communications and disrupt decision-making, and to supply fast-moving forces. Despite a balance of military power, the right offensive strategy can bring victory. Equally, defending forces must pay attention to the ability to locate and move quickly to counter the opponent's massing forces, to prevent the attacker's air force achieving superiority in the skies, to launch unexpected counteroffensives, to maintain communication and orderly retreats and regrouping, and to supply even embattled and surrounded units. An offence can be blunted by a nimble defence.

Assuming that China is not interested in a war of outright conquest in Ladakh or even in Arunachal Pradesh (despite its claims to the entire state), its options along the border come down to three possibilities. The first is an attack along a broad front as in 1962. The second is to attack in key sectors where its forces can concentrate and achieve local superiority. The third is to go behind India's lines using infiltrating or air-dropped special forces, even as a frontal attack serves to distract and to pin down Indian border units. An attack across a broad front would be a punitive war or bargaining war. It is hard to imagine any goals other than to get India to accept certain kinds of economic or political conditions, to diminish its status internationally, or to occupy territory as a bargaining chip towards a final settlement of the border on China's terms. An attack in key sectors would aim to better protect Chinese infrastructure and to put Indian infrastructure at a disadvantage: this seems to have been one of the objectives of the Ladakh incursions in April 2020. A special forces attack would be motivated by the same objective as a limited sectoral attack but would use a different instrument, namely, an attack to surprise and overwhelm Indian border positions from behind rather than in a sustained frontal attack.

What are India's options in defending against these three types of attacks? Let's deal with the least likely attack first – the use of special forces behind India's border forces in combination with a frontal attack. This is China's riskiest option. The first difficulty is getting behind Indian forces either by ground infiltration or by airdrop in the hazardous Himalayan terrain. The second is that even if the infiltration succeeds, it must evade Indian special forces and other units deployed in a layered defence that are primed to react quickly and hunt down intruders. Should the Chinese special forces fail to evade Indian counterattacks, they would be captured and destroyed, handing India a strategic and public relations victory. More likely, then, is a Chinese push against Indian forces along a broad front or a grab of strategic ground in key sectors. Either way, the difficulties for China are terrain and Indian counterattacks. In many places the fighting will occur at heights of 4000 metres and above, where no armies have ever fought before (except the Indians and Pakistanis at Siachen and the Indians and Chinese in 1962). Even with acclimatized troops, any extended military operations will test troop endurance to the limit. In the winter, operations will be almost impossible given the cold and the snow.

If the Chinese make any significant gains or breakthroughs, they will confront the problem of supplying their units. The further they come, the greater their supply problems, and the easier it will be for the Indian Army to sustain its forces: in military parlance, the Chinese will have the 'exterior lines' while the Indians will have the 'interior lines'. Furthermore, despite China's massive developments in infrastructure in Tibet, logistical problems will hobble Chinese forces. The Tibetan Plateau with its flat terrain enables road and rail communications; but the flatness of the terrain means its facilities are difficult to hide and are therefore vulnerable to air and missile attacks. India's infrastructure is relatively weak, but it has one advantage. Many of the key roads leading to the front are narrow and twisting. This slows Indian supplies, but if the Chinese broke through Indian lines they would have to slowly weave their way down these very same roads, making them highly vulnerable. Indian air, artillery, and missile fire would be able to decimate the incoming force. In addition, the further the Chinese come, the more vulnerable they will be to counterattacks. The Indian counterattacks could come against positions where the Chinese have made gains but also in other areas where India has local superiority. The result would be a chequerboard, where the Chinese gain here and the Indians gain there. Overall, China might not be in a better position.

Naval Balance

While India and China primarily worry about a land war involving ground forces and air power, the two sides could find themselves embroiled in a naval conflict. In 2019, India had a total of twenty-seven key surface combatants (aircraft carriers, destroyers, and frigates) and seventeen submarines, while China had eighty-four key surface combatants and fifty-six submarines.[22] That is, China had roughly three to four times the number of surface and submarine combatants. This somewhat underestimates the imbalance. India has two nuclear-powered submarines: one nuclear-powered attack submarine or SSN (armed with conventional weapons) and one nuclear-powered ballistic missile submarine or SSBN (capable of launching a nuclear-tipped ballistic missile). China has six SSNs and four SSBNs. These are vital since they can stay below the surface for long periods of time and therefore escape detection. The SSNs can hunt down other submarines as well as surface vessels. The SSBNs on the other hand can carry nuclear weapons and so are crucial for deterrence: since they are difficult to find below the surface, they can survive a first strike by an adversary.

The other asymmetry that India may soon have to confront is in respect of aircraft carriers. The Indian Navy is aiming for a three-carrier force (two on active duty, one in port for maintenance), though a clear timetable to achieve this goal has not been announced. Delivery of a second carrier has faced repeated delays and is expected to be ready only in 2022.[23] There have been indications that approval for a third carrier may not be forthcoming given the huge financial costs.[24] China on the other hand is accelerating efforts to have six carriers by 2035.[25] Overall, India will struggle to keep up with China's shipbuilding, which is the most ambitious in the world. Estimates are tricky for a variety of reasons, but India may have a total fleet strength (which goes beyond the surface and submarine combatants referred to earlier to include smaller vessels) of 175 vessels by 2027 while China could have as many as 425 vessels by 2030.[26]

These numbers suggest that China has overwhelming naval superiority. The Indian and Chinese navies could come into conflict when China is able to establish a larger presence in the Indian Ocean. However, once again, the numbers can be misleading. The Chinese navy must be distributed between several duties: offshore patrolling and deterrence (primarily of the US Navy); possible actions against Taiwan should it declare outright independence from the mainland; and defending China's claims in the East China Sea (against Japan) and the South China Sea (against various Southeast Asian countries). In addition, where the Himalaya have stopping power on land, distances and straits have stopping power at sea. Despite China's huge numbers of vessels, its navy will have to operate a long way from home base, which means long interior supply lines stretching back to eastern China and contending with narrow straits that can be closed in time of war.

China's supply problem may be eased by establishing a string of overseas bases in and around the Indian Ocean. The difficulty for its navy is that the bases would in turn be susceptible to Indian disruption, particularly if they are in East Africa, the Gulf of Aden, the Persian Gulf, or even coastal Pakistan. India's navy could intercept Chinese resupply missions from the mainland to these bases (the mainland bases are 2500 miles away), and backed by air power could blockade and raid China's overseas ports. In any case, the bulk of the Chinese navy will have to transit the Malacca, Sunda, Lombok, and other straits. The Malacca Strait is particularly important because it has deep waters, and it cuts sailing times to the Indian Ocean the most. On the other hand, it is a narrow strip of water and is nearest to India. It is therefore vulnerable to being closed by the Indian navy. This would not be an easy operation, and much depends on how long and effectively closure can be enforced, yet the threat of bottling up the strait is another reason that the Chinese navy's superiority is exaggerated.

Nuclear Balance

Beyond conventional weapons, what is the tally of nuclear weapons? In 2020, India had about 150 nuclear weapons of various sizes whereas China had 320. Both countries have a triad – nuclear weapons that can be launched from the air, land, and sea. India's triad is very new, and most of its nuclear force is on air- and land-based platforms: 118 of 150 devices are air- and ground-launched. China's triad is much older, and the overwhelming part of it is land- and sea-based: 220 of 320 devices are on land and sea.[27] In total, China has twice the number of devices as India, but this may not constitute a decisive edge. With nuclear weapons, it does not take a large arsenal to deter the other side from launching an attack. Nuclear weapons can be used against population centres and against the other side's nuclear weapons – or both at the same time. Attacking India's population centres is suicidal because it would invite Indian retaliation against Chinese cities and towns. Attacking India's nuclear weapons is just as suicidal. Since China cannot destroy India's nuclear arsenal in a first strike, it must once again be prepared to face a retaliatory strike targeting its population centres. Finally, following from the above, China does not have enough nuclear weapons to simultaneously attack major Indian population centres and disarm India's nuclear arsenal. If it tried to do so, it would be devastated by retaliatory strikes.

The survivability of India's arsenal and therefore the credibility of its retaliation depend on an array of factors beyond the numbers – most fundamentally, advance warning of an incoming attack, the dispersal of the weapons, their mobility or their safety in hardened silos, the survival of command-and-control systems, and the numbers, size, and accuracy of the attacker's nuclear weapons. If India has taken the necessary precautions, its arsenal should be secure despite China's lead in numbers of weapons. India's nuclear forces can bolster its conventional forces. Nuclear weapons have been called the great equalizers because they can compensate for the lack of sufficient conventional weapons. If China were to threaten to overwhelm Indian defences on either land or sea, it must worry about the possibility of nuclear weapons being used to stop its forces.

Four Caveats . . . And a Final Comparison

While China certainly has greater military power than India, its ability to coerce or defeat India appears limited for the reasons given earlier: geography and strategy. However, four caveats are important.

The first caveat is that logistics count. India's ability to defend itself depends on supplies of ammunition and other vital inputs and the ability to deliver those to the fighting arm in time and for the duration of the war. India has improved its infrastructure and its military transport, particularly for land warfare. Less is known about its stock of ammunition and related supplies. Understandably, the Indian government will not make public how long war supplies will last. Estimates vary, but in a recent assessment of a two-front war, the defence expert Sushant Singh reports that in case of an 'intense' war with Pakistan, India has sufficient stocks for ten days' fighting. With China, the Indian military expects to fight for up to thirty days.[28] If a war with China becomes a two-front war, with Pakistan opening another front in Kashmir, then Indian defences will be stretched and its supplies perilous. That India's logistics are wafer-thin is in part because it depends on foreign supplies, particularly for key weapon systems.

The second caveat on India's ability to construct a robust defence is related to the point just made, namely, its massive dependence on foreign weapon systems. The Indian defence industry does not produce a single major conventional armament, with the partial exception of naval vessels. Automatic rifles and artillery, combat aircraft, helicopters, and transport planes, and even most of its naval vessels are imported or made under licence. The only systems that are largely indigenously designed and produced are nuclear weapons and missiles. Why so? Because no one will sell these to India. They are so-called strategic weapons – because of their decisive nature in war – and no one, not even allies, are prone to share them. They therefore had to be produced at home. When the crisis with China in the summer of 2020 deepened, India's nervousness over its conventional forces was evident. In June, India's defence minister, Rajnath Singh, went to Russia to participate in its Victory Day celebrations, but the larger purpose was to ensure that Moscow fulfilled its contracts with India for the delivery of the S-400 missiles and spare parts for India's Russian-made aircraft, tanks, and helicopters. While Russia promised to honour its commitments, the question that hung in the air was: what would happen in the case of an India–China war given Moscow's close relations with Beijing?

The third caveat on India's military capacities relates to nuclear weapons. As argued earlier, Chinese advantages in conventional weapons could be offset not just by geography and appropriate conventional defence, they could also be compensated for by nuclear weapons. Yet, India's resort to nuclear weapons must face the same challenge that Pakistan faces in nuclearizing the battlefield. It has been argued by Indian strategists that Islamabad is unlikely to use nuclear weapons against larger Indian forces because India has 'escalation dominance' – Delhi can 'up the ante' and increase the level of violence beyond anything that Pakistan can throw at it including nuclear weapons (though now that Pakistan is reported to have more nuclear weapons than India, this may no longer be a sustainable argument). The problem for India in a conflict with China is that the situation will be reversed:

the Chinese will have escalation dominance including in respect of nuclear weapons.

A final caveat relates to military technologies not dealt with earlier, namely, cyber, automated, and remotely operated devices married to artificial intelligence (AI) – what the Chinese call 'informatized warfare' and what the US calls 'net-centric capability'. The future battlefield is in a sense already here. The advanced militaries around the world have and are developing capabilities in all these areas. In essence, in addition to conventional and nuclear weapons, militaries will depend on cyber communications and the internet to orchestrate attack and defence using humans but also automated devices such as robots and drones. In the mix will be AI capabilities which will process huge volumes of data, interpret them, and use them to provide real-time options to humans and machines in the field. The AI systems may even be programmed to make decisions.

The battlefield will not just be on land, air, and sea but also in the virtual realm, with computers attacking and deceiving each other to disrupt enemy decision-making and actions. War will involve terrestrial and virtual battlefields as also hostilities in the exo-atmosphere and deep space. Operating such a system requires well-educated personnel at every level, organizational changes in the military, and integration of new technologies into expanded command-and-control systems. Indications are that the Chinese military is ahead on all counts. These new systems are 'force multipliers' and can enhance firepower and military effectiveness massively. In this sense, the relatively even military balance between India and China could rapidly become imbalanced.

How much difference the new technologies can make in the remote Himalaya at extremely low temperatures and at great heights is unknown, but their existence complicates strategy. Also, of course, the Chinese have not been at war since 1979 (when they invaded Vietnam) and therefore have not used their systems in real conditions. All in all, though, India must be counted as being at a considerable disadvantage in this domain. Lora Saalman, an expert on Indian and Chinese AI capabilities, in a recent assessment, concludes: 'The difference in [AI] capacity between India and China is immense: India earmarked $150 million in AI, compared with a Chinese effort to generate $150 billion, and Indian start-ups have been able to raise $87 million, in contrast with an estimated $28 billion raised by Chinese start-ups in 2017.'[29] For an Indian military planner, the sheer magnitude of China's investments must be sobering.

One final view on how the two militaries compare. During the peak of the Ladakh crisis in 2020, some Indian commentators argued that the combat effectiveness of Chinese ground forces is questionable. China's one-child policy means that many recruits – perhaps most – are the only child of their parents. The nervousness of Chinese parents over the safety of their sons would apparently communicate to the young men serving in Ladakh who would be hesitant to fight. Again, the fact that China has not fought a war since 1979 would add to the fragility of Chinese units in actual combat. Indian troops, by contrast, are presumably expendable because their families have more than one child. They are able therefore to fight without worry. Also, the Indian military has recent war experience to draw on. It fought in Kargil in 1999 and has been on almost continuous counter-insurgency duty since the early 1980s.

This rather reassuring argument deserves a thought or two. First, judging by the fight at Galwan, it would be hard to conclude that the Chinese fought any less effectively than the Indian troops. In any case, this perspective fundamentally misunderstands why troops fight: they fight for the safety and regard of 'buddies' and officers in their small units and perhaps for the honour of their communities or families at home. They fight for survival and self-respect, in those desperate moments, and it is very doubtful that parental concerns over their safety hold them back. Second, given that the ordinary Indian soldier on average has roughly fifteen years of active service in a combat role, very few have any war experience behind them – those who fought in Kargil twenty years ago are no longer front-line troops, if indeed they are still with the army. Third, counter-insurgency is very different from war, where Indian troops will fight a professional army backed by the full panoply of modern arms and logistics. The experience in one form of combat does not necessarily transfer to the other. Fourth, the combat effectiveness of troops depends in good part on officer leadership. Is there any reason to think that Chinese officers are lacking in the qualities needed to lead their units? Finally, and perhaps most importantly, if the Chinese military relies heavily on weapons that can be deployed and manipulated remotely, this may compensate for any weaknesses in the combat effectiveness of their troops. As noted earlier, the utility of these technologies at those heights and in difficult terrain of the Himalaya is unknown, but it would be imprudent to discount their impact.

Soft Power

China has a massive economic lead over India, and there is no prospect of India reducing the gap significantly in the next three decades. The Chinese military is superior in key areas, but the difference is not decisive given the limitations arising out of geography and strategy. The most marked difference in military power is due to China's indigenous defence production and possibly the new technologies and forms of warfare that it is developing. India could reduce the military gap over the next two or three decades with the new self-reliance programme of Atmanirbhar Bharat Abhiyan. If China leads India in hard power, above all in economic power, what about soft power, the ability to persuade without force or coercion? Here too, surprisingly, China has a lead over India, one that looks set to persist for a good long time.

In 2012, the Indian politician and former UN official Shashi Tharoor spoke at the Lee Kuan Yew School of Public Policy in Singapore. He drew on his book *Pax Indica: India and the World of the 21st Century*, which had just been published. Among the propositions he advanced for India's greater role in the world was its soft power – its ability to persuade by attracting others to its values, institutions, and achievements. When challenged on this score, including on the issue of admiration for India's democracy in Asia, Tharoor inimitably and humorously responded that the questioner – this author – was assessing the regard for India's democratic achievements sitting in the wrong country! He was convinced, though, that India already had a respectable amount of soft power and could develop its attractiveness further. He did not essay a comparison with China, but it was the 'dragon' in the room.

Five years later, Parama Sinha Palit published a book comparing Indian and Chinese soft power and came to a rather different conclusion from Tharoor.[30] Palit assiduously tracked Chinese soft power initiatives in every region of the world and then cast a briefer look at Indian efforts. Included in her view of soft power are high-level visits, various forms of economic assistance and cooperation including infrastructure and connectivity projects, cultural and public diplomacy, and education cooperation and outreach. In her wide-ranging and sober assessment, she concluded the following: 'India, despite being compared incessantly with China, is yet to command a similar global pull . . . China is engaging the world on a much bigger scale and faster pace than India . . . The sheer scale of China's initiatives dwarfs those of India . . . While not emulating Chinese initiatives in size, the "visibility" quotient of India's soft power is likely to become larger over time.'[31]

India's and China's Soft Power Measured

Joseph Nye suggests we can assess India's and China's soft power in three broad dimensions: foreign policy influence; cultural influence; and political influence. The foreign policy dimension asks how others see a country's foreign policy – is its conduct regarded as legitimate and moral? The cultural dimension asks whether others are attracted to or respect another country's culture (high or classical culture, popular culture, its heritage sites, its brands, etc.). The political values/institutions dimension asks to what extent others are attracted to or respect, even emulate, another society's political system (democracy, justice, governance, etc.).

The great difficulty of estimating and comparing soft power is that in the end it requires information on the perceptions and then behaviour of people. We need to know three things: first, what soft power resources or capabilities does a country possess (in foreign policy, culture, and politics); are foreigners attracted, repulsed, or neutral towards the foreign policy, culture, or political values of another country; and do those perceptions affect their actual behaviour? In the end, this three-step logic would require getting inside the heads of large numbers of people (and particularly government officials) and then tracking their actions towards the country in question – an almost impossible task. The focus in this section therefore is largely on the first element: what kind of soft power resources or capabilities do India and China possess? Even this is a challenging task since the data is scattered and incomplete. Fortunately, the Lowy Institute in Australia, in its comprehensive measure of Asian power, has produced various measures of soft power which correspond roughly to foreign policy influence, cultural influence, and political influence.[32]

How, then, do India and China compare on foreign policy influence? According to the Lowy Institute's measure of 'diplomatic influence', which is an aggregate of several other measures, India ranks sixth and China ranks first among twenty-five Asian powers which include the US (Lowy includes the US as an Asian power given its massive military, diplomatic, economic, and cultural interests and presence in the continent). A closer look at the Lowy measure shows that it distinguishes between two elements of diplomatic influence: diplomatic networks; and perceived foreign policy leadership, ambition, and effectiveness. Broadly, India does well on the networks component, often nearly matching China; but, crucially for the purposes of estimating soft power, it does much less well on perceptions of its willingness and ability to lead other countries in international affairs.[33]

What about cultural influence? Lowy's overall measure of 'cultural influence' ranks India in fourth place and China in second place in Asia (with the US in first place by a considerable distance). Lowy divides cultural influence into three elements: cultural projection; information flows; and people exchanges (including in- and out-migration).In cultural projection, India scores better on Google searches abroad of its newspapers and its television/radio broadcasts, and it exports more of its 'cultural services'. China does better on virtually all of the other indicators. For instance, on the number of World Heritage sites in the UNESCO listings, India has thirty-seven sites compared to China's fifty-three. In terms of information flows, in 2016–17, India hosted a mere 24,000 foreign students in its tertiary education institutions whereas China hosted 225,000, nine times the Indian number. In people exchanges, as of 2017, India had 5 million regional immigrants (presumably from neighbouring South Asian states such as Bangladesh, Nepal, and Sri Lanka), while China had only 800,000. As far as tourist arrivals is concerned, in 2017 India clocked 5 million arrivals from Asia. China on the other hand clocked 41 million arrivals and ranked first among twenty-five Asian countries.[34] In terms of total tourist arrivals from all over the world, India received 17 million while China received 63 million.[35]

Finally, what about India's and China's relative standing in terms of the attraction to or respect for their political values? Perhaps surprisingly, in 2017, the two were not ranked that far apart. A conventional view is that federal and democratic India's governance effectiveness is low and that centralized and authoritarian China's governance effectiveness is high. In fact, the governance effectiveness index shows that the difference may not be that great: in 2017, India scored in the 57th percentile and ranked 12th while China scored in the 68th percentile and ranked 10th. Neither country scored impressively on 'political stability and absence of violence/terrorism': India ranked 21st with a 17th percentile score and China ranked 15th with a 37th percentile score. Nor were they that far apart on 'civil unrest'.[36] With respect to the quality of their regulatory systems, rule of law, and control of corruption, too, India and China were close. On the other hand, on voice and accountability, which is a measure of the extent to which citizens can express their grievances and demand that officials and politicians are held responsible for their actions (and inactions), India was substantially ahead, averaging a score of roughly 60 (on a scale of 100) over a four-year period while China averaged less than seven.[37]

This is not an exhaustive assessment of India's and China's soft power. For instance, the extent of public and cultural diplomacy (including training foreign officials and workers), humanitarian and development assistance (including peacekeeping, aid), and infrastructure and connectivity projects abroad matter as well. In cultural influence, the reputation of one's classical and modern art, one's cuisine, music, and films, and one's popular cultural products have an impact on foreigners. In modern mass societies, sports achievements too have a huge impact. In terms of political influence, respect for political diversity, rights, and tolerance also attract or repulse others. These other elements are only very partially measured by the Lowy assessment. Most importantly, though, the Lowy study only gives us a comparison of soft power *resources*. To get a more convincing estimate of soft power *outcomes* would require getting into people's heads by means of surveys and polls to establish whether India's and China's foreign policies, their cultural products, and their political values actually do attract or repulse. In any case, what can we say about their soft power beyond the numbers?

Soft Power Beyond the Numbers

Having said that the Lowy figures and numeric comparisons have their limitations, a broad conclusion is that India is behind in terms of its perceived international diplomatic and cultural attraction but does better, by some distance, on political attraction (openness or 'voice and accountability'). Even here, we should be careful, for at least two contradictory reasons. First, in the eyes of many around the world, India's political openness is the problem and not the solution. John Kenneth Galbraith, the US ambassador to India during the 1962 India–China war, in a backhanded compliment remarked that India is a 'functioning anarchy'. For many in Southeast and Northeast Asia, India's openness is anarchy, plain and simple. They see little that is functional. After a decade of living and working in East Asia, I have yet to hear a fulsome endorsement of India's political system. Southeast and Northeast

Asians are not attracted to it and hold India's politics responsible for the country's policy incoherence, governance ineffectiveness, and stuttering economic growth and backwardness.

Second, since 2014, particularly in the eyes of the West, India's claim to political openness is increasingly under question. If Western critics are right, India's lead in the one soft power dimension where it did better is eroding. Indeed, to the extent that India is becoming politically more centralized and less democratic, it appears to be moving in the direction of the Chinese model. India's liberal decline suggests that in the contest over political values it is China that may prevail. Indians may choose to be governed more like China rather than the other way round. If so, China will have swept the soft power contest altogether.

Most observers of international relations would say that India does not, and at least in the foreseeable future cannot, match China's soft power. The narrative around China's rise is a global one. Any mention of China usually evokes a conversation about its size, astonishing economic and military rise, ubiquitous presence in the global marketplace, the burgeoning and modernity of its cities and infrastructure, the ambition and energy of its people, the far-seeing and technocratic abilities of its leadership at many levels (not just at the very top), the single-minded pursuit of power and influence, its dedicated long-term strategic vision, the magnificence of its classical culture and heritage, and the driving spirit of its contemporary culture. Virtually all discussions of China in other words exhibit a sense of awe and fascination. Few would choose to describe India in the same way.

Even Indians who read about China or have visited the country, no matter how patriotic, develop that sense of awe and fascination, and feel deflated about India. Years ago, a hard-nosed Indian diplomat friend was invited to China under a Sino-Indian agreement. Before he left, he was studiously blasé. He had, he said, read all the stories and seen all the shiny pictures of the new China, especially its cities and special economic zones. He was prepared to be underwhelmed or at least not terribly surprised. We met soon after he returned. He now confessed to being 'blown away' (or words to that effect). Of course, the Chinese had led him by the nose to see what they wanted him to see. He was rarely out of the sight of his 'minders' who kept a close eye on him and the other Indian diplomats. Yet, allowing for the carefully curated programme and the effort to impress, he had come away shocked at just how far ahead China was in its development and modernity. While he had not changed his negative view of Chinese foreign policy and strategy, he admitted that the challenge for India was greater than he had imagined.

At the risk of caricature, we can say that it is a vital part of Chinese soft power initiatives to influence others by demonstrating the magnificence and inevitability of China's rise. Indian soft power initiatives rely on almost the opposite. Where China seeks to immediately overwhelm, to overawe by its size and (supposed) homogeneity, and to fascinate by carefully controlled revelations, India seeks to unfold gradually, to impress by its profusion and heterogeneity, and to disclose its soul completely. China is a seamless and material experience; India is a discontinuous and sensual experience. China evokes orderliness; India evokes fluidity. India does not signal inevitability, but it has its own magnificence: a British friend of mine who studied India and lived and travelled there explains her interest in India saying it features both 'the best and the worst of everything'. Few would choose to describe China in the same way.

It is almost certainly the case that China fits the spirit of the times and India never quite does. As a result, China has a soft power advantage that India will find difficult to attenuate. In 1958, the American social psychologist Harold Isaacs wrote a book on

US attitudes towards India and China.[38] Isaacs interacted with Americans from academic life, the mass media, serving and former government officials, business, 'groups concerned with public opinion and education', and church and missionary groups. At the height of the Cold War and just five years after Chinese and American troops had fought a bloody war in Korea, Isaacs reports his findings: 'There has been over time a consistently heavy weight of favorable images of the Chinese stored in American minds . . . The sources of this difference are dealt with at length in this book. They are rooted partly in the effect of relative cultural values, the Chinese being long seen – for purposes of this comparison – as 'closer' – pragmatic, down-to-earth, hardheaded – and the Indians, or more particularly, the Hindus, as much more exotic, much more violently different, as indeed Hindu culture is from Anglo-Protestant and most other forms of Western culture.'[39]

Isaacs' study was of American views of India and China. But many would testify that these images exist in varying degrees in other societies around the world. This is not surprising. The Western media, particularly the American, and Western publishing more broadly, has played an enormous role. Perhaps the single most damning book on India over the past one hundred years was the American Katherine Mayo's 1927 book, *Mother India*, which was so critical of Indian society that Mahatma Gandhi was moved to call it 'the report of a drain inspector'. On the other hand, influential Westerners in political, social, and economic life constantly reinforce the image of the pragmatic, civic-minded Chinese. Ironically, Indians, particularly educated middle-class Indians, have their own version of the image: the Chinese are prepared to take 'hard decisions' and make sacrifices for the collective good while Indians are prone to choose 'soft options' and selfishly pursue their own advancement. Whether these images are 'true' is not the point. They exist, and they colour the view foreigners, Indians, and Chinese have of the two societies.

Over the past two decades, China has appeared in a related guise: as an international, global, and secular setting, particularly in its big cities. Beijing, Shanghai, Chongqing, Tianjin, Guangzhou, and Shenzhen feel like modern, perhaps even ultra-modern, metropolises: if one forgets the Chinese faces on the streets, they could be located on any continent. India never feels like that. It feels very national and local, with religiosity conspicuously on display in its many places of worship, religious processions, and other public marks of faith. Its cities are a mix of civic amenities that could be simultaneously of the nineteenth, twentieth, and twenty-first centuries: they have a distinctly South Asian look and feel. Indian cities have their own attractions, but they are not those of Prada-lined global cities. Not surprisingly, foreigners of all kinds flock to China – to visit, to work, to invest, and to study, in modular cities laid out in American-style grids. Expatriates are highly visible in at least half a dozen Chinese cities. Soft power (and economic power) brings foreigners into China, and their presence in turn reinforces Chinese soft power. That is the not the case for India. Indians may or may not want to have global cities; but China's global cities are a growing source of soft power.

~

Even China's secondary cities are impressively modern. In 2017, I suddenly decided to fly to the ancient city of Xi'an to see its famous terracotta warriors from the third century BCE. Not having done my homework on the city (or indeed on the excavation of the terracotta figures), I was left to do it on the airplane journey. In my ignorance, I had imagined a quaint tourist town, something along the lines of Siem Reap in Cambodia which has become the tourist hub for Angkor Wat – I pictured wandering out to the site and then strolling back for beer and local food. My hastily printed Google documents on Xi'an shook me out of my reverie. The city had once been one of China's great capital cities and was now home to over 12 million residents.

As I drove to my hotel some hours later, it struck me that no Indian city could match this second-tier Chinese city – not Mumbai, Bengaluru, or Hyderabad. In the days that followed, I saw not just the excavated terracotta warriors which are outside the city proper, but also attractions within the inner city. Downtown Xi'an had broad, clean streets, a convenient and user-friendly public transport system (especially the suburban trains), heavy but disciplined motorized traffic, well-dressed and healthy-looking people, and everywhere the facilities and resources one would encounter in a modern metropolitan environment.

At the terracotta excavations, the huge crowds were systematically channelled through the site in a way I had never experienced in India. Perhaps even more impressive was our guide. He was a dignified forty-year-old man dressed in a neat guide's uniform, spoke excellent English, and, above all, could quote the latest archaeological research on the site. How do you know so much, I asked? It turned out the guides are licensed (and presumably paid) by the government. To keep their licences, they attend short courses on the latest research on the artefacts and history of the burial grounds. No Indian guide I had ever encountered could match this smiling, proud, erudite man. The visit was a telling soft power moment. Exposed to ancient and modern Xi'an, I was left simultaneously admiring and deflated – admiring of Chinese infrastructure and attention to detail and deflated at how India, with its rich legacies, does such an underwhelming job of marketing and curating them.

As I walked around Xi'an, I remembered what a Chinese

colleague often said to me. He had visited India several times, been to many of the usual tourist spots, in and around Delhi, and loved Indian food and company. When we travelled in China and India together as part of our research, he would frequently shake his head: 'India has much more to showcase than China. So many things in China were destroyed by war and modernization. You have kept your monuments, but Indian tourist facilities are so horrible!' I thought back, too, to a shocking fact that a JNU graduate student working on tourism policy had shared during the defence of his thesis proposal in the late 1990s: that Bangkok had more hotel rooms than all of India combined. Years later, when tourism in India was doing better, it turned out a lot more hotel rooms were available. The Indian hotel industry had now caught up with Shanghai!

On my final day in Xi'an, I was to get another surprise. In the middle of the city, somewhere near the famous Bell Tower of the fourteenth century, was a row of little shops, rather like Janpath in Delhi. In a consumerist fever, wanting to memorialize my trip to Xi'an, I decided to buy some souvenirs. A smiling old lady waved me into her stall. Armed with a basket, I went round and loaded up. As she totted up the bill, I flourished my yuan, Singapore dollars, and US bills. 'No, no, no money!' I put away the currency and brought out my plastic. 'No, no, no card, no card.' At this point, I was nonplussed. I was from rich, advanced Singapore: what was going on? In effect, here was high-tech at ground zero, and I was 'out of it'. The shop only accepted WeChat payments or Alipay or other equivalents. I had read about Chinese fintech and the spread of online payments but had dismissed them as state propaganda and popular hype – much as, years before, I had laughed at the idea of buying a smartphone. The truth was that it was not propaganda or hype but rather a street reality in Xi'an. In the end, awkwardly and with due apologies, I left empty-handed. The stall owner, much less twinkly-eyed by then, waved me out of her store grumbling at the 'Xinjiapo' – Singapore – hick who was making her re-shelve a basket of unsold souvenirs.

Conclusion

India and China are far apart on power. The most visible and basic difference is in economic power, where the GDP gap is nearly $12 trillion. The second area of asymmetry is in soft power, the power of attraction. Here too, though more difficult to measure, the gap is substantial. Surprisingly, in military terms, the difference between the two powers, given geography and strategy, is not as large as the raw numbers might suggest. Leaving aside the question of why and whether China would choose to attack India, the Chinese military will find that the Himalaya and the Indian Ocean as well as Indian defensive options constitute a major limitation.

Power differences, as suggested earlier, matter. India as the weaker power is unwilling to make concessions. It does not want to further embolden China. China as the stronger power is also unwilling to make concessions. It does not see why it should do so given its strength. Shyam Saran, the former Indian foreign secretary and former chairman of the National Security Advisory Board who has served in China, in an interview in October 2020 had this judgement on the implications of the power gap: 'Today they [the Chinese] feel, "Why should we give anything?" You know, "We are so powerful, the other side has to accept what we are trying to say."'[40] In 2010, in a revealing moment, the Chinese foreign minister, Yang Jiechi, in discussions with Southeast Asian countries on the South China Sea, justified Beijing's unyielding attitude: 'China is a big country, and you are small countries, and that is a fact.'[41] The implication of what Saran and Yang are saying is clear: until India substantially closes the power gap, there is little prospect of a lasting rapprochement.

Can India close the gap? With difficulty. If comprehensive national power (a concept much in vogue over the past two decades) is equal to a combination of economic, military, and soft power, where do India and China come out? Assuming, as was suggested earlier, that the three elements of power are synergistically related and that they affect each other, then comprehensive national power is the mathematical product of economic, military, and soft power (economic power times military power times soft power). Since it is hard to multiply unlike things – for example, GDP times numbers of weapons times numbers of movies produced in a year – we can instead multiply the ratios between India and China. Assuming China's GDP is five times the size of India's, its military (say) 1.2 times the size of the Indian military (on the land border), and its soft power also 1.2 times the size of India's (based on the 'cultural influence' scores of the two countries in the Lowy Index 2019), then we can say that China's comprehensive national power is about seven times that of India (5 times 1.2 times 1.2, equals 7.2). China's economy is five times India's, but its comprehensive national power may be seven times India's. That may be the truer gap between the two countries. Is it any wonder that the Chinese patronize India and that Indians fear China?

Conclusion

Looking Ahead: Perceptions, Perimeters, Partnerships, and Power

The crisis in Ladakh in the summer of 2020 showed how quickly India–China differences can turn violent. Indian analysts are still trying to understand why Chinese troops moved into areas in Ladakh, particularly in the Galwan area, that have been peaceful since 1962. Was the crisis triggered by Chinese *perceptions* that a series of Indian policies were attempts by an 'inferior' power to embarrass China, including Amit Shah's remarks on Aksai Chin, Delhi's criticism of Chinese connectivity projects, and India's tough military posture during the Doklam confrontation? Was it due to continuing differences over *perimeters* and Chinese worries over Indian infrastructure expansion? Was it, instead, Beijing's response to Delhi's increasing strategic *partnership* with Washington? Or, finally, was it a demonstration of *power* in consonance with China's growing assertiveness in the Indo-Pacific with Taiwan, Japan, Southeast Asia, and Australia, part of its 'wolf warrior' diplomacy? It is too early to tell conclusively, but as the earlier chapters have suggested, India–China relations always seem to be framed by a combination of these four elements. What is the future of mutual perceptions, differences over perimeters, rival partnerships, and the power gap? Does the future look positive or negative?

Perceptions, Perimeters, and Partnerships

If India and China are to mend their relations, if not end the border quarrel and deal with other differences, their deeply rooted negative perceptions of each other will have to change. Unfortunately, the changes have been in the wrong direction. Indeed, the Ladakh crisis, the worst since 1962, could be a turning point for the worse. *India Today* magazine's 'Mood of the Nation' survey of public opinion in August 2020 is revealing. Nearly 60 per cent surveyed wanted India to go to war over Ladakh, and 70 per cent thought that it could win a war. Nearly half held China responsible for the crisis. Indians overwhelmingly did not trust Xi Jinping and China: 84 per cent said that Xi had betrayed Modi. Ninety per cent favoured boycotting Chinese products, and 91 per cent supported the measures against Chinese apps and contracts in India. Sixty-seven per cent were even prepared to pay more for goods not made in China.[1]

As it turns out, the Chinese public was polled about India, also in August 2020. *Global Times* and the China Institutes of Contemporary International Relations (CICIR) reported that 70 per cent of those surveyed thought that India was being too hostile in the wake of Ladakh. Ninety per cent supported strong retaliatory action against India if it were to provoke China. On the other hand, 57 per cent felt that India was no threat to China militarily, and 50 per cent noted that India was heavily dependent on Chinese products. More than half thought that in terms of comprehensive national power, India would never surpass China. Interestingly, over 70 per cent said they 'had a clear understanding' of or were very familiar with India. And in a list of 'most favourable neighbours' of China (that is, most liked), India surprisingly ranked fourth, ahead of South Korea.[2] Allowing for the possible unreliability of the Indian and Chinese surveys, given that they were conducted at a time of crisis between India and China, they mostly present a discouraging picture of mutual perceptions.

The original quarrel over perimeters has been made worse by India's reorganization of Jammu and Kashmir in August 2019 and China's rejection of it. After India's decision to abrogate Article 370 of the Constitution and remove Jammu and Kashmir's special status, Home Minister Amit Shah was quoted as having said, 'Kashmir is an integral part of India, there is no doubt over it. When I talk about Jammu and Kashmir, Pakistan occupied Kashmir and Aksai Chin are included in it . . . This country's Parliament cannot be stopped from making any law on J&K.'[3] Shah's statement on Indian claims is consistent with Delhi's formal stand going back to the 1950s, but his abrasive tone probably provoked Beijing to immediately say: 'China is always opposed to India's inclusion of the Chinese territory [i.e. Ladakh] in the western sector of the China-India boundary into its administrative jurisdiction. Recently India has continued to undermine China's territorial sovereignty by unilaterally changing its domestic law. Such practice is unacceptable and will not come into force.'[4]

Well into the crisis in Ladakh, in September 2020, Beijing very publicly insisted that 'the China-India border LAC is very clear, [and] that is the LAC on November 7, 1959. China announced it in the 1950s, and the international community including India are also clear about it.'[5] That claim line includes all of Aksai Chin and territories up to the foothills of the mountains in Arunachal Pradesh. China first invoked the line back in 1959 as the basis for a mutual pullback of forces to stabilize the deteriorating military situation. Beijing followed up the September 2020 statement by repeating its opposition to the changes in Jammu and Kashmir: 'China doesn't recognize the so-called "Ladakh Union Territory" illegally set up by India and opposes infrastructure building aimed at military contention in disputed border areas.'[6] By going so public on its claims, and by its continued rejection of India's reorganization of Jammu and Kashmir, Beijing has indicated a firm position, from which it will be difficult to retreat. Delhi had rejected the 1959 proposal and is adamant on the reorganization of Jammu and Kashmir. If and when Indian and Chinese negotiators sit down to discuss a border settlement, they will have to find a way to deal with a new set of mutually contradictory and very public stands.

Beyond the border but related to it is the issue of Tibet. The Dalai Lama's advanced age is bringing Tibet once again into focus in India–China relations. Beijing has said it will find a new Dalai Lama from among Tibetans in Tibet. At times, the Dalai Lama has said that he might be the last to hold office. At other times, he has suggested that if there is to be a new Dalai Lama he could be found anywhere in the world – including, presumably, among Tibetans in India. The possibility that the next Dalai Lama would be India-born would be worrying to Chinese authorities. Delhi has remained silent on the issue of a post–Dalai Lama Tibet and the future of Tibetans on Indian soil. Yet it must think about how to deal with Tibet and Tibetan exiles after the present Dalai Lama departs the stage. If, as suggested earlier, the 1962 war was related to developments in Tibet after the rebellion of 1956, India could find itself in an awkward position.

In the meantime, Beijing seems to have stepped up its campaign in Tibet. In late August 2020, it warned against 'splittism' (separatism) in Tibet. At a Central Committee symposium on 29 August on Tibet, Xinhua reported President Xi as calling for 'continuous efforts to enhance recognition of *the great motherland, the Chinese nation, the Chinese culture*, the CPC and socialism with Chinese characteristics by people of all ethnic groups . . . Tibetan Buddhism should be guided in adapting to the socialist society and *should be developed in the Chinese context*' (emphasis added).[7] Reports suggest that Xinjiang-style re-education has begun in Tibet – military-style training for rural labour mostly – accompanied by the forced transfer of labour to other parts of Tibet or other provinces. Conditions in Tibet always colour China's view of India. Beijing has never shed the view that Delhi interferes in Tibetan affairs, and it is certain that in a post–Dalai Lama period the two countries will find themselves eyeing each other suspiciously.

Beyond India's and China's long-standing tensions over their perimeters is the question of their strategic partnerships with the Great Powers. As we saw, it is non-aligned India that has repeatedly sought alignments against China. China too has aligned with both Russia and the US, but it has done so to balance against those two powers. This pattern looks set to continue. India has drifted closer to the US in order to balance China, while China has partnered Russia to balance the US. The Ladakh crisis has accelerated Delhi's closeness to Washington. As noted earlier, India has signed three foundational military agreements with the US since 2002. The fourth and final one, the Basic Exchange and Cooperation Agreement (BECA), was signed in October 2020. Taken together these allow for access to each other's intelligence, secure communications, logistical facilities upon request, and US surveillance systems. After a fairly tepid Indian response to the US's and Japan's Free and Open Indo-Pacific, Delhi has warmed up to both the FOIP and the associated Quad. It now agrees that the meetings of the FOIP and the Quad with Australia, Japan, and the US should be held at the ministerial level. It has also finally invited Australia to the Malabar naval exercises along with Japan and the US. The Ladakh crisis and a desire to signal greater closeness to the US certainly played a role in tipping India over into inviting the Australian Navy.

If India has been slow to align with the US, this is because it has wanted to avoid provoking China and alienating Russia beyond a point. After the Ladakh crisis, the reluctance to irk China has diminished considerably. On the other hand, keeping Russia friendly is crucial. Russian arms, particularly major weapon systems, are still the preferred option for the Indian military. Besides, in Delhi's view, Moscow must be stopped from going completely over to Beijing's side. However, in the long term, given the power gap with China and the several confrontations at the border since 2013, India has little option but to partner the US. Indian decision-makers know that the US will stay away from being directly involved in an India–China fight, but they are counting on American intelligence, arms, military technologies, and diplomatic support to enhance Indian material capabilities as also its bargaining power with China.

Predictably, China is suspicious of India's partnership with the US. The standard Chinese view is that the two powers are teaming up to 'contain' China's rise and that India's talk of 'strategic autonomy' and 'non-alignment' is just that – mere talk. Delhi is in fact working with the US and other powers in Asia including the Quad powers to 'encircle' China. Chinese views are not uniform. An alternative perspective in China is that Delhi's robust sense of independence, plus the contradictions in the India–US relationship over Iran, Russian arms, trade, and immigration, will limit its drift towards Washington. There is also a recognition that Chinese actions such as the Belt and Road Initiative and the Ladakh crisis may have pushed India closer to the US. China is therefore torn on how to deal with India, just as India is still somewhat divided on quite how close it wants to get to the US once the Ladakh situation stabilizes.

Having said that, an India–US alignment against China seems inescapable in the years ahead. If India and China were not in conflict over the border, they might have teamed up against the US: a balance-of-power logic would seem to suggest that two weaker powers would combine against the more powerful. Yet this has never really happened. The border conflict has ensured that global balance-of-power considerations have been trumped by bilateral differences. Even if the border conflict were resolved, the power gap between neighbouring India and China would likely push Delhi towards Washington – for the simple reason that China's power is on India's doorstep and therefore much more threatening than US power.

The only way the India–US partnership might be disrupted is if China and the US were to call a truce or decide to run the world together. The Australian strategist Hugh White's well-known book *The China Choice* is subtitled: *Why America Should Share Power*. White proposes a power-sharing future between a rising China and a declining US as a way of stabilizing Asia.[8] If that were to happen, India would be left to face China on its own, unless the power-sharing deal included a Chinese commitment to leave India alone. How likely is a China–US rapprochement? The general view all over the world is that rapprochement is unlikely given the hardening of US views across the political divide in Washington. If so, in addition to their negative perceptions of each other and differences over their perimeters, India's partnership with the US will constitute a third layer of friction between Delhi and Beijing, for as long as we can see into the future.

Power

What about the final P – power? Given the power gap and the prospect that China will pull even further away from India, how far can China go? What is the future of China's power and its role in the international system? Will it challenge and then surpass the US to become the global hegemon?

Virtually all assessments of the Chinese economy are that it will surge past the American economy in nominal GDP terms – the latest projections are that it may move into first place by 2028 as a result of China's continuing economic growth and the US economy's intermittent slowdowns.[9] Most analysts accept that China's GDP has already passed the US's in purchasing power parity or PPP terms: PPP is a method for adjusting nominal GDP figures based on what it costs to buy a similar basket of goods across countries. International relations scholars generally assume economic superiority will gradually turn into military superiority. For Asia, this would mean that China will be not only economically but also militarily dominant and that the US will be under pressure to retrench from the continent.

Opinions are divided on how large the gap between China and the US could become. Among the China optimists is the British journalist Martin Jacques, who argues the inevitability of Chinese hegemony in his book, *When China Rules the World*.[10] Is China destined to be number one and to rule the world? The Princeton political scientist and expert on US grand strategy Aaron L. Friedberg, in his book *A Contest for Supremacy*, thinks Chinese hegemony is not inevitable. Instead, he sees a 'struggle for mastery in Asia' and concludes that the US with various partners can balance China.[11] In June 2016, at a meeting organized by the German Marshall Fund (GMF) and the International Institute of Strategic Studies (IISS), I not very originally argued that

Chinese power was advancing steadily and sometimes stealthily. At the end of the session, a tall, rather stern man strode up to me and put a book in my hand, saying, 'You might like to read this.' Before I could react, he was already giving someone else a copy of the book. In my hand was Michael Pillsbury's *The Hundred-Year Marathon: China's Secret Strategy to Replace America as the Global Superpower.*[12] The bearer of the book turned out to be the author himself. In it, like Friedberg, he argues that the US still has a chance to stop Chinese hegemony. Pillsbury went on to advise the Trump administration on China and is credited with the hardening of US policy since 2016. All three analysts share the more or less conventional and accepted view that China is likely to overtake the US – in Friedberg's book, the focus is on who will be dominant in Asia, not globally.

The inexorable rise of China is the orthodox position, and by now most well-educated schoolchildren can recite some version of it. It is useful here to consider the contrasting view. One of the most clearly articulated is that of Michael Beckley, a professor of political science at Tufts University in the US, who has questioned China's supposedly unstoppable rise to number one. His 2016 book is titled *Unrivaled: Why America Will Remain the Sole Superpower.*[13] More than the others, Beckley weighs up the prospects of the two countries carefully, using an array of metrics, and he accepts that the gap is closing in some areas and that the US maintaining its lead is not a given for all time.

In an article published in 2020 in the US journal *Foreign Affairs*, titled 'Rogue Superpower: Why This Could Be an Illiberal American Century', Beckley presents his most recent argument for why China will not match the US in the twenty-first century. The argument rests on demography and automation. According to Beckley, in the next fifty years, the US will be the only country among the top twenty economic powers, along with Australia and Canada, to have a growing population of adults between the age of twenty and forty-nine. His estimate is that China will lose 225 million workers and consumers in that age group, which is more than one-third of the current total (due largely to its ageing population which in turn is the result of its one-child policy going back to 1979). In the US on the other hand those cohorts will grow by ten per cent. As a result, America will have a huge and growing internal market and will be less reliant on foreign trade and investment than China.[14]

Beckley suggests that demography will adversely affect China's military as well. Expenditures on pensions and health for the ageing Chinese population will triple by 2050 whereas this will only increase by 35 per cent in the US. The amount of money China can spend on the military will be under pressure. Within China's military budget, about 50 per cent of expenditures already go to personnel costs; that figure will increase. Technologically, Beckley argues that AI and automation will change the US's economy. The US, he claims, has five times the number of AI companies and experts as China. This will make American manufacturing and services vastly more efficient and 're-shore' many US businesses (including call centres). China's (and India's) labour cost advantages therefore will slip away. Militarily, the US will be able to replace costly systems with cheap and effective drones and other automated weapons. While China will need a standing army of size to conquer and control areas that it claims, the US will only have to stop Chinese forces. Its AI and automated systems could be decisive in doing that.[15]

In earlier writings, Beckley lists other hurdles facing China: slowing growth, the burgeoning of its debt, dwindling export markets, water and food scarcities, labour protests, and elite emigration, among others. At the same time, he estimates that the US stock of 'produced capital' (that is, machines), human capital, and natural capital (that is, natural resources) will further outdistance China's in the decades ahead.[16] He notes, too, the US's geographical advantage: it is separated from its rivals by the oceans and is unthreatened in its hemisphere. At the same time, the US transcends its geography through hundreds of bases and facilities abroad and a freewheeling navy.[17] The worry for Beckley is not Chinese hegemony but rather increasing domestic troubles in China leading to growing aggression abroad.[18] The US can counter this in East Asia by continuing its alliance with Japan, by drawing in militarily to protect only its closest allies in the region, and by defending others on a strictly transactional basis.[19]

That the US will continue to be the greatest power will be reassuring to India, which has no prospect of catching up with China in the foreseeable future. Given the power gap with China, India must rely on what international relations scholars call 'external balancing', that is, alliances and strategic partnerships. But, as Beckley notes, a dominant US may be increasingly reluctant to come to the aid of others. Given its self-sufficiency and geographic distance from its rivals, it could well restrict its exertions to homeland and hemispheric defence, the security of Australia and the UK, and the protection of Japan. Even this limited international role is open to question in light of something that Beckley largely ignores: the US's massive internal political polarization and its susceptibility to foreign interference and influence operations.

In 2012, in my column for the *Times of India* just days after Barack Obama was elected president for the second time, I wrote this about the US: 'Perhaps the greatest worry is the white middle class and upper middle class. A very large proportion of this class has become ever more resentful of Obama, the Democratic Party, minorities, government, and liberal values. Some sections of it are feeling the bite of an increasingly unequal America . . . A middle class that is on the slide downwards is a dangerous force . . . Could the unthinkable eventually happen in the US? Could a large chunk of the US choose to secede . . .?'[20] Eight years later, the internal churn of the US is even greater. Writing in the *New York Times* on 29 September 2020, after the presidential debate between Donald Trump and Joe Biden, Thomas Friedman, the American columnist, sounded a desperate warning bell:

> I can't say this any more clearly: Our democracy is in terrible danger – more danger than it has been since the Civil War, more danger than after Pearl Harbor, more danger than during the Cuban missile crisis and more danger than during Watergate . . . I began my career as a foreign correspondent covering Lebanon's second civil war . . . I saw what happens in a country when everything becomes politics, when a critical mass of politicians put party before country, when responsible people, or seemingly responsible people, think that they can bend or break the rules – and go all the way – and that the system won't break . . . But when extremists go all the way, and moderates just go away, the system can break. And it will break. I saw it happen.[21]

The Lebanonization of the US, helped along as Lebanon was by foreign interference, is perhaps not as far-fetched as I had imagined in 2012.

Weeks after Friedman wrote his despairing column, Donald Trump lost the US presidential elections. It would be naive to think, though, that with his defeat the dangers to America's democracy and internal peace have disappeared: the storming of the US Capitol by Trump supporters on 6 January 2021 and the unremorseful view of the participants show how far America's Lebanonization has gone. Joe Biden as president will lead a deeply divided country: over 70 million Americans voted for Trump, only

3–4 million less than for Biden. Trump or a Trumpist Republican including a member of his family may run for election in 2024 – and who is to say that he or a political clone will not win? Before then, we can imagine a period of upheaval and violence, including against the US leadership and its legislators.

What about China's internal politics? Are Xi and the communist party firmly in control? It is hard to know. Chinese politics is so far removed from public scrutiny that all kinds of views exist about the future of China. A high-level communist party official who for years was an influential professor at the Central Party School in Beijing recently fled to the US. In late 2020, Cai Xia published an account of her career and her disillusionment with China's government including President Xi. In her essay in the influential American journal *Foreign Affairs*, she argues that Xi is brutally authoritarian, divorced from political and economic and perhaps even geopolitical realities, and unwilling to commit to the next generation of reforms. She writes: 'China's long-standing problems of corruption, excessive debt, and unprofitable state enterprises are rooted in party officials' power to meddle in economic decisions without public supervision.'[22] These are the standard ills that critics of China have long highlighted. Will they lead to large-scale unrest and the collapse of the present regime? Cai Xia avoids that conclusion, but she gestures at the possibility of growing internal dissatisfaction. Another dissident now living in the US, Deng Yuwen, also formerly of the Central Party School, suggests that reformists may be biding their time: 'Based on my observations, a considerable number of reformists inside the party are despairing, like Cai Xia . . . But for the most part they put the blame on Xi Jinping and are waiting for some kind of error by Xi to reinvigorate reformist forces within the party.'[23]

A contrary view relies less on the disillusionment of party insiders and elites and more on popular opinion to gauge internal stability. According to Sungmin Cho, professor at the Daniel K. Inouye Asia Pacific Center for Security Studies in Hawaii, during the early days of the Covid-19 crisis ordinary Chinese were quite openly critical of their central government. They soon split their view, turning their ire against local and provincial officials and voicing increasing support for Beijing and Xi. As the pandemic unfolded, Xi's popularity rose to unprecedented levels.[24] A survey by the Canadian researcher Cary Wu of nearly 20,000 Chinese in thirty-one provinces showed that 81–89 per cent of those surveyed were satisfied with the central government's performance in disseminating relevant information and making available daily necessities and protective gear.[25] At least part of this is attributable to China's relative success in handling the pandemic compared to the disastrous response of the West (as well as Brazil, India, and Russia). Cho argues, though, that the more telling fact is that ordinary Chinese including the youth are 'liberal nationalists' – liberal in holding local and provincial leaders to account and nationalists in defending China and the central government against any foreign criticism.[26] This suggests systemic strength not fragility – a 'safety valve' at the local and provincial levels where citizen dissatisfaction is vented, and a 'lid' at the central government level that will not permit dissent beyond a point.

Beyond the snapshot of Chinese views at a time of crisis, what is the long-term prognosis on internal stability? To get a better sense of the government's ability to handle serious internal troubles, the crucial issue is the attitude of ordinary Chinese people in the densely populated parts of the country. The future of communist party rule and internal stability is not so much related to what happens in Hong Kong, Tibet, and Xinjiang, which are in the periphery; it is the attitude of the population in the heartland areas that counts.

To get a sense of those attitudes, let us look at the trend in popular protests. Official figures show that between 1993 and 2004 so-called mass incidents rose from 8700 to 74,000. An unofficial estimate is that between 1993 and 2010 'protests' grew from about 10,000 to 180,000.[27] Another unofficial estimate, for a slightly later period, is that between June 2013 and June 2016 the total number of protests was nearly 75,000.[28] Clearly, between 1993 and at least 2010, protests of various kinds, including mass incidents, increased. They may have peaked around 2010 and then declined. Still, 75,000 protests from 2013 to 2016 is a large number of disruptive events per year.

The question is: what kind of protests occur, and are they aimed at the government, particularly the central government and communist party rule? It appears that 70 per cent of the protests were related to labour, real estate, and land issues, with labour protests accounting for the largest segment.[29] The labour protests are apparently mostly over financial compensation, and they happen around the Chinese New Year when millions of workers go home to celebrate.[30] Real estate protests are between homeowners on one side and real estate developers and property managers on the other, over matters such as fraudulent dealings, delays in construction, poor quality of workmanship, and provision of utilities (for example, water, electricity). Land issues, particularly land-grabs, evictions, and relocations of people, are in decline as a cause of protest. Overall, protests are mostly in the cities, in the eastern part of China, and are small (involving between ten and 100 people), with an average of thirty people.[31]

A lot more needs to be known about protests in China. Scholars who study them acknowledge that the data is uneven and of questionable quality. From what is known, though, labour protests and homeowners' real-estate protests are the most significant. This would suggest that Chinese authorities could have a problem. The working population of China is massive, in the hundreds of millions, and nearly ninety per cent of Chinese urban households own the leasehold to their homes.[32] Labour protests plus homeowner protests could therefore be explosive. However, indications are that the majority of protests are non-political and therefore not a great threat. In addition, the central government has been able to manage the problem by acknowledging protester grievances, avoiding heavy-handed repression, and publicly calling for local and provincial authorities to 'temper' their response to the protests. As a result, protesters blame non-government entities or local governments for their difficulties, but they do not clamour for civil and political rights and they do not question the legitimacy of the central government.[33] In sum, China seems to be quite stable internally in the sense that system-wide disaffection against the communist party is absent.

What if anything, then, could tip China over into nationwide instability? Four possibilities exist: a sustained and significant economic downturn after a long period of growth and betterment; defeat in war (or even in a big crisis); poor government handling of a natural or ecological disaster; and an increasing feeling that fundamental lifestyle preferences are unavailable to a large part of the population.

Historians and social theorists have argued that a period of economic growth followed by a period of downturn against the expectation of long-term advancement can produce widespread unrest, even revolution. Defeat in war or surrender in a crisis could also spark popular anger. A massive natural disaster that threatens millions of people by itself may not trigger revolt, but an ineffective response to it could. Climate change is one candidate for such a disaster. Huge water scarcities – always a fear in China historically – could also mobilize a revolt. A pandemic, if not controlled, has the potential to become a nationwide disaster.

Covid-19 was controlled, and the vaccines promise that the end of the story will be a happy one. The next pandemic may be less tractable. Finally, comparisons with lifestyles in other countries could fan large-scale disaffection, particularly among the elite. In the USSR, the Soviet elite, led by Mikhail Gorbachev and the reformists, acknowledged that their system of governance was simply not delivering the kind of lifestyles that Western people enjoyed and that the gap was widening. Those lifestyle preferences were not just economic; they were also political and social. The spread of the social media helps publics become aware of how others live and could suddenly make the Chinese more aspirational in large numbers.

That Xi and the communist party have significantly tightened their grip on Chinese politics since 2012 suggests that in their view there are huge challenges ahead. Competition with the US is one reason for the tighter grip – Chinese society must be disciplined for the rigours of the US challenge. But surely nervousness about China's domestic stability is also a reason for Xi's increasing authoritarianism. The very fact that he and the leadership have chosen increasingly centralized and repressive means of rule suggests that they know something that we do not about China's prospects, and they are worried. The problem for the party leadership is: will authoritarianism in the long run make China more competitive or less able to compete? Will it stifle political dissent, or will it intensify it?

A broad conclusion about China's place in the world then is the following: it will continue to strengthen, but it will not be dominant. Its increasing centralization and authoritarianism betray worries among the leadership about its future. The US is likely to remain number one in comprehensive national power even if not in strict GDP terms. All the signs, though, are that it will be a troubled society. Its effective lead over China may therefore become quite narrow. A safe bet in other words is that the world will be bipolar, with two more or less equal Great Powers. The question is what role the US will play. If it retreats from Asia to focus on domestic challenges and security closer to home, then the continent could become a Chinese sphere of influence. In 2019, China's GDP was twice the size of India's and Japan's combined. If India does not grow its power rapidly, twenty-five years from now that ratio will be even bigger. If so, no coalition in Asia will be able to match Chinese power.

India's Challenge

The challenge for India in its dealings with China is clear enough. The persistently negative perceptions of each other's societies, the stubbornness of the border quarrel and suspicions over Tibet, and the questionable reliability of the US as a partner suggest that the power balance is the most dynamic element of the India–China relationship: it is the one thing that India can change by its own policies and choices. Diplomacy has helped stabilize the relationship between the two countries but only succeeded in producing what Jeff Smith in his perceptive book on India–China relations has described as a 'cold peace'.[34] The determined, responsible pursuit of power is the challenge ahead.

Will India embark on such a course? Perhaps, but much will depend on how desperately Indians want to be powerful. Nye's work on the components of power – hard power (economic and military capabilities) and soft power (the ability to attract and persuade) – misses a key element of power: the *desire* for power and a channelling of social effort towards the attainment of power. This desire for power is part of the argument of Manjari Chatterjee Miller's new book, *Why Nations Rise: Narratives and the Path to Great Power*.[35] Indians after the economic reforms of 1991 have in some measure developed a desire for power – 'in some measure' because the preoccupation of tens of millions of Indians is with the challenges of daily survival and betterment. The desire for power is therefore largely restricted to an urban elite. In any case, though, the will to power is not simply a matter of burning desire. It also requires a systematic social effort led by the government to 'produce' power. Great Powers arose in the past without the will to power: the population did not necessarily thirst for power, and the government did not have a clear and dedicated plan for power. The rise to power 'happened'. Modern mass societies, since Napoleon, have been different. If they have had a will to power, it is because popular and government ambitions were fused.

What was the key turning point? In all probability it was the emergence of total war. Total war is the mobilization of a nation's entire resources and population in the service of warfare. Europe increasingly fought total wars after Napoleon. The US and Russia (and later the USSR) in their time experienced total war: the US in its civil war, and Russia and the USSR after the 1917 revolutions. In Asia, the first country to prepare for and fight total war was Japan, beginning in the early twentieth century. China followed, living with total war from its republican and then communist revolutions to the fight against Japan from 1937 onward. Most of Asia was a theatre of total war in the sense that it was thrown into the midst of the Second World War and lived through the Japanese occupation. It is only India (and what we now call South Asia) that has never experienced total war.

This is not to wish total war on India. It is to suggest that the country has yet to develop the soft, hard, and social infrastructure for the determined, responsible pursuit of power which it will need if it wants to catch up with China. Soft infrastructure consists of ideas, data, bureaucracies, rules, laws, and other politico-administrative structures that allow for the mobilization of tens of millions of people and their coordination towards collective goals. Hard infrastructure consists of all the material elements of power – mass education facilities (school and universities), affordable health care, skilled and healthy populations, energy and transport, agricultural and industrial capabilities, communication and computing systems, science and technology, and military capabilities.

Soft and hard infrastructure are not enough. A country that wants to attain power globally must also have social infrastructure: a mass population that has been emancipated from feudal servitude and debilitating forms of stratification (for example, class, caste). That in turn means radical political reform and, in all probability, a society that has changed from predominantly or substantially rural to largely urban. It is impossible to build a modern Great Power on deep, enduring inequalities and a huge rural population. Just reading through this list of necessary social infrastructure should give the reader a sense of the challenges that will have to be faced to reduce the power gap with China. All this must be accomplished, it bears saying, at the same time as India and the rest of the world enter a period of extraordinary planetary change that will set limits on what can be done and how quickly (to put it mildly): China made its power moves before the onset of climate change; India will have to do so in the middle of the biggest crisis that modern humans have faced.

The road ahead for India is not an impossible one. But it would be fanciful to think that matching China is just a matter of attaining double-digit rates of growth, doubling GDP every decade, producing indigenous weapon systems, and external balancing by aligning with Great Powers. Far more fundamental change will be needed, almost a civilizational change. China underwent a civilizational change with the communist revolution.

India will need a near-civilizational change too: not back to some golden, almost mythical era but forward to a society that is more equal, experimental, and ecological. These are not just feel-good values; they are the essential attributes of a society that wants to imagine and accrue power in the twenty-first century.

Notes

Introduction

1. Jawaharlal Nehru, *The Discovery of India* (New Delhi: Penguin, 2004), p. 48.
2. Ranjit Singh Kalha, *India–China Boundary Issues: Quest for Settlement* (New Delhi: Indian Council of World Affairs and Pentagon Press, 2014, p. 182) suggests that Indian deaths in the largest confrontation after 1962 – at Nathu La in 1967 – were 88. The number of deaths in the Galwan incident was 25, with one subsequent death a few weeks later. The number of Indian deaths since 1967 therefore is 113 plus 4 killed in the Tulung La incident of 1975, for a total of 117.
3. Kanti Bajpai, 'Modi's China Policy and the Road to Confrontation', *Pacific Affairs* 91, no. 2 (June 2018): 260.

1. Perceptions: From Regard to Disdain

1. Prabodh Chandra Bagchi, *India and China: A Thousand Years of Cultural Relations* (Delhi: Munshiram Manoharlal, 2008), pp. 81–82.
2. Bagchi, pp. 35–59.
3. Tansen Sen, 'Changes and Exchanges', in *India–China: Neighbours Strangers*, edited by Ira Pande (New Delhi: HarperCollins and India International Centre, 2010), pp. 35–36.

4. Bagchi, *India and China*, pp. 199–200.
5. Rudolf G. Wagner, 'China and India, Pre-1939', in *Routledge Handbook of China–India Relations*, edited by Kanti Bajpai, Selina Ho, and Manjari Chatterjee Miller (New York: Routledge, 2020), p. 37.
6. Wagner, pp. 37–38. On the use of the word 'Zhongguo' ('Middle Kingdom') to refer to 'Madhyadesh' (India), see Bagchi, *India and China*, fn. 8, p. 29.
7. Wagner, 'China and India, Pre-1939', p. 38.
8. Wagner, pp. 39–40.
9. This draws on Tansen Sen, *India, China, and the World: A Connected History* (New York: Rowman and Littlefield, 2017), pp. 168–86.
10. Sen, *India, China, and the World*, p. 128.
11. Sen, pp. 176–93.
12. This draws on Sen, *India, China, and the World*, pp. 168–86.
13. Sen, *India, China, and the World*, p. 220.
14. Sen, p. 233.
15. Sen, p. 274.
16. Sen, pp. 273–79.
17. Wagner, 'China and India, Pre-1939', p. 44.
18. Murray's Encyclopedia entry of 1837 quoted in Wagner, 'China and India, Pre-1939', p. 44.
19. Wagner, 'China and India, Pre-1939', pp. 47–48.
20. Wagner, pp. 48–51.
21. Quoted in Wagner, 'China and India, Pre-1939', pp. 52–53.
22. Wagner, 'China and India, Pre-1939', pp. 54–55.
23. Wagner, pp. 55–56.
24. Wagner, p. 57.
25. Ramachandra Guha, 'Travelling with Tagore', an essay that inspired his speech on Tagore on 18 March 2015, International House, Tokyo, pp. 28–29.
26. Sen, *India, China, and the World*, pp. 272–73.
27. Xing Zhang, 'The Bowbazar Chinatown', in *India–China: Neighbour Strangers*, edited by Ira Pande (New Delhi: HarperCollins India and the India International Centre, 2010), p. 398.

28. Xing, pp. 396–405.
29. Sen, *India, China, and the World*, pp. 272–73.
30. Xing, 'The Bowbazar Chinatown', pp. 407–08.
31. Rita Chowdhury, *Chinatown Days* (New Delhi: Macmillan, 2018), p. 398.
32. Sen, *India, China, and the World*, pp. 297–337.
33. See Ideas of India, https://www.ideasofindia.org/, accessed on 7 October 2020.
34. Vikram Seth, *From Heaven Lake: Travels Through Xinjiang and Tibet* (London: Phoenix Books, 1993).
35. Seth, pp. 11–14.
36. Seth, pp. 39–40.
37. Seth, pp. 49–50.
38. Seth, pp. 104–05.
39. Seth, pp. 104–06.
40. Seth, pp. 177–78.
41. Anurag Vishwanath, *Finding India in China: Travels to the Lesser Known* (Singapore: Chindia Publishing, 2015).
42. Vishwanath, p. 45.
43. Vishwanath, p. 55.
44. Vishwanath, pp. 164–66.
45. Reshma Patil, *Strangers Across the Border: Indian Encounters in Boomtown China* (New Delhi: HarperCollins India, 2014).
46. Patil, pp. 4–5.
47. Patil, p. 15.
48. Patil, p. 23.
49. Patil, pp. 23–24.
50. Patil, pp. 55–56.
51. Patil, p. 115.
52. Patil, p. 217.
53. Quoted in Patil, *Strangers Across the Border*, pp. 9–10.
54. Patil, *Strangers Across the Border*, pp. 98–101.
55. Patil, pp. 111–12.
56. Patil, pp. 114–16.

57. Patil, pp. 27–28.
58. Patil, p. 29.
59. Patil, p. 37.
60. Patil, p. 47.
61. Patil, p. 20.
62. Patil, p. 221.
63. Patil, p. 255.
64. Patil, p. 24.
65. Patil, p. 238.
66. Patil, p. 243.
67. Patil, p. 24.
68. Patil, p. 83.
69. Patil, p. 26.
70. Patil, p. 104.
71. Patil, pp. 109–26.
72. Patil, pp. 56–57.
73. Simon Shen, 'Exploring the Neglected Constraints on Chindia: Analysing the Online Chinese Perception of India and Its Interaction with China's Indian Policy', *China Quarterly* 207 (September 2011): 541–60.
74. Shen, p. 547.
75. Shen, pp. 547–52.
76. Shen, pp. 552–55.
77. Simon Shen and Debasish Roy Chowdhary, 'The Alien Next Door: Media Images in China and India', in *Routledge Handbook of China–India Relations*, edited by Kanti Bajpai, Selina Ho, and Manjari Chatterjee Miller (New York: Routledge, 2020), p. 120.
78. Shen and Roy Chowdhary, pp. 124–27.
79. Shen and Roy Chowdhary, pp. 127–28.
80. Shen and Roy Chowdhary, pp. 127–30.
81. Compiled from Pew Global Surveys between 2014 and 2019. See https://www.pewresearch.org/global/2017/11/15/india-and-the-world/; https://www.pewresearch.org/global/2019/12/05/views-of-the-balance-of-power-between-u-s-and-china-2019; and https://www.pewresearch.org/global/.

82. Jwala Gutta, 'Growing Up in India with a Chinese Mother Hasn't Been Easy, Covid Makes It Worse', *Indian Express*, 7 April 2020, https://indianexpress.com/article/opinion/columns/coronavirus-outbreak-north-eastern-racism-jwala-gutta-6348807/.
83. Thongkolal Haokip, 'From "Chinky" to "Coronavirus": Racism Against Northeast Indians During the Covid-19 Pandemic', *Asian Ethnicity*, 18 May 2020, DOI: 10.1080/14631369.2020.1763161.
84. Liu Chuen Chen, 'Can You See Me as I Am, an Indian Chinese?' *Indian Express*, 29 June 2020, https://indianexpress.com/article/opinion/columns/india-china-galwan-valley-faceoff-ladakh-indian-chinese-6479479/.
85. Manoj Kewalramani, 'Survey Findings: Perceptions of PRC amid Covid-19 Pandemic', Takshashila Institution, April 2020, https://takshashila.org.in/survey-findings-perceptions-of-prc-amid-covid-19-pandemic/.
86. Kunal Purohit, 'Coronavirus: Anti-Chinese Conspiracy Theories Go Viral in India, Amid Frayed Ties', *South China Morning Post*, 16 March 2020.
87. Akash Sriram, 'Chinese Scientists Now Say India Is Origin of Coronavirus', *Deccan Herald*, 28 November 2020, https://www.deccanherald.com/national/chinese-scientists-now-say-india-is-origin-of-coronavirus-921072.html, accessed on 24 February 2021. The Chinese paper is available on the website.
88. Denise Jia, 'Scientists Slam Indian Study that Fueled Coronavirus Rumors', *Nikkei Asia*, 14 February 2020, https://asia.nikkei.com/Spotlight/Caixin/Scientists-slam-Indian-study-that-fueled-coronavirus-rumors, accessed on 24 February 2021.
89. John Berger, *Ways of Seeing* (London: Penguin, 1972).
90. Shyam Saran, *How India Sees the World* (New Delhi: Juggernaut, 2017), p. 14.
91. Pratap Bhanu Mehta, 'Still Under Nehru's Shadow? The Absence of Foreign Policy Frameworks in India', *India Review* 8, no. 3 (2009): 213–14.
92. Jawaharlal Nehru, *The Discovery of India* (New Delhi: Penguin

Books India, 2004), pp. 596–97; and Jawaharlal Nehru, *India's Foreign Policy: Selected Speeches, September 1946–April 1961* (New Delhi: Publications Division, Ministry of Information and Broadcasting, Government of India, 1961), pp. 1–50.

93. Nehru, *India's Foreign Policy*, p. 38.
94. Madhav Sadashiv Golwalkar, 'The Elixir of National Life-I', in *India, the West, and International Order*, edited by Kanti Bajpai and Siddharth Mallavarapu, (New Delhi: Orient Blackswan, 2019), p. 255.
95. This is the tenor of M.S. Golwalkar, *Bunch of Thoughts*, 4th impression (Bangalore: Vikrama Prakashan, 1968), pp. 1–21.
96. S. Jaishankar, *The India Way: Strategies for an Uncertain World* (New Delhi: HarperCollins India, 2020), Kindle edition, p. 186.
97. Bharat Karnad, *Why India Is Not a Great Power (Yet)* (New Delhi: Oxford University Press, 2015), p. 20.
98. Shishir Arya, 'India's Reaction to Aggression Left China Rattled: RSS Chief', *Times of India*, 26 October 2020, https://timesofindia.indiatimes.com/india/indias-reaction-to-aggression-left-china-rattled-rss-chief/articleshow/78863604.cms.
99. Tingyang Zhao, 'Rethinking Empire from a Chinese Concept: "All-Under-Heaven" (Tian-xia)', *Social Identities* 12, no. 1 (January 2006): 29–41.
100. Zhang Weiwei, *The China Wave: Rise of a Civilizational State* (Hackensack, NJ: World Century Publishing Corporation, 2012); and Zhang Weiwei, *The China Horizon: Glory and Dream of a Civilizational State* (Hackensack, NJ: World Century Publishing Corporation, 2016).
101. Zhang, *The China Horizon*, p. 157.
102. Zhang, p. 164.
103. Zhang, *The China Wave*, pp. 139–41.
104. Hu Xijin, 'De-Escalating Tensions on China–India Border Paramount', *Global Times*, 22 June 2020, https://www.globaltimes.cn/content/1192382.html.

2. Perimeters: From Cooperation to Conflict

1. Charles Glaser, 'The Security Dilemma Revisited', *World Politics* 50, no. 1 (October 1997): 171–201.
2. Srinath Raghavan, *War and Peace in Modern India: A Strategic History of the Nehru Years* (Ranikhet: Permanent Black, 2010), pp. 230–31.
3. Quoted in Raghavan, *War and Peace*, p. 233.
4. Raghavan, *War and Peace*, p. 236.
5. Raghavan, p. 238; and Steven A. Hoffmann, *India and the China Crisis* (Delhi: Oxford University Press, 1990), p. 3.
6. Raghavan, *War and Peace*, p. 237.
7. Raghavan, p. 237.
8. Raghavan, pp. 237–38.
9. Dai Chaowu, 'From "Hindi Chini Bhai Bhai" to "International Class Struggle" Against Nehru: China's India Policy and the Frontier Dispute, 1950–1962', in *The Sino-Indian War of 1962: New Perspectives*, edited by Amit R. Das Gupta and Lorenz M. Luthi (New York: Routledge, 2017), p. 71.
10. Dai, p. 71.
11. Dai, p. 72.
12. Dai, p. 72.
13. Dai, p. 70.
14. Dai, p. 71.
15. Raghavan, *War and Peace*, p. 243.
16. Ranjit Singh Kalha, *India–China Boundary Issues: Quest for Settlement* (New Delhi: Indian Council of World Affairs and Pentagon Press, 2014), pp. 73–75.
17. Kalha, p. 76.
18. I draw on Kalha, *India–China Boundary Issues*, pp. 81–82.
19. Kalha, *India–China Boundary Issues*, pp. 115–16.
20. Kalha, p. 118.
21. Quoted in Raghavan, *War and Peace*, p. 235.
22. Kalha, *India–China Boundary Issues*, p. 72, on the British era maps.
23. Quotes from Raghavan, *War and Peace*, p. 243; and Kalha, *India–China Boundary Issues*, p. 73.

24. Quoted in Kalha, *India–China Boundary Issues*, p. 109.
25. Raghavan, *War and Peace*, pp. 252–53.
26. Kalha, *India–China Boundary Issues*, p. 121.
27. Kalha, pp. 119–29.
28. Raghavan, *War and Peace*, p. 256.
29. Raghavan, p. 260.
30. Hoffmann, *India and the China Crisis*, p. 85.
31. Raghavan, *War and Peace*, p. 261.
32. Hoffmann, *India and the China Crisis*, p. 86.
33. Raghavan, *War and Peace*, pp. 261–64.
34. Raghavan, pp. 261–63; Kalha, *India–China Boundary Issues*, pp. 133–34; and Hoffmann, *India and the China Crisis*, pp. 86–87.
35. On Zhou's attitude before the summit and China's post-summit response, see Dai, 'From "Hindi Chini Bhai Bhai" to "International Class Struggle" Against Nehru', p. 77.
36. Kalha, *India–China Boundary Issues*, pp. 134–35.
37. Eric Hyer, 'The Strategic and Regional Contexts of the Sino-Indian Border Conflict: China's Policy of Conciliation with Its Neighbours', in *The Sino-Indian War of 1962: New Perspectives*, edited by Amit R. Das Gupta and Lorenz M. Luthi (New Delhi: Routledge, 2017), p. 93.
38. Quoted in Kalha, *India–China Boundary Issues*, p. 99.
39. Quoted in Kalha, *India–China Boundary Issues*, p. 99.
40. Kalha, *India–China Boundary Issues*, pp. 145–46.
41. Kalha, p. 147.
42. Dai, 'From "Hindi Chini Bhai Bhai" to "International Class Struggle" Against Nehru', pp. 74–75.
43. Rana Mitter, *China's War with Japan, 1937–1945: The Struggle for Survival* (London: Penguin, 2014), p. 5.
44. Ramachandra Guha, *India After Gandhi: The History of the World's Largest Democracy*, 2nd edition (London: Macmillan, 2017), Kindle, pp. 363–64.
45. Raghavan, *War and Peace*, p. 258.
46. Guha, *India After Gandhi*, p. 367.

47. Guha, pp. 367–71.
48. Guha, pp. 381–82.
49. Kalha, *India–China Boundary Issues*, p. 106.
50. John W. Garver, 'China's Decision for War with India in 1962', in *New Directions in the Study of China's Foreign Policy*, edited by Alastair Iain Johnston and Robert S. Ross (Stanford: Stanford University Press, 2006), p. 123.
51. Hyer, 'The Strategic and Regional Contexts of the Sino-Indian Border Conflict', pp. 86–87.
52. Hyer, p. 88.
53. Garver, 'China's Decision for War with India in 1962', pp. 86–130.
54. Kalha, *India–China Boundary Issues*, p. 79.
55. Kalha, p. 80.
56. Garver, 'China's Decision for War with India in 1962', p. 101.
57. Kalha, *India–China Boundary Issues*, p. 90.
58. Tien-sze Fan, *Asymmetrical Threat Perceptions in India–China Relations* (New Delhi: Sage, 2014), pp. 54–55.
59. Kalha, *India–China Boundary Issues*, pp. 98–99.
60. Hoffmann, *India and the China Crisis*, pp. 64–65.
61. Garver, 'China's Decision for War with India in 1962', p. 93.
62. Garver, pp. 93–95.
63. Garver, pp. 95–96.
64. Garver, pp. 92–93.
65. Hoffmann, *India and the China Crisis*, p. 66.
66. Bruce O. Riedel, *JFK's Forgotten Crisis: Tibet, the CIA, and the Sino-Indian War* (New Delhi: HarperCollins, 2016), pp. 21–42 and pp. 55–65 on CIA operations related to Tibet.
67. Garver, 'China's Decision for War with India in 1962', pp. 96–98 including on Zhou's remarks on the Dalai's possible asylum in India. On the 1954 and 1960 remark, see Kalha, *India–China Boundary Issues*, p. 91.
68. Garver, 'China's Decision for War with India in 1962', pp. 96–101.
69. Garver, p. 106.
70. Kalha, *India–China Boundary Issues*, pp. 129–32.

71. Kalha, pp. 107–08.
72. Raghavan, *War and Peace*, p. 288.
73. Garver, 'China's Decision for War with India in 1962', pp. 111–12.
74. Garver, pp. 114–19.
75. Garver, pp. 110–11.
76. Garver, pp. 120–21.
77. Raghavan, *War and Peace,* p. 271.
78. Raghavan, p. 275.
79. Hoffmann, *India and the China Crisis*, p. 168, indicates that early in the war Nehru felt that the Chinese would not push into India beyond a point. He may have held this view before the war too.
80. Hoffmann, p. 124.
81. Quoted in Raghavan, *War and Peace*, p. 279.
82. Raghavan, *War and Peace*, pp. 280–82.
83. Kalha, *India–China Boundary Issues*, p. 138.
84. Kalha, p. 147.
85. On the size of the two forces in 1962, see Larry M. Worzel, 'Concentrating Forces and Audacious Action: PLA Lessons from the Sino-Indian War', in *The Lessons of History: The Chinese People's Liberation Army at 75*, edited by Laurie Burkitt, Andrew Scobell, and Larry M. Wortzel, pp. 339–42, Strategic Studies Institute, US Army War College, Carlisle, July 2003, https://www.globalsecurity.org/jhtml/jframe.html#https://www.globalsecurity.org/military/library/report/2003/ssi_burkitt-scobell-wortzel.pdf|||The%20Lessons%20of%20History:%20The%20Chinese%20people's%20Liberation%20Army%20at%2075, accessed on 24 November 2020.
86. Kalha, *India–China Boundary Issues*, p. 182; and M. Taylor Fravel, *Strong Borders, Secure Nation: Cooperation and Conflict in China's Territorial Disputes* (Princeton: Princeton University Press, 2008), p. 197.
87. On the 1967 clash, see Vandana Menon and Nayanika Chatterjee, 'Remembering the War We Forgot: 51 Years Ago, How India Gave China a Bloody Nose', The Print, 1 October 2018, https://theprint.in/defence/remembering-the-war-we-forgot-51-years-

ago-how-india-gave-china-a-bloody-nose/127356/, accessed on 25 October 2020; and on the 1975 clash, see Srijan Shukla, '1975 Arunachal Ambush: The Last Time Indian Soldiers Died in Clash with China at LAC', The Print, 16 June 2020, https://theprint.in/india/1975-arunachal-ambush-the-last-time-indian-soldiers-died-in-clash-with-china-at-lac/442674/, accessed on 25 October 2020.

88. Kalha, *India–China Boundary Issues*, p. 199.
89. Shastri Ramachandran, 'Nehru Did Not Trust the Chinese "One Bit", Reveals New Book', *Times of India*, 18 March 2018, https://timesofindia.indiatimes.com/india/nehru-did-not-trust-the-chinese-one-bit-reveals-new-book/articleshow/63348548.cms, accessed on 24 November 2020.
90. Shyam Saran, *How India Sees the World: Kautilya to the 21st Century* (New Delhi: Juggernaut, 2017), pp. 136–39.
91. I rely on Kalha, *India–China Boundary Issues*, pp. 192–99, on the eight rounds of border negotiations.
92. Quoted in John W. Garver, *Protracted Contest: Sino-Indian Rivalry in the Twentieth Century* (Seattle: University of Washington Press, 2011), p. 102.
93. Garver, p. 106.
94. Garver, p. 106.
95. Garver, p. 108.
96. Kalha, *India–China Boundary Issues*, pp. 196–98; and Saran, *How India Sees the World*, p. 140.
97. Garver, *Protracted Contest*, p. 103.
98. Personal email communication from Kishore Mahbubani, Singapore, 24 November 2020.
99. Sun Yun, 'The Ladakh Clash: China's India Dilemma', *GlobalAsia* 15, no. 3 (September 2020), https://www.globalasia.org/v15no3/debate/the-ladakh-clash-chinas-india-dilemma_sun-yun, accessed on 24 February 2021.
100. Atul Aneja, 'LAC Clarification Not the Only Route to Enhance Border Peace, Says China', *The Hindu*, 4 June 2015, https://www.thehindu.com/news/national/lac-clarification-not-the-only-route-

to-enhance-border-peace-says-china/article7281620.ece, accessed on 24 February 2021.

101. Quoted in Kanti Bajpai, 'Modi's China Policy and the Road to Confrontation', *Pacific Affairs* 91, no. 2 (June 2018): 254–55.
102. Quoted in Bajpai, 'Modi's China Policy and the Road to Confrontation', pp. 254–55.
103. 'Read Full Text: PM Modi's Speech at Tsinghua University, Beijing', *Times of India*, 15 May 2015, https://timesofindia.indiatimes.com/india/Read-full-text-PM-Modis-speech-at-Tsinghua-University-Beijing/articleshow/47295807.cms, accessed on 24 February 2021.
104. 'Joint Statement Between the People's Republic of China and the Republic of India', *News from China* 27, no. 5 (2015): 19, https://www.fmprc.gov.cn/ce/cein/chn/xwfw/zgxw/P020150721003177543529.pdf, accessed on 24 February 2021.
105. Garver, *Protracted Contest*, pp. 62–63.
106. Lobsang Sangay, 'Tibet: Exiles' Journey', *Journal of Democracy* 14, no. 3 (July 2003): 121.
107. Garver, *Protracted Contest*, pp. 62–63.
108. Sangay, 'Tibet: Exiles' Journey', p. 123.
109. See Garver, *Protracted Contest*, pp. 67–68.
110. The Office of Tibet – Pretoria, 'Text of Statement Issued to the Press by His Holiness the Dalai Lama on Sep 4, 1993', http://www.officeoftibet.com/index.php/statetments/2014-09-01-19-38-03/text-of-statement-issued-to-the-press-by-his-holiness-the-dalai-lama-on-sep-4-1993, accessed on 25 October 2020.
111. See Rajiv Sikri, 'The Tibet Factor in China–India Relations', *Journal of International Affairs* 64, no. 2 (Spring/Summer 2011): 65–66.
112. For the full text, refer to Ministry of External Affairs, Government of India, 'Joint Communiqué of the Republic of India and the People's Republic of China', 16 December 2010, http://mea.gov.in/bilateral-documentshtm?dtl/5158/Joint+Communiqu+of+the+Republic+of+India+and+the+Peoples+Republic+of+China, accessed on 24 February 2021.
113. See Siddharth Varadarajan, 'India Tells China: Kashmir Is to Us What Tibet, Taiwan Are to You', *The Hindu*, 15 November 2010,

http://www.thehindu.com/news/national/india-tells-china-kashmir-is-to-us-what-tibet-taiwan-are-to-you/article886483.ece, accessed on 24 February 2021.

114. See 'Arunachal Pradesh Is Our Territory: Chinese Envoy', Rediff.com, 14 November 2006, http://www.rediff.com/news/2006/nov/14china.htm, accessed on 24 February 2021.
115. See Diwakar, 'Settle Border Dispute Without Displacing People, PM Tells Hu', *Times of India*, 8 June 2007, https://timesofindia.indiatimes.com/world/europe/Settle-border-dispute-without-displacing-people-PM-tells-Hu/articleshow/2107711.cms.
116. Prem Shankar Jha, 'Shadow Over the Himalayas: India's Tibet Problem', *Asie Visions*, no. 28, 6–10, Institut Français des Relations Internationals (IFRI), Paris, https://www.ifri.org/sites/default/files/atoms/files/av28psjha.pdf, accessed on 24 October 2020.
117. Mohan Malik, *China and India: Great Power Rivals* (New Delhi: Viva Books, 2012), pp. 152–54.
118. Shivshankar Menon, *Choices: Inside the Making of Indian Foreign Policy* (New Delhi: Penguin Random House, 2016), p. 41; and Pravin Sawhney and Ghazala Wahab, *Dragon on Our Doorstep: Managing China Through Military Power* (New Delhi: Aleph, 2017), p. 58.
119. '"We Are Prepared to Meet Any Kind of Threat from Pakistan and China" – General V.K. Singh, Chief of the Army Staff', *The Tribune*, 17 October 2010, https://www.tribuneindia.com/2010/20101017/edit.htm#1, accessed on 24 November 2020.
120. M. Taylor Fravel, 'Stability in a Secondary Strategic Direction: China and the Border Dispute with India after 1962', in *Routledge Handbook of China–India Relations*, edited by Kanti Bajpai, Selina Ho, and Manjari Chatterjee Miller (New York: Routledge, 2020), pp. 174–75.
121. Srijan Shukla, 'How India and China Resolved Three Major Stand-Offs in the Modi Era', The Print, 27 May 2020, https://theprint.in/defence/how-india-and-china-resolved-three-major-stand-offs-in-the-modi-era/430594/, accessed on 17 September 2020.
122. Raghavan, *War and Peace*, p. 260.

3. Partnerships: From Entente to Rivalry to Cold War

1. 'Remarks of Senator John F. Kennedy, Conference on India and the United States, Washington, D.C., May 4, 1959', John F. Kennedy Presidential Library and Museum, https://www.jfklibrary.org/archives/other-resources/john-f-kennedy-speeches/india-and-the-us-conference-washington-dc-19590504, accessed on 24 February 2021.
2. Paul M. McGarr, *The Cold War in South Asia: Britain, the United States and the Indian Subcontinent, 1945–1965* (Delhi: Cambridge University Press, 2013), p. 35.
3. In 1952, India had signed a deal for 200 Sherman tanks (but had its request for aircraft turned down). It later bought 29 C-119 transport aircraft (but had its request for the Sidewinder missiles rejected). See Dennis Kux, *Estranged Democracies: India and the United States, 1941–1991* (New Delhi: Sage, 1993), p. 86.
4. Ranjit Singh Kalha, *India–China Boundary Issues: Quest for Settlement* (New Delhi: Indian Council of World Affairs and Pentagon Press, 2014), p. 25, on Stalin's remark about Han settlement in Tibet.
5. Quoted in Kalha, *India–China Boundary Issues*, p. 103.
6. McGarr, *The Cold War in South Asia*, p. 227.
7. P.R. Chari, 'Indo-Soviet Military Cooperation: A Review', *Asian Survey* 19, no. 3 (March 1979): 237.
8. Quoted in Andreas Hilger, 'The Soviet Union and the India–China Border War, 1962', in *The Sino-Indian War of 1962: New Perspectives,* edited by Amit R. Das Gupta and Lorenz M. Luthi (New Delhi: Routledge, 2017), p. 151.
9. Kux, *Estranged Democracies*, pp. 150–51.
10. Bruce O. Riedel, *JFK's Forgotten Crisis: Tibet, the CIA, and the Sino-Indian War* (New Delhi: HarperCollins, 2016), p. 120.
11. Riedel, pp. 120–21, 135–38.
12. Riedel, pp. 120–46. The quote is from pages 145–46.
13. Jaw-ling Joanne Chang, 'United States–China Normalization: An Evaluation of Foreign Policy Decision Making', Occasional

Papers/Reprints Series in Contemporary Asian Studies, Number 4-1986 (75), School of Law, University of Maryland, p. 26, https://digitalcommons.law.umaryland.edu/cgi/viewcontent.cgi?article=1074&context=mscas, accessed on 23 August 2020.
14. Chang, p. 27.
15. Richard M. Nixon, 'Asia After Viet Nam', *Foreign Affairs*, October 1967, pp. 121–23.
16. John Pomfret, *The Beautiful Country and the Middle Kingdom: America and China, 1776 to the Present* (New York: Henry Holt, 2016), Kindle edition, p. 443.
17. Chang, 'United States–China Normalization', pp. 30–31.
18. Pomfret, *The Beautiful Country and the Middle Kingdom*, p. 444.
19. William Burr, 'The Sino-Soviet Border Conflict, 1969: U.S. Reactions and Diplomatic Maneuvers', National Security Archive Electronic Briefing Book No. 49, https://nsarchive2.gwu.edu/NSAEBB/NSAEBB49/, accessed on 24 February 2021, has the US archival material on this fascinating episode.
20. Xia Yafeng, 'China's Elite Politics and Sino-American Rapprochement, January 1969–February 1972', *Journal of Cold War Studies* 8, no. 4 (Fall 2006): 3–28.
21. Quoted in Srinath Raghavan, *1971: A Global History of the Creation of Bangladesh* (Ranikhet: Permanent Black, 2013), p. 104.
22. Raghavan, *1971*, pp. 106–07.
23. Rajan Menon, 'India and the Soviet Union: A New Stage of Relations?' *Asian Survey* 18, no. 7 (July 1978): 744–45.
24. Chari, 'Indo-Soviet Military Cooperation: A Review', pp. 236–37.
25. Pomfret, *The Beautiful Country and the Middle Kingdom*, p. 477.
26. Pomfret, p. 486.
27. Pomfret, p. 489; Chang, 'United States–China Normalization', pp. 178–80; and Zhang Guangrui, 'Ten Years of Chinese Tourism: Profile and Assessment', *Tourism Management*, March 1989, p. 52.
28. Amit Gupta, 'The Indian Arms Industry: A Lumbering Giant?' *Asian Survey* 30, no. 9 (September 1990): 855–56.
29. Vladislav Zubok, 'The Soviet Union and China in the 1980s: Reconciliation and Divorce', *Cold War History* 17, no. 2 (2017): 134.

30. This paragraph draws on Pomfret, *The Beautiful Country and the Middle Kingdom*, pp. 514–19.
31. Pomfret, *The Beautiful Country and the Middle Kingdom*, p. 545.
32. World Integrated Trade Solutions (WITS), https://wits.worldbank.org/CountryProfile/en/Country/CHN/Year/2001/TradeFlow/EXPIMP/Partner/by-country, accessed on 24 February 2021.
33. On the military sales and cooperation, see Paul Schwartz, 'Evolution of Sino-Russian Defense Cooperation since the Cold War', *Open Forum*, 13 June 2014, http://www.theasanforum.org/evolution-of-sino-russian-defense-cooperation-since-the-cold-war/, accessed on 15 August 2020.
34. Atal Bihari Vajpayee, 'India, USA and the World: Let Us Work Together to Solve the Political-Economic Y2K Problem', Asia Society, New York, 28 September 1998, https://asiasociety.org/india-usa-and-world-let-us-work-together-solve-political-economic-y2k-problem, accessed on 24 February 2021.
35. Rudra Chaudhuri, *Forged in Crisis: India and the United States since 1947* (London: C. Hurst, 2014), p. 189.
36. Chaudhuri, p. 200.
37. Condoleezza Rice, 'Campaign 2000: Promoting the National Interest', *Foreign Affairs* 79, no. 1 (January/February 2000): 56.
38. 'Report of the India–Russia Joint Study Group', Moscow–Delhi, 2007, Ministry of Commerce, Government of India, https://commerce.gov.in/writereaddata/uploadedfile/MOC_635567636562814678_Report_India_Russia_Joint_Study_Group_10_9_2007.pdf, p. 13, accessed on 16 August 2020.
39. PHD Research Bureau, 'India–China Trade Relationship: The Trade Giants of Past, Present and Future', PHD Chamber of Commerce and Industry, January 2018, p. 4, https://www.phdcci.in/wp-content/uploads/2018/11/India-China-Trade-Relationship_The-Trade-Giants-of-Past-Present-and-Future.pdf, accessed on 24 February 2021.
40. These are computed from the World Bank.
41. 'US Looking to Ramp Up Arms Sales to India, Including Heavy-Lifting Drones: Report', *Economic Times*, 5 August 2020, https://

economictimes.indiatimes.com/news/defence/us-looking-to-ramp-up-arms-sales-to-india-including-heavy-lifting-drones-report/articleshow/77363224.cms, accessed on 17 August 2020.

42. 'Foreign Trade', US Census Bureau, https://www.census.gov/foreign-trade/balance/c5330.html, accessed on 17 August 2020 on India–US trade. On India–China, see PHD Research Bureau, 'India–China Trade Relationship: The Trade Giants of Past, Present, Future', 4, and Embassy of India, Beijing, 'India–China Trade and Economic Relations', https://www.eoibeijing.gov.in/economic-and-trade-relation.php, accessed on 17 August 2020.
43. Nivedita Kapoor, 'India–Russia Ties in a Changing World Order: In Pursuit of a "Special Strategic Partnership"', ORF Occasional Paper 2019, October 2018, https://www.orfonline.org/research/india-russia-ties-in-a-changing-world-order-in-pursuit-of-a-special-strategic-partnership-56877/, accessed on 19 August 2020, pp. 10–12; and Katherine Foshko Tsan, 'Re-Energizing the Indian–Russian Relationship: Opportunities and Challenges for the 21st Century', *Jindal Journal of International Affairs* 2, no. 1 (August 2012): 148–49.
44. World Integrated Trade Solutions (WITS), https://wits.worldbank.org/CountryProfile/en/Country/CHN/Year/2017/TradeFlow/EXPIMP/Partner/by-country, accessed on 24 February 2021.

4. Power: From Parity to Asymmetry

1. Joseph S. Nye, *Soft Power: The Means to Success in World Politics* (New York: PublicAffairs, 2005).
2. Angus Maddison, 'Maddison Database 2010', Groningen Growth and Development Centre, Faculty of Economics and Business, University of Groningen, https://www.rug.nl/ggdc/historicaldevelopment/maddison/releases/maddison-database-2010, accessed on 24 February 2021.
3. Data compiled from World Intellectual Property Organization (WIPO), 'Statistical Country Profiles', https://www.wipo.int/

ipstats/en/statistics/country_profile/, accessed on 8 October 2020.

4. 'Global 500', *Fortune*, https://fortune.com/global500/, accessed on 24 February 2021.
5. 'Top 50 Richest People in the World: Mark Zuckerberg Is the Youngest Billionaire', *Business Insider India*, 2 March 2020, https://www.businessinsider.in/finance/news/list-of-top-50-richest-people-in-the-world/articleshow/74439071.cms, accessed on 24 February 2021.
6. On highways, see CEIC, 'India Length of Roads: Highways', https://www.ceicdata.com/en/india/roads-and-highways-statistics-length-of-roads/length-of-roads-highways, accessed on 8 October 2020; and Gao Jiayin, et al., 'Influence of Expressway Construction on the Ecological Environment and the Corresponding Treatment Measures: A Case Study of Changyu (ChangchunFuyu Lalin River) Expressway, China', *Nature Environment and Pollution Technology* 19, no. 3, 1195. On total road length, see Ministry of Road Transport and Highways, Transport Research Wing, Government of India, *Basic Road Statistics of India 2016–2017*, https://morth.gov.in/sites/default/files/Basic%20_Road_Statics_of_India.pdf, p. 1, accessed on 5 October 2020; and National Bureau of Statistics of China, People's Republic of China, 'Basic Conditions of Transport', https://data.stats.gov.cn/english/tablequery.htm?code=AC0L, accessed on 5 October 2020.
7. Neha L.M. Tripathi, 'India's Commercial Airline Fleet Grew 29% in 2019', *Hindustan Times*, 2 January 2020, https://www.hindustantimes.com/mumbai-news/india-s-commercial-airline-fleet-grew-29-in-2019/story-xMCTziU5SsLcDgR5TrxecO.html#:~:text=From%20520%20in%202018%2C%20the,104%20new%20aircraft%20in%202018, accessed on 8 October 2020; and Lu Hui, 'China's Civil Aviation Fleet Exceeds 3,700', Xinhua.net, 18 July 2019, http://www.xinhuanet.com/english/2019-07/18/c_138237617.htm, accessed on 8 October 2020.
8. India Brand Equity Foundation, *Indian Aviation Industry Report*, August, https://www.ibef.org/download/Aviation-August-2020.

pdf, p. 7; and Xinhua, 'China's Civil Airports Register Robust Growth in 2019', Xinhua.net, 9 March 2020, http://www.xinhuanet.com/english/2020-03/09/c_138859303.htm, accessed on 5 October 2020.

9. United Nations Conference on Trade and Development, 'Statistics: Data Center', https://unctadstat.unctad.org/wds/ReportFolders/reportFolders.aspx?sCS_ChosenLang=en, accessed on 8 October 2020.
10. India and China's energy figures are from the International Energy Agency. On India see https://www.iea.org/countries/india; and on China see https://www.iea.org/countries/china, accessed on 20 October 2020.
11. Ella Hurworth, 'India to Overtake China as the World's Most Populous Country: UN', CNN, 20 June 2019, https://edition.cnn.com/2019/06/19/health/india-china-world-population-intl-hnk/index.html, accessed on 24 February 2021.
12. United Nations Department of Economic and Social Affairs, 'Graphs and Profiles', World Population Prospects 2019, https://population.un.org/wpp/Graphs/DemographicProfiles/Line/156, accessed on 24 February 2021.
13. Asian Productivity Organization, *APO Productivity Databook 2018* (Tokyo: Keio University Press, 2018), p. 56.
14. World Bank, 'Literacy Rate, Adult Total (% of People Ages 15 and Above)', https://data.worldbank.org/indicator/SE.ADT.LITR.ZS?locations=IN-CN, accessed on 11 October 2020.
15. World Bank, 'Persistence to Last Grade of Primary, Total (% of Cohort)', https://data.worldbank.org/indicator/SE.PRM.PRSL.ZS?locations=IN-CN, accessed on 11 October 2020.
16. Kritika Sharma, 'Study Shows How India's Higher Education Enrollment Can Jump to 65% from 27%', The Print, 15 June 2020, https://theprint.in/india/education/study-shows-how-indias-higher-education-enrollment-can-jump-to-65-from-27/441582/, accessed on 11 October 2020.
17. Times Higher Education, 'World University Rankings', https://www.timeshighereducation.com/world-university-rankings; 'QS

World University Rankings', https://www.topuniversities.com/university-rankings/world-university-rankings/2019; and 'QS Asia University Rankings', https://www.topuniversities.com/university-rankings/asian-university-rankings/2019, accessed on 13 October 2020.

18. 'QS World University Rankings 2021', https://www.topuniversities.com/university-rankings/world-university-rankings/2021, accessed on 13 October 2020.
19. Global Hunger Index, '2020 Global Hunger Index, By Severity', https://www.globalhungerindex.org/results.html, accessed on 12 October 2020.
20. NCD–RisC, 'Evolution of Height Over Time', https://www.ncdrisc.org/height-mean-ranking.html, accessed on 24 February 2021.
21. All figures are from International Institute of Strategic Studies (IISS), *The Military Balance 2020* (New York: Routledge, 2020).
22. IISS, *The Military Balance 2020*, pp. 271–72; and Office of the Secretary of Defense (2020), *Annual Report to Congress: Military and Security Developments Involving the People's Republic of China*, September 2020, https://media.defense.gov/2020/Sep/01/2002488689/-1/-1/1/2020-DOD-CHINA-MILITARY-POWER-REPORT-FINAL.PDF, accessed on 24 February 2021, p. 165.
23. Press Trust of India, 'Navy's Long-Term Plan Is to Have 3 Aircraft Carriers: Navy Chief', *Economic Times*, 3 December 2019, https://economictimes.indiatimes.com/news/defence/navys-long-term-plan-is-to-have-3-aircraft-carriers-navy-chief/articleshow/72344794.cms, accessed on 24 February 2021.
24. Press Trust of India, 'Approval for Third Aircraft Carrier May Not Come Soon, Indicates Gen Bipin Rawat', *Times of India*, 17 February 2020, https://timesofindia.indiatimes.com/india/approval-for-third-aircraft-carrier-may-not-come-soon-indicates-gen-bipin-rawat/articleshow/74178436.cms, accessed on 24 February 2021.

25. Minnie Chan, 'China Steps Up Shipbuilding with Two More Aircraft Carriers Under Construction Towards 2035 Navy Goal', *South China Morning Post*, 18 July 2020, https://www.scmp.com/news/china/military/article/3093656/china-steps-shipbuilding-two-more-aircraft-carriers-under, accessed on 24 February 2021.
26. Manu Pubby, 'Indian Navy Cutting Down on Procurement Due to Budget Cuts', *Economic Times*, 16 January 2020, https://economictimes.indiatimes.com/news/defence/indian-navy-trims-acquisition-list-due-to-budget-cuts/articleshow/73281243.cms, accessed on 24 February 2021; and Congressional Research Service, 'China Naval Modernization: Implications for U.S. Navy Capabilities – Background and Issues for Congress', *CRS Reports*, p. 2, updated 1 September 2020, https://crsreports.congress.gov/product/pdf/RL/RL33153, accessed on 24 February 2021.
27. Stockholm International Peace Research Institute (SIPRI), *SIPRI Yearbook 2020: Armaments, Disarmament and International Security* (Oxford: Oxford University Press, 2020), pp. 356, 364.
28. Sushant Singh, 'Can India Transcend Its Two-Front Challenge?' War on the Rocks, 14 September 2020, https://warontherocks.com/2020/09/can-india-transcend-its-two-front-challenge/, accessed on 19 October 2020.
29. Lora Saalman, 'China and India: Two Models for AI Military Acquisition and Integration', in *Routledge Handbook of China–India Relations*, edited by Kanti Bajpai, Selina Ho, and Manjari Chatterjee Miller (New York: Routledge, 2020), p. 281.
30. Parama Sinha Palit, *Analysing China's Soft Power Strategy and Comparative Indian Initiatives* (New Delhi: Sage, 2017).
31. Palit, pp. 295–96.
32. Lowy Institute, *Asia Power Index 2019* (Sydney: Lowy Institute, 2019); and Chris Ogden (with Marcus Ioannou), *Great Power Attributes: A Compendium of Historical Data*, Fifth Hammer, Edinburgh, 2020, https://chrisogdendotorg.files.wordpress.com/2020/10/chris-ogden-markos-ioannou-2020-great-power-attributes-edinburgh-fifth-hammer.pdf, accessed on 10 October 2020.

33. Lowy Institute, *Asia Power Index 2019*, pp. 43–47.
34. Lowy Institute, pp. 57–64.
35. World Bank, 'International Tourism, Number of Arrivals', https://data.worldbank.org/indicator/ST.INT.ARVL, accessed on 2 October 2020.
36. Lowy Institute, *Asia Power Index 2019*, p. 30.
37. World Bank, 'Worldwide Governance Indicators', https://databank.worldbank.org/reports.aspx?source=worldwide-governance-indicators#, accessed on 8 October 2020.
38. Harold Isaacs, *Scratches on Our Mind: American Views of China and India* (Abingdon: Routledge, 2015), Kindle. It was originally published by John Day in 1958.
39. Isaacs, pp. 11–12.
40. Shyam Saran, 'China Wants Everyone to Accept That This Is an Asian Order Dominated by China', *Indian Express,* 14 October 2020, https://indianexpress.com/article/explained/china-wants-everyone-to-accept-that-this-is-an-asian-order-dominated-by-china-6723981/, accessed on 14 October 2020.
41. Quoted in Ravi Velloor, 'The Yang Factor, Admiral Harris, and Trump–Modi Summit', *Straits Times*, 23 June 2017, https://www.straitstimes.com/opinion/the-yang-factor-admiral-harris-and-trump-modi-summit, accessed on 14 October 2020.

Conclusion

1. 'Mood of the Nation', *India Today*, August 2020, https://www.indiatoday.in/mood-of-the-nation-survey-2020, accessed on 17 October 2020.
2. Yang Sheng, Chu Daye, Zhan Hui, and Liu Caiy, 'India Unable to Threaten China Militarily, Economically: Survey', *Global Times*, 27 August 2020, https://www.globaltimes.cn/content/1199027.shtml, accessed on 17 October 2020.
3. 'PoK, Aksai Chin Integral Part of India, Can Die for It: Amit Shah in Lok Sabha', *Times of India*, 6 August 2019, https://timesofindia.

indiatimes.com/india/we-will-sacrifice-our-lives-for-kashmir-amit-shah/articleshow/70549004.cms, accessed on 15 October 2020.

4. Ministry of Foreign Affairs of the People's Republic of China, 'Foreign Ministry Spokesperson Hua Chunying's Remarks on the Indian Government's Announcement of the Establishment of the Ladakh Union Territory Which Involves Chinese Territory', 6 August 2019, https://www.fmprc.gov.cn/mfa_eng/xwfw_665399/s2510_665401/2535_665405/t1686549.shtml, accessed on 24 February 2021.
5. Quoted in The Wire Staff, 'After China Brings up "1959 LAC Alignment", India Says that Proposal Wasn't Accepted', The Wire, 29 September 2020, https://thewire.in/diplomacy/after-china-brings-up-1959-lac-alignment-india-says-that-proposal-wasnt-accepted, accessed on 24 February 2021.
6. Sreemoy Talukdar, 'By Insisting on 1959 LAC, China Seeks to Justify Recent Intrusion, Put Pressure on India to Accept Redrawing of Border', Firstpost, https://www.firstpost.com/india/by-insisting-on-1959-lac-china-seeks-to-justify-recent-intrusion-put-pressure-on-india-to-accept-redrawing-of-border-8868471.html, accessed on 16 October 2020.
7. Xinhua, 'Xinhua Headlines: China Sets Policy Directions for Developing Tibet', 29 August 2020, http://www.xinhuanet.com/english/2020-08/29/c_139327831.htm, accessed on 16 October 2020.
8. Hugh White, *The China Choice: Why America Should Share Power* (Collingwood, Victoria, Australia: Black Inc., 2012).
9. Reuters, 'China Set to Surpass U.S. as World's Biggest Economy by 2028, Says Report', CNBC, 25 December 2020, https://www.cnbc.com/2020/12/26/china-set-to-surpass-us-as-worlds-biggest-economy-by-2028-says-report.html, accessed on 24 February 2021.
10. Martin Jacques, *When China Rules the World: The End of the Western World and the Birth of a New Order* (New York: Penguin Random House, 2009).

11. Aaron L. Friedberg, *A Contest for Supremacy: China, America, and the Struggle for Mastery in Asia* (New York: W.W. Norton, 2011).
12. Michael Pillsbury, *The Hundred-Year Marathon: China's Secret Strategy to Replace America as the Global Superpower* (New York: St. Martin's, 2016).
13. Michael Beckley, *Unrivaled: Why America Will Remain the Sole Superpower* (Ithaca: Cornell University Press, 2016), Kindle.
14. Michael Beckley, 'Rogue Superpower: Why This Could Be an Illiberal American Century', *Foreign Affairs* 99, no. 6 (October–December 2020): 73–86.
15. Beckley, pp. 76–78.
16. Michael Beckley, 'Stop Obsessing About China: Why Beijing Will Not Imperil U.S. Hegemony', *Foreign Affairs*, 21 September 2018, https://www.foreignaffairs.com/articles/china/2018-09-21/stop-obsessing-about-china, accessed on 24 February 2021.
17. Beckley, *Unrivaled*, chapter 5.
18. Michael Beckley, 'The United States Should Fear a Faltering China: Beijing's Assertiveness Betrays Its Desperation', *Foreign Affairs*, 28 October 2019, https://www.foreignaffairs.com/articles/china/2019-10-28/united-states-should-fear-faltering-china, accessed on 24 February 2021.
19. Beckley, 'Rogue Superpower', pp. 80–84.
20. Kanti Bajpai, *India in the World: Trials of the Republic* (New Delhi: Times Group Books, 2017), pp. 70–71.
21. Thomas L. Friedman, 'Trump Sent a Warning. Let's Take It Seriously', *New York Times*, 29 September 2020, https://www.nytimes.com/2020/09/29/opinion/trump-election-fraud-2020.html?searchResultPosition=1, accessed on 16 October 2020.
22. Cai Xia, 'The Party That Failed: An Insider Breaks with Beijing', *Foreign Affairs* 100, no. 1 (January/February 2012): 93.
23. Chris Buckley, 'She Was a Communist Party Insider in China. Then She Denounced Xi', *New York Times*, 18 August 2020, https://www.nytimes.com/2020/08/18/world/asia/china-cai-xia-expelled-communist-party.html, accessed on 24 February 2021.

24. Sungmin Cho, 'COVID-19 Has Dimmed Xi's Approval Ratings Abroad – But Not in China', *The Diplomat*, 9 October 2020, https://thediplomat.com/2020/10/covid-19-has-dimmed-xis-approval-ratings-abroad-but-not-in-china/, accessed on 24 February 2021.
25. Cary Wu, 'How Chinese Citizens View Their Government's Coronavirus Response', *The Conversation*, 5 June 2020, https://theconversation.com/how-chinese-citizens-view-their-governments-coronavirus-response-139176, accessed on 24 February 2021.
26. Cho, 'COVID-19 Has Dimmed Xi's Approval Ratings Abroad'.
27. H. Christoph Steinhardt, 'Discursive Accommodation: Popular Protest and Strategic Elite Communication in China', *European Political Science Review* 9, no. 4 (2017): 543–44.
28. Christian Gobel, 'Social Unrest in China: A Bird's-Eye View', in *Handbook of Protest and Resistance in China*, edited by Theresa Wright (Cheltenham, UK: Edward Elgar, 2019), p. 27.
29. Gobel, p. 41.
30. Gobel, pp. 38–29.
31. Gobel, pp. 30–38.
32. Gobel, p. 29.
33. Steinhardt, 'Discursive Accommodation', pp. 545–54.
34. Jeff Smith, *Cold Peace: China–India Rivalry in the Twenty-First Century* (New York: Lexington Books, 2014).
35. Manjari Chatterjee Miller, *Why Nations Rise: Narratives and the Path to Great Power* (New York: Oxford University Press, 2021).

Bibliography

Aneja, Atul. 'LAC Clarification Not the Only Route to Enhance Border Peace, Says China'. *The Hindu*, 4 June 2015. https://www.thehindu.com/news/national/lac-clarification-not-the-only-route-to-enhance-border-peace-says-china/article7281620.ece.

'Arunachal Pradesh Is Our Territory: Chinese Envoy'. Rediff.com, 14 November 2006. http://www.rediff.com/news/2006/nov/14china.htm.

Arya, Shishir. 'India's Reaction to Aggression Left China Rattled: RSS Chief'. *Times of India*, 26 October 2020. https://timesofindia.indiatimes.com/india/indias-reaction-to-aggression-left-china-rattled-rss-chief/articleshow/78863604.cms.

Asian Productivity Organization. *APO Productivity Databook 2018*. Tokyo: Keio University Press, 2018.

Bagchi, Prabodh Chandra. *India and China: A Thousand Years of Cultural Relations*. Delhi: Munshiram Manoharlal, 2008.

Bajpai, Kanti. *India in the World: Trials of the Republic*. New Delhi: Times Group Books, 2017.

———. 'Modi's China Policy and the Road to Confrontation'. *Pacific Affairs* 91, no. 2 (June 2018): 245–60.

Beckley, Michael. 'Rogue Superpower: Why This Could Be an Illiberal American Century'. *Foreign Affairs* 99, no. 6 (October–December 2020): 73–86.

———. 'Stop Obsessing About China: Why Beijing Will Not Imperil U.S. Hegemony'. *Foreign Affairs*, 21 September 2018. https://www.foreignaffairs.com/articles/china/2018-09-21/stop-obsessing-about-china.

———. 'The United States Should Fear a Faltering China: Beijing's Assertiveness Betrays Its Desperation'. *Foreign Affairs*, 28 October 2019. https://www.foreignaffairs.com/articles/china/2019-10-28/united-states-should-fear-faltering-china.

———. *Unrivaled: Why America Will Remain the Sole Superpower*. Ithaca: Cornell University Press, 2016. Kindle.

Berger, John. *Ways of Seeing*. London: Penguin, 1972.

Buckley, Chris. 'She Was a Communist Party Insider in China. Then She Denounced Xi'. *New York Times*, 18 August 2020. https://www.nytimes.com/2020/08/18/world/asia/china-cai-xia-expelled-communist-party.html.

Burr, William. 'The Sino-Soviet Border Conflict, 1969: U.S. Reactions and Diplomatic Maneuvers'. National Security Archive Electronic Briefing Book No. 49. https://nsarchive2.gwu.edu/NSAEBB/NSAEBB49/.

Cai, Xia. 'The Party That Failed: An Insider Breaks with Beijing'. *Foreign Affairs* 100, no. 1 (January/February 2012): 78–96.

CEIC. 'India Length of Roads: Highways'. https://www.ceicdata.com/en/india/roads-and-highways-statistics-length-of-roads/length-of-roads-highways.

Chan, Minnie. 'China Steps Up Shipbuilding with Two More Aircraft Carriers Under Construction Towards 2035 Navy Goal'. *South China Morning Post*, 18 July 2020. https://www.scmp.com/news/china/military/article/3093656/china-steps-shipbuilding-two-more-aircraft-carriers-under.

Chang, Jaw-ling Joanne. 'United States–China Normalization: An Evaluation of Foreign Policy Decision Making'. Occasional Papers/Reprints Series in Contemporary Asian Studies, Number 4-1986 (75), School of Law, University of Maryland, https://digitalcommons.law.umaryland.edu/cgi/viewcontent.cgi?article=1074&context=mscas.

Chari, P.R. 'Indo-Soviet Military Cooperation: A Review'. *Asian Survey* 19, no. 3 (March 1979): 230–44.

Chaudhuri, Rudra. *Forged in Crisis: India and the United States since 1947*. London: C. Hurst, 2014.

Cho, Sungmin. 'COVID-19 Has Dimmed Xi's Approval Ratings Abroad – But Not in China'. *The Diplomat*, 9 October 2020. https://thediplomat.com/2020/10/covid-19-has-dimmed-xis-approval-ratings-abroad-but-not-in-china/.

Chowdhury, Rita. *Chinatown Days*. New Delhi: Macmillan, 2018.

Congressional Research Service. 'China Naval Modernization: Implications for U.S. Navy Capabilities – Background and Issues for Congress'. *CRS Reports*, updated 1 September 2020. https://crsreports.congress.gov/product/pdf/RL/RL33153.

Dai, Chaowu. 'From "Hindi Chini Bhai Bhai" to "International Class Struggle" Against Nehru: China's India Policy and the Frontier Dispute, 1950–1962'. In *The Sino-Indian War of 1962: New Perspectives*, edited by Amit R. Das Gupta and Lorenz M. Luthi, pp. 68–84. New York: Routledge, 2017.

Diwakar. 'Settle Border Dispute Without Displacing People, PM Tells Hu'. *Times of India*, 8 June 2007. https://timesofindia.indiatimes.com/world/europe/Settle-border-dispute-without-displacing-people-PM-tells-Hu/articleshow/2107711.cms.

Embassy of India, Beijing. 'India–China Trade and Economic Relations'. https://www.eoibeijing.gov.in/economic-and-trade-relation.php.

Fang, Tien-sze. *Asymmetrical Threat Perceptions in India–China Relations*. New Delhi: Sage, 2014.

Fortune. *Global 500* (2020). https://fortune.com/global500/.

Fravel, M. Taylor. 'Stability in a Secondary Strategic Direction: China and the Border Dispute with India after 1962'. In *Routledge Handbook of China–India Relations*, edited by Kanti Bajpai, Selina Ho, and Manjari Chatterjee Miller, pp. 169–79. New York: Routledge, 2020.

———. *Strong Borders, Secure Nation: Cooperation and Conflict in China's Territorial Disputes*. Princeton: Princeton University Press, 2008.

Friedberg, Aaron L. *A Contest for Supremacy: China, America, and the Struggle for Mastery in Asia*. New York: W.W. Norton, 2011.

Friedman, Thomas L. 'Trump Sent a Warning. Let's Take It Seriously'. *New York Times*, 29 September 2020. https://www.nytimes.com/2020/09/29/opinion/trump-election-fraud-2020.html?searchResultPosition=1.

Gao, Jiayin; Zhang Mingfei; Hu Zhaoguang; and Shan Wei. 'Influence of Expressway Construction on the Ecological Environment and the Corresponding Treatment Measures: A Case Study of Changyu (ChangchunFuyu Lalin River) Expressway, China'. *Nature Environment and Pollution Technology* 19, no. 3, 1195–1201.

Garver, John W. 'China's Decision for War with India in 1962'. In *New Directions in the Study of China's Foreign Policy*, edited by Alastair Iain Johnston and Robert S. Ross, pp. 86–130. Stanford: Stanford University Press, 2006.

———. *Protracted Contest: Sino-Indian Rivalry in the Twentieth Century*. Seattle: University of Washington Press, 2011.

Glaser, Charles. 'The Security Dilemma Revisited'. *World Politics* 50, no. 1 (October 1997): 171–201.

Global Hunger Index. '2020 Global Hunger Index, By Severity'. https://www.globalhungerindex.org/results.html.

Gobel, Christian. 'Social Unrest in China: A Bird's-Eye View'. In *Handbook of Protest and Resistance in China*, edited by Theresa Wright, pp. 27–45. Cheltenham, UK: Edward Elgar, 2019.

Golwalkar, M.S. *Bunch of Thoughts*. 4th impression. Bangalore: Vikrama Prakashan, 1968.

———. 'The Elixir of National Life-I'. In *India, the West, and International Order*, edited by Kanti Bajpai and Siddharth Mallavarapu, pp. 231–56. New Delhi: Orient Blackswan, 2019.

Guha, Ramachandra. *India After Gandhi: The History of the World's Largest Democracy*. 2nd edition. London: Macmillan, 2017. Kindle.

———. 'Travelling with Tagore'. International House, Tokyo. https://www.i-house.or.jp/programs/wp-content/uploads/2015/06/Tagore-essay_R.Guha_.pdf.

Gupta, Amit. 'The Indian Arms Industry: A Lumbering Giant?' *Asian Survey* 30, no. 9 (September 1990): 846–61.

Gutta, Jwala. 'Growing Up in India with a Chinese Mother Hasn't Been Easy, Covid Makes It Worse'. *Indian Express*, 7 April 2020. https://indianexpress.com/article/opinion/columns/coronavirus-outbreak-north-eastern-racism-jwala-gutta-6348807/.

Haokip, Thongkolal. 'From "Chinky" to "Coronavirus": Racism Against Northeast Indians During the Covid-19 Pandemic'. *Asian Ethnicity*, 18 May 2020. DOI: 10.1080/14631369.2020.1763161.

Hilger, Andreas. 'The Soviet Union and the India–China Border War, 1962'. In *The Sino-Indian War of 1962: New Perspectives*, edited by Amit R. Das Gupta and Lorenz M. Luthi, pp. 142–59. New Delhi: Routledge, 2017.

Hoffmann, Steven A. *India and the China Crisis*. Delhi: Oxford University Press, 1990.

Hu, Xijin. 'De-Escalating Tensions on China–India Border Paramount'. *Global Times*, 22 June 2020. https://www.globaltimes.cn/content/1192382.shtml.

Hurworth, Ella. 'India to Overtake China as the World's Most Populous Country: UN'. CNN, 20 June 2019. https://edition.cnn.com/2019/06/19/health/india-china-world-population-intl-hnk/index.html.

Hyer, Eric. 'The Strategic and Regional Contexts of the Sino-Indian Border Conflict: China's Policy of Conciliation with Its Neighbours'. In *The Sino-Indian War of 1962: New Perspectives*, edited by Amit R. Das Gupta and Lorenz M. Luthi, pp. 85–102. New Delhi: Routledge, 2017.

Ideas of India. https://www.ideasofindia.org/.

India Brand Equity Foundation. *Indian Aviation Industry Report*, August 2020. https://www.ibef.org/download/Aviation-August-2020.pdf.

International Energy Agency. 'China'. https://www.iea.org/countries/china.

———. 'India'. https://www.iea.org/countries/india.

International Institute of Strategic Studies (IISS). *The Military Balance 2020*. New York: Routledge, 2020.

Isaacs, Harold. *Scratches on Our Mind: American Views of China and India*. Abingdon: Routledge, 2015. Kindle.

Jacques, Martin. *When China Rules the World: The End of the Western World and the Birth of a New Order*. New York: Penguin Random House, 2009.

Jaishankar, S. *The India Way: Strategies for an Uncertain World*. New Delhi: HarperCollins India, 2020. Kindle.

Jha, Prem Shankar. 'Shadow Over the Himalayas: India's Tibet Problem'. *Asie Visions*, no. 28. Institut Français des Relations Internationals (IFRI), Paris. https://www.ifri.org/sites/default/files/atoms/files/av28psjha.pdf.

Jia, Denise. 'Scientists Slam Indian Study That Fueled Coronavirus Rumors'. *Nikkei Asia*, 14 February 2020. https://asia.nikkei.com/Spotlight/Caixin/Scientists-slam-Indian-study-that-fueled-coronavirus-rumors.

'Joint Statement Between the People's Republic of China and the Republic of India'. *News from China* 27, no. 5 (2015): 19. https://www.fmprc.gov.cn/ce/cein/chn/xwfw/zgxw/P020150721003177543529.pdf.

Kalha, Ranjit Singh. *India–China Boundary Issues: Quest for Settlement*. New Delhi: Indian Council of World Affairs and Pentagon Press, 2014.

Kapoor, Nivedita. 'India–Russia Ties in a Changing World Order: In Pursuit of a "Special Strategic Partnership"'. ORF Occasional Paper 2019, October 2018. https://www.orfonline.org/research/india-russia-ties-in-a-changing-world-order-in-pursuit-of-a-special-strategic-partnership-56877/.

Karnad, Bharat. *Why India Is Not a Great Power (Yet)*. New Delhi: Oxford University Press, 2015.

Kewalramani, Manoj. 'Survey Findings: Perceptions of PRC Amid Covid-19 Pandemic'. Takshashila Institution, April 2020. https://takshashila.org.in/survey-findings-perceptions-of-prc-amid-covid-19-pandemic/.

Kux, Dennis. *Estranged Democracies: India and the United States, 1941–1991*. New Delhi: Sage, 1993.

Liu, Chuen Chen. 'Can You See Me as I Am, an Indian Chinese?' *Indian Express*, 29 June 2020. https://indianexpress.com/article/opinion/columns/india-china-galwan-valley-faceoff-ladakh-indian-chinese-6479479/.

Lowy Institute. *Asia Power Index 2019*. Sydney: Lowy Institute, 2019.

Lu, Hui. 'China's Civil Aviation Fleet Exceeds 3,700'. Xinhua.net, 18 July 2019. http://www.xinhuanet.com/english/2019-07/18/c_138237617.htm.

Maddison, Angus. 'Maddison Database 2010'. Groningen Growth and Development Centre, Faculty of Economics and Business, University of Groningen. https://www.rug.nl/ggdc/historicaldevelopment/maddison/releases/maddison-database-2010.

Malik, Mohan. *China and India: Great Power Rivals*. New Delhi: Viva Books, 2012.

McGarr, Paul M. *The Cold War in South Asia: Britain, the United States and the Indian Subcontinent, 1945–1965*. Delhi: Cambridge University Press, 2013.

Mehta, Pratap Bhanu. 'Still Under Nehru's Shadow? The Absence of Foreign Policy Frameworks in India'. *India Review* 8, no. 3 (2009): 209–33.

Menon, Rajan. 'India and the Soviet Union: A New Stage of Relations?' *Asian Survey* 18, no. 7 (July 1978): 731–50.

Menon, Shivshankar. *Choices: Inside the Making of Indian Foreign Policy*. New Delhi: Penguin Random House, 2016.

Menon, Vandana, and Nayanika Chatterjee. 'Remembering the War We Forgot: 51 Years Ago, How India Gave China a Bloody Nose'. The Print, 1 October 2018. https://theprint.in/defence/remembering-the-war-we-forgot-51-years-ago-how-india-gave-china-a-bloody-nose/127356/.

Miller, Manjari Chatterjee. *Why Nations Rise: Narratives and the Path to Great Power*. New York: Oxford University Press, 2021.

Ministry of External Affairs, Government of India. 'Joint Communiqué of the Republic of India and the People's Republic of China',

16 December 2010. http://mea.gov.in/bilateral-documents.htm?dtl/5158/Joint+Communiqu+of+the+Republic+of+India+and+the+Peoples+Republic+of+China.

Ministry of Foreign Affairs of the People's Republic of China. 'Foreign Ministry Spokesperson Hua Chunying's Remarks on the Indian Government's Announcement of the Establishment of the Ladakh Union Territory Which Involves Chinese Territory', 6 August 2019. https://www.fmprc.gov.cn/mfa_eng/xwfw_665399/s2510_665401/2535_665405/t1686549.shtml.

Ministry of Road Transport and Highways, Transport Research Wing, Government of India. 'Basic Road Statistics of India 2016–2017'. https://morth.gov.in/sites/default/files/Basic%20_Road_Statics_of_India.pdf.

Mitter, Rana. *China's War with Japan, 1937–1945: The Struggle for Survival* (London: Penguin, 2014).

'Mood of the Nation'. *India Today*, August 2020. https://www.indiatoday.in/mood-of-the-nation-survey-2020.

National Bureau of Statistics of China, People's Republic of China. 'Basic Conditions of Transport'. https://data.stats.gov.cn/english/tablequery.htm?code=AC0L.

NCD-RisC. 'Evolution of Height Over Time'. https://www.ncdrisc.org/height-mean-ranking.html.

Nehru, Jawaharlal. *India's Foreign Policy: Selected Speeches, September 1946–April 1961*. New Delhi: Publications Division, Ministry of Information and Broadcasting, Government of India, 1961.

———. *The Discovery of India*. New Delhi: Penguin Books India, 2004.

Nixon, Richard M. 'Asia After Viet Nam'. *Foreign Affairs*, October 1967, pp. 121–23.

Nye, Joseph S. *Soft Power: The Means to Success in World Politics*. New York: PublicAffairs, 2005.

Office of the Secretary of Defense. *Annual Report to Congress: Military and Security Developments Involving the People's Republic of China*, September 2020. https://media.defense.gov/2020/

Sep/01/2002488689/-1/-1/1/2020-DOD-CHINA-MILITARY-POWER-REPORT-FINAL.PDF.

Office of Tibet – Pretoria. 'Text of Statement Issued to the Press by His Holiness the Dalai Lama on Sep 4, 1993'. http://www.officeoftibet.com/index.php/statetments/2014-09-01-19-38-03/text-of-statement-issued-to-the-press-by-his-holiness-the-dalai-lama-on-sep-4-1993.

Ogden, Chris, with Marcus Ioannou. *Great Power Attributes: A Compendium of Historical Data*. Fifth Hammer, Edinburgh, 2020. https://chrisogdendotorg.files.wordpress.com/2020/10/chris-ogden-markos-ioannou-2020-great-power-attributes-edinburgh-fifth-hammer.pdf.

Palit, Parama Sinha. *Analysing China's Soft Power Strategy and Comparative Indian Initiatives*. New Delhi: Sage, 2017.

Patil, Reshma. *Strangers Across the Border: Indian Encounters in Boomtown China*. New Delhi: HarperCollins, 2014.

Pew Global Surveys. 'India and the World', 15 November 2017. https://www.pewresearch.org/global/2017/11/15/india-and-the-world/.

———. 'Views of the Balance of Power Between U.S. and China', 5 December 2019. https://www.pewresearch.org/global/2019/12/05/views-of-the-balance-of-power-between-u-s-and-china-2019.

PHD Research Bureau. 'India–China Trade Relationship: The Trade Giants of Past, Present and Future'. PHD Chamber of Commerce and Industry, January 2018. https://www.phdcci.in/wp-content/uploads/2018/11/India-China-Trade-Relationship_The-Trade-Giants-of-Past-Present-and-Future.pdf.

Pillsbury, Michael. *The Hundred-Year Marathon: China's Secret Strategy to Replace America as the Global Superpower*. New York: St. Martin's, 2016.

'PoK, Aksai China Integral Part of India, Can Die for It: Amit Shah in Lok Sabha'. *Times of India*, 6 August 2019. https://timesofindia.indiatimes.com/india/we-will-sacrifice-our-lives-for-kashmir-amit-shah/articleshow/70549004.cms.

Pomfret, John. *The Beautiful Country and the Middle Kingdom: America and China, 1776 to the Present*. New York: Henry Holt, 2016. Kindle.

Press Trust of India. 'Approval for Third Aircraft Carrier May Not Come Soon, Indicates Gen Bipin Rawat'. *Times of India*, 17 February 2020. https://timesofindia.indiatimes.com/india/approval-for-third-aircraft-carrier-may-not-come-soon-indicates-gen-bipin-rawat/articleshow/74178436.cms.

———. 'Navy's Long-Term Plan Is to Have 3 Aircraft Carriers: Navy Chief'. *Economic Times*, 3 December 2019. https://economictimes.indiatimes.com/news/defence/navys-long-term-plan-is-to-have-3-aircraft-carriers-navy-chief/articleshow/72344794.cms.

Pubby, Manu. 'Indian Navy Cutting Down on Procurement Due to Budget Cuts'. *Economic Times*, 16 January 2020. https://economictimes.indiatimes.com/news/defence/indian-navy-trims-acquisition-list-due-to-budget-cuts/articleshow/73281243.cms.

Purohit, Kunal. 'Coronavirus: Anti-Chinese Conspiracy Theories Go Viral in India, Amid Frayed Ties'. *South China Morning Post*, 16 March 2020.

'QS Asia University Rankings 2019'. https://www.topuniversities.com/university-rankings/asian-university-rankings/2019.

'QS World University Rankings 2019'. https://www.topuniversities.com/university-rankings/world-university-rankings/2019.

'QS World University Rankings 2021'. https://www.topuniversities.com/university-rankings/world-university-rankings/2021.

Raghavan, Srinath. *1971: A Global History of the Creation of Bangladesh*. Ranikhet: Permanent Black, 2013.

———. *War and Peace in Modern India: A Strategic History of the Nehru Years*. Ranikhet: Permanent Black, 2010.

Ramachandran, Shastri. 'Nehru Did Not Trust the Chinese "One Bit", Reveals New Book'. *Times of India*, 18 March 2018. https://timesofindia.indiatimes.com/india/nehru-did-not-trust-the-chinese-one-bit-reveals-new-book/articleshow/63348548.cms.

'Read Full Text: PM Modi's Speech at Tsinghua University, Beijing'. *Times of India*, 15 May 2015. https://timesofindia.indiatimes.com/

india/Read-full-text-PM-Modis-speech-at-Tsinghua-University-Beijing/articleshow/47295807.cms.

'Remarks of Senator John F. Kennedy, Conference on India and the United States, Washington, D.C., May 4, 1959'. John F. Kennedy Presidential Library and Museum. https://www.jfklibrary.org/archives/other-resources/john-f-kennedy-speeches/india-and-the-us-conference-washington-dc-19590504.

'Report of the India–Russia Joint Study Group'. Moscow–Delhi, 2007, Ministry of Commerce, Government of India. https://commerce.gov.in/writereaddata/uploadedfile/MOC_635567636562814678_Report_India_Russia_Joint_Study_Group_10_9_2007.pdf.

Reuters. 'China Set to Surpass U.S. as World's Biggest Economy by 2028, Says Report'. CNBC, 25 December 2020. https://www.cnbc.com/2020/12/26/china-set-to-surpass-us-as-worlds-biggest-economy-by-2028-says-report.html.

Rice, Condoleezza. 'Campaign 2000: Promoting the National Interest'. *Foreign Affairs* 79, no. 1 (January/February 2000).

Riedel, Bruce O. *JFK's Forgotten Crisis: Tibet, the CIA, and the Sino-Indian War*. New Delhi: HarperCollins, 2016.

Saalman, Lora. 'China and India: Two Models for AI Military Acquisition and Integration'. In *Routledge Handbook of China–India Relations*, edited by Kanti Bajpai, Selina Ho, and Manjari Chatterjee Miller, pp. 266–88. New York: Routledge, 2020.

Sangay, Lobsang. 'Tibet: Exiles' Journey'. *Journal of Democracy* 14, no. 3 (July 2003): 119–30.

Saran, Shyam. 'China Wants Everyone to Accept That This Is an Asian Order Dominated by China'. *Indian Express*, 14 October 2020. https://indianexpress.com/article/explained/china-wants-everyone-to-accept-that-this-is-an-asian-order-dominated-by-china-6723981/.

———. *How India Sees the World: Kautilya to the 21st Century*. New Delhi: Juggernaut Books, 2017.

Sawhney, Pravin, and Ghazala Wahab. *Dragon on Our Doorstep: Managing China Through Military Power*. New Delhi: Aleph, 2017.

Schwartz, Paul. 'Evolution of Sino-Russian Defense Cooperation since the Cold War'. *Open Forum*, 13 June 2014. http://www.theasanforum.org/evolution-of-sino-russian-defense-cooperation-since-the-cold-war/.

Sen, Tansen. 'Changes and Exchanges'. In *India–China: Neighbours Strangers*, edited by Ira Pande, pp. 34–47. New Delhi: HarperCollins and the India International Centre, 2010.

———. *India, China, and the World: A Connected History*. New York: Rowman and Littlefield, 2017.

Seth, Vikram. *From Heaven Lake: Travels Through Xinjiang and Tibet*. London: Phoenix Books, 1993.

Sharma, Kritika. 'Study Shows How India's Higher Education Enrollment Can Jump to 65% from 27%'. The Print, 15 June 2020. https://theprint.in/india/education/study-shows-how-indias-higher-education-enrollment-can-jump-to-65-from-27/441582/.

Shen, Simon. 'Exploring the Neglected Constraints on Chindia: Analysing the Online Chinese Perception of India and Its Interaction with China's Indian Policy'. *China Quarterly* 207 (September 2011): 541–60.

Shen, Simon, and Debasish Roy Chowdhary. 'The Alien Next Door: Media Images in China and India'. In *Routledge Handbook of China–India Relations*, edited by Kanti Bajpai, Selina Ho, and Manjari Chatterjee Miller, pp. 119–38. New York: Routledge, 2020.

Sheng, Yang, Chu Daye, Zhan Hui, and Liu Caiyu. 'India Unable to Threaten China Militarily, Economically: Survey'. *Global Times*, 27 August 2020. https://www.globaltimes.cn/content/1199027.shtml.

Shukla, Srijan. '1975 Arunachal Ambush: The Last Time Indian Soldiers Died in Clash with China at LAC'. The Print, 16 June 2020. https://theprint.in/india/1975-arunachal-ambush-the-last-time-indian-soldiers-died-in-clash-with-china-at-lac/442674/.

———. 'How India and China Resolved Three Major Stand-Offs in the Modi Era'. The Print, 27 May 2020. https://theprint.in/defence/how-india-and-china-resolved-three-major-stand-offs-in-the-modi-era/430594/.

Sikri, Rajiv. 'The Tibet Factor in China–India Relations'. *Journal of International Affairs* 64, no. 2 (Spring/Summer 2011): 55–71.

Singh, Sushant. 'Can India Transcend Its Two-Front Challenge?' War on the Rocks, 14 September 2020. https://warontherocks.com/2020/09/can-india-transcend-its-two-front-challenge/.

Smith, Jeff. *Cold Peace: China–India Rivalry in the Twenty-First Century*. New York: Lexington Books, 2014.

Sriram, Akash. 'Chinese Scientists Now Say India Is Origin of Coronavirus'. *Deccan Herald*, 28 November 2020. https://www.deccanherald.com/national/chinese-scientists-now-say-india-is-origin-of-coronavirus-921072.html.

Steinhardt, H. Christoph. 'Discursive Accommodation: Popular Protest and Strategic Elite Communication in China'. *European Political Science Review* 9, no. 4 (2017): 539–60.

Stockholm International Peace Research Institute (SIPRI). *SIPRI Yearbook 2020: Armaments, Disarmament and International Security*. Oxford: Oxford University Press, 2020.

Talukdar, Sreemoy. 'By Insisting on 1959 LAC, China Seeks to Justify Recent Intrusion, Put Pressure on India to Accept Redrawing of Border'. Firstpost, 1 October 2020. https://www.firstpost.com/india/by-insisting-on-1959-lac-china-seeks-to-justify-recent-intrusion-put-pressure-on-india-to-accept-redrawing-of-border-8868471.html.

Times Higher Education. 'World University Rankings'. https://www.timeshighereducation.com/world-university-rankings.

'Top 50 Richest People in the World: Mark Zuckerberg Is the Youngest Billionaire'. *Business Insider India*, 2 March 2020. https://www.businessinsider.in/finance/news/list-of-top-50-richest-people-in-the-world/articleshow/74439071.cms.

Tripathi, Neha L.M. 'India's Commercial Airline Fleet Grew 29% in 2019'. *Hindustan Times*, 2 January 2020. https://www.hindustantimes.com/mumbai-news/india-s-commercial-airline-fleet-grew-29-in-2019/story-xMCTziU5SsLcDgR5TrxecO.html#:~:text=From%20520%20in%202018%2C%20the,104%20new%20aircraft%20in%202018.

Tsan, Katherine Foshko. 'Re-Energizing the Indian–Russian Relationship: Opportunities and Challenges for the 21st Century'. *Jindal Journal of International Affairs* 2, no. 1 (August 2012): 140–84.

United Nations Conference on Trade and Development. 'Statistics: Data Center'. https://unctadstat.unctad.org/wds/ReportFolders/reportFolders.aspx?sCS_ChosenLang=en.

United Nations Department of Economic and Social Affairs. 'Graphs and Profiles'. World Population Prospects 2019. https://population.un.org/wpp/Graphs/DemographicProfiles/Line/156.

'US Looking to Ramp Up Arms Sales to India, Including Heavy-Lifting Drones: Report'. *Economic Times*, 5 August 2020. https://economictimes.indiatimes.com/news/defence/us-looking-to-ramp-up-arms-sales-to-india-including-heavy-lifting-drones-report/articleshow/77363224.cms.

Vajpayee, Atal Bihari. 'India, USA and the World: Let Us Work Together to Solve the Political-Economic Y2K Problem'. Asia Society, New York, 28 September 1998. https://asiasociety.org/india-usa-and-world-let-us-work-together-solve-political-economic-y2k-problem.

Varadarajan, Siddharth. 'India Tells China: Kashmir Is to Us What Tibet, Taiwan Are to You'. *The Hindu*, 15 November 2010. http://www.thehindu.com/news/national/india-tells-china-kashmir-is-to-us-what-tibet-taiwan-are-to-you/article886483.ece.

Velloor, Ravi. 'The Yang Factor, Admiral Harris, and Trump–Modi Summit'. *Straits Times*, 23 June 2017. https://www.straitstimes.com/opinion/the-yang-factor-admiral-harris-and-trump-modi-summit.

Vishwanath, Anurag. *Finding India in China: Travels to the Lesser Known*. Singapore: Chindia Publishing, 2015.

Wagner, Rudolf G. 'China and India, Pre-1939'. In *Routledge Handbook of China–India Relations*, edited by Kanti Bajpai, Selina Ho, and Manjari Chatterjee Miller, pp. 35–62. New York: Routledge, 2020.

'"We Are Prepared to Meet Any Kind of Threat from Pakistan and China" – General V.K. Singh, Chief of the Army Staff'. *The Tribune*, 17 October 2010. https://www.tribuneindia.com/2010/20101017/edit.htm#1.

White, Hugh. *The China Choice: Why America Should Share Power*. Collingwood, Victoria, Australia: Black Inc., 2012.

Wire Staff. 'After China Brings up "1959 LAC Alignment", India Says That Proposal Wasn't Accepted'. The Wire, 29 September 2020. https://thewire.in/diplomacy/after-china-brings-up-1959-lac-alignment-india-says-that-proposal-wasnt-accepted.

World Bank. 'International Tourism, Number of Arrivals'. https://data.worldbank.org/indicator/ST.INT.ARVL.

———. 'Literacy Rate, Adult Total (% of People Ages 15 and Above)'. https://data.worldbank.org/indicator/SE.ADT.LITR.ZS?locations=IN-CN.

———. 'Persistence to Last Grade of Primary, Total (% of Cohort)'. https://data.worldbank.org/indicator/SE.PRM.PRSL.ZS?locations=IN-CN.

———. 'Worldwide Governance Indicators'. https://databank.worldbank.org/reports.aspx?source=worldwide-governance-indicators#.

World Integrated Trade Solutions (WITS). 'China Trade Balance, Exports and Imports by Country 2001.' https://wits.worldbank.org/CountryProfile/en/Country/CHN/Year/2001/TradeFlow/EXPIMP/Partner/by-country.

———. 'China Trade Balance, Exports and Imports by Country 2017'. https://wits.worldbank.org/CountryProfile/en/Country/CHN/Year/2017/TradeFlow/EXPIMP/Partner/by-country.

World Intellectual Property Organization. 'Statistical Country Profiles'. https://www.wipo.int/ipstats/en/statistics/country_profile/.

Worzel, Larry M. 'Concentrating Forces and Audacious Action: PLA Lessons from the Sino-Indian War.' In *The Lessons of History: The Chinese People's Liberation Army at 75*, edited by Laurie Burkitt, Andrew Scobell, and Larry M. Wortzel, pp. 327–52. Strategic Studies Institute, US Army War College, Carlisle, July 2003. https://www.globalsecurity.org/jhtml/jframe.html#https://www.globalsecurity.org/military/library/report/2003/ssi_burkitt-scobell-wortzel.

pdf|||The%20Lessons%20of%20History:%20The%20Chinese%20people's%20Liberation%20Army%20at%2075.

Wu, Cary. 'How Chinese Citizens View Their Government's Coronavirus Response'. *The Conversation*, 5 June 2020. https://theconversation.com/how-chinese-citizens-view-their-governments-coronavirus-response-139176.

Xia, Yafeng. 'China's Elite Politics and Sino-American Rapprochement, January 1969–February 1972'. *Journal of Cold War Studies* 8, no. 4 (Fall 2006): 3–28.

Xing, Zhang. 'The Bowbazar Chinatown'. In *India–China: Neighbours Strangers*, edited by Ira Pande, pp. 396–413. New Delhi: HarperCollins and the India International Centre, 2010.

Xinhua. 'China's Civil Airports Register Robust Growth in 2019', 9 March 2020. http://www.xinhuanet.com/english/2020-03/09/c_138859303.htm.

———. 'Xinhua Headlines: China Sets Policy Directions for Developing Tibet', 29 August 2020. http://www.xinhuanet.com/english/2020-08/29/c_139327831.htm.

Yun, Sun. 'The Ladakh Clash: China's India Dilemma'. *GlobalAsia* 15, no. 3 (September 2020). https://www.globalasia.org/v15no3/debate/the-ladakh-clash-chinas-india-dilemma_sun-yun.

Zhang, Guangrui. 'Ten Years of Chinese Tourism: Profile and Assessment'. *Tourism Management*, March 1989, pp. 51–62.

Zhang, Weiwei. *The China Horizon: Glory and Dream of a Civilizational State*. Hackensack, NJ: World Century Publishing Corporation, 2016.

———. *The China Wave: Rise of a Civilizational State*. Hackensack, NJ: World Century Publishing Corporation, 2012.

Zhao, Tingyang. 'Rethinking Empire from a Chinese Concept: "All-Under-Heaven" (Tian-xia)'. *Social Identities* 12, no. 1 (January 2006): 29–41.

Zubok, Vladislav. 'The Soviet Union and China in the 1980s: Reconciliation and Divorce'. *Cold War History* 17, no. 2 (2017): 121–41.

Acknowledgements

This book began and was seen through to the end with the encouragement and skill of Nandini Mehta at Juggernaut. So my greatest thanks are to her. She is not responsible for what is in its pages beyond the usual editorial comments and suggestions, but she insisted on a more personalized, informal book than an academic would usually write and the final product bears the imprint of her thought. I also want to thank others at Juggernaut who reacted to the original outline of the book including Chiki Sarkar – I didn't deliver on the long list of topics I began with, but I hope that this more focused account of India–China relations goes some way towards what they wanted. Finally, Jaishree Ram Mohan saw the manuscript to completion with her careful editing and patience, and so my deep thanks to her as well.

The book is dedicated to my children and extended family, but I also want to record my gratitude to them. Over the years, they have been wonderfully supportive, urging me to write something longer than I usually do. I finally did, partly out of my great affection for them. The book was done quickly, as this Juggernaut series requires, and it was done in the middle of a semi-lockdown in Singapore due to the Covid pandemic. Regular Zoom and other conversations with the Bajpai clan helped me to 'grin and bear it' and keep writing.

I also want to record my thanks to Dean Danny Quah and Vice Deans Suzaina Kadir and Yuen Foong Khong at the Lee Kuan Yew School, National University of Singapore, for giving me a semester-long break from teaching in order to write the book. My previous Dean, Kishore Mahbubani, brought me to the School to think and write about India–China relations. Kishore kept pushing me along on the project, and I have tried to 'deliver'. He makes writing these kinds of books look easy. I know now that it is by no means easy! In 2012, he nominated me to the Rockefeller Bellagio Center for a six-week stint where I worked on a more academic book on India–China relations. This book owes something to the beautiful surroundings and the calm of the Center, the other Fellows in residence, and the tremendous support of the staff. I want to record my thanks to everyone there during those idyllic days.

I could not have written the book without the always cheerful and unstinting help of Esther Yeoh, Serene Teang, Byron Chong, and Jassie Cheng at the Centre on Asia and Globalisation at the LKY School. Esther and Serene keep the Centre humming along administratively so that I hardly need to do anything beyond signing a few papers. Byron is invaluable as a research assistant and read the entire manuscript with a sharp eye. Jassie, our most recent addition to the Centre, brings a quiet, efficient energy.

Finally, since I have not said it before in print, the LKY School is a wonderful academic home, and I will always be grateful for having packed my bags and come here back in 2011.

Click the QR Code with a QR scanner app
or type the link into the Internet browser
on your phone to download the app.